SAA: A Guide to Implementing
IBM's Systems Application Architecture

Selected titles from the YOURDON PRESS COMPUTING SERIES
Ed Yourdon, *Advisor*

BAUDIN Manufacturing Systems Analysis with Application to Production Scheduling
BELLIN AND SUCHMAN Structured Systems Development Manual
BLOCK The Politics of Projects
BODDIE Crunch Mode: Building Effective Systems on a Tight Schedule
BOULDIN Agents of Change: Managing the Introduction of Automated Tools
BRILL Building Controls into Structured Systems
BRILL Techniques of EDP Project Management: A Book of Readings
CHANG Principles of Visual Programming Systems
COAD AND YOURDON Object-Oriented Analysis
CONNELL AND SHAFER Structured Rapid Prototyping: An Evolutionary Approach to Software Development
CONSTANTINE AND YOURDON Structured Design: Fundamentals of a Discipline of Computer Program and Systems Design
DeMARCO Concise Notes on Software Engineering
DeMARCO Controlling Software Projects: Management, Measurement, and Estimates
DeMARCO Structured Analysis and System Specification
DeSALVO AND LIEBOWITZ Managing Artificial Intelligence and Expert Systems
DICKINSON Developing Structured Systems: A Methodology Using Structured Techniques
FLAVIN Fundamental Concepts in Information Modeling
FOLLMAN Business Applications with Microcomputers: A Guidebook for Building Your Own System
FRANTZEN AND McEVOY A Game Plan for Systems Development: Strategy and Steps for Designing Your Own System
GROCHOW SAA: A Guide to Implementing IBM's Systems Application Architecture
INMON Information Engineering for the Practitioner: Putting Theory into Practice
KELLER Expert Systems Technology: Development and Application
KELLER The Practice of Structured Analysis: Exploding Myths
KING Creating Effective Software: Computer Program Design Using the Jackson Method
KING Current Practices in Software Development: A Guide to Successful Systems
LIEBOWITZ AND DeSALVO Structuring Expert Systems: Domain, Design, and Development
McMENAMIN AND PALMER Essential System Analysis
ORR Structured Systems Development
PAGE-JONES Practical Guide to Structured Systems Design, 2/E
PETERS Software Design: Methods and Techniques
RIPPS An Implementation Guide to Real-Time Programming
RODGERS UNIX Database Management Systems
RUHL The Programmer's Survival Guide: Career Strategies for Computer Professionals
SCHMITT The OS/2 Programming Environment
SCHLAER AND MELLOR Object-Oriented Systems Analysis: Modeling the World in Data
SHILLER Software Excellence
THOMSETT People and Project Management
TOIGO Disaster Recovery Planning: Managing Risk and Catastrophe in Information Systems
VESELY Strategic Data Management: The Key to Corporate Competitiveness
WARD Systems Development Without Pain: A User's Guide to Modeling Organizational Patterns
WARD AND MELLOR Structured Development for Real-Time Systems. Volumes I, II, and III
WEAVER Using the Structured Techniques: A Case Study
WEINBERG Structured Analysis
YOURDON Classics in Software Engineering
YOURDON Managing the Structured Techniques, 4/E
YOURDON Managing the System Life Cycle, 2/E
YOURDON Modern Structured Analysis
YOURDON Structured Walkthroughs, 4/E
YOURDON Techniques of Program Structure and Design
YOURDON Writing of the Revolution: Selected Readings on Software Engineering

SAA: A Guide to Implementing

IBM's Systems Application Architecture

Being an Exposition on the Concepts of Common User Access, Common Programming Interface, Common Communications Support, and Common Applications, and Their Relation To Software Quality and Productivity, Strategic Systems Planning, Software Architectures, Cooperative Processing, Distributed Processing, Client-Server Processing, Software Engineering, Computer Aided Software Engineering, Application Development Environments, Software Methodologies, Structured Design, Object Oriented Design, Computer Hardware Planning, Programmable Workstations, Host Processors, Computer Networks, and Associated Topics

Jerrold M. Grochow

YOURDON PRESS
Prentice Hall Building
Englewood Cliffs, New Jersey 07632

Library of Congress Cataloging-in-Publication Data

Grochow, Jerrold M.
SAA : a guide to implementing IBM's systems application architecture / Jerrold M. Grochow.
p. cm.
Includes bibliographical references and index.
ISBN 0-13-785759-4
1. IBM computers. 2. Computer software. 3. Computer architecture. 4. OfficeVision (Computer program) I. Title.
QA76.8.I1015G76 1991
004.2'525--dc20 90-7999
CIP

Editorial/production supervision: Karen Bernhaut
Cover design: Wanda Lubelska
Manufacturing buyer: Kelly Behr/Susan Brunke

Published by Prentice-Hall, Inc.
A division of Simon & Schuster
Englewood Cliffs, New Jersey 07632

The publisher offers discounts on this book when ordered in bulk quantities. For more information, write:

Special Sales/College Marketing
Prentice-Hall, Inc.
College Technical and Reference Division
Englewood Cliffs, New Jersey 07632

Printed in the United States of America

10 9 8 7 6 5 4 3 2

ISBN 0-13-785759-4

Prentice-Hall International (UK) Limited, *London*
Prentice-Hall of Australia Pty. Limited, *Sydney*
Prentice-Hall Canada Inc., *Toronto*
Prentice-Hall Hispanoamericana, S.A., *Mexico*
Prentice-Hall of India Private Limited, *New Delhi*
Prentice-Hall of Japan, Inc., *Tokyo*
Simon & Schuster Asia Pte. Ltd., *Singapore*
Editora Prentice-Hall do Brasil, Ltda., *Rio de Janeiro*

To Louise, Rebecca, and Joshua

Overview

Contents

List of Figures

Foreword

IBM's Systems Application Architecture (SAA), although introduced only three and a half years ago, has generated exceptional interest in the data processing community. Computer users see it as a way to make their tasks easier. Application developers recognize its potential for dramatically improving their productivity. And information systems managers know that SAA can effectively and efficiently link their diverse computer systems. Yet the broad scope of SAA which makes possible its potential for resolving many of the most difficult computing challenges can also make it difficult to understand. That's why I welcome this outstanding book.

Jerry Grochow, as an expert in software development, is eminently qualified to discuss both the technical and managerial aspects of SAA. But, equally important, he can write about them in a way that is clear to a broad-based audience. So *SAA: A Guide to Implementing IBM's Systems Applications Architecture* will be useful to many; software providers, software implementers, and software users alike.

For many readers, the key word in the title of this book will be "implementing." As a growing number of computer users experience the benefits of SAA applications, there will be increasing demand for SAA platforms. This book will be a valuable guide to the successful implementation of SAA applications on these platforms. It provides many insights into the wide range of topics that will be the province of the SAA implementer.

No one company can by itself satisfy the demand for all SAA solutions. IBM has formed business partnerships with several leading companies, such as American Management Systems, Inc., that are offering their own SAA-based solutions. As AMS's Vice President, Corporate Technology, Jerry exemplifies with this book the kind of partnership needed to move the data processing industry forward. Everyone with an interest in the evolution and progress of the industry can benefit from reading it.

Earl Wheeler
IBM Senior Vice President
and General Manager
Programming Systems
IBM Corporation
Purchase, N.Y.

Preface (Revised for Second Printing)

IBM announced Systems Application Architecture on St. Patrick's Day, March 17, 1987. On April 22, after having read that announcement about a dozen times (it was the only document available from IBM at the time) and having digested every news article and study available, I was with Ivan Selin, then Chairman of AMS, on my way to Atlanta to visit with the top SAA marketing executives. This was the beginning of what, so far, has been a three year effort to understand SAA from both technical and managerial points of view, to find out what it means for the thousands of computer professionals and computer users who will need to know something about the "common view."

We knew then that SAA was important to us as software developers, although how far reaching it would be remained to be seen. We knew that it would have profound impacts on computer users, but how soon was uncertain. What we didn't anticipate is how much uncertainty, misunderstanding, and general confusion there would be about how to react to what IBM was doing. Hence, the reason for this book.

SAA: A Guide to Implementing IBM's Systems Application Architecture is a book written for multiple audiences. Whether you consider yourself a part of the professional data processing community or view the computer as simply a tool to use in performing your job, you will find something of interest. It will provide you with a balanced discussion of technical and managerial perspectives on IBM's Systems Application Architecture and the impact it will have on your organization. The primary objective is to help you to formulate a strategy for dealing with that impact.

What follows is divided into two parts. The first answers the question "What is SAA?" at a mid-technical level. This part of the book can be viewed as an interpretive summary of the SAA concepts presented in the IBM manuals that make up the SAA "bible." Chapters on OfficeVision and AD/Cycle address these important adjuncts of the SAA concept.

The second part of the book deals with the wide range of issues that must be addressed in formulating an "enterprise" computing strategy. This part offers practical help in getting you beyond the jargon of "common user access" and "cooperative processing" and "common programming interfaces." Its chapters are intended for both technical and managerial readers, although some sections contain details that can be skipped by the less technical person.

On September 5, 1990, IBM announced the System 390 and with it ushered in a new generation of hardware and software for enterprise systems. 140 product announcements were made on that day, including new releases of every major operating system, communications monitor, and database management system in use on IBM's then current System 370 hardware architecture. New software products to make it easier to develop and manage distributed computing sytems were announced. Strategic directions for transaction management and distributed relational data were clarified and expanded. It was a grand set of announcements, all advancing the Systems Application Architecture strategy.

The new hardware and software, with its emphasis on Enterprise Systems Architecture, will make it easier to implement the cooperative and distributed processing approaches underlying the SAA strategy. They will better support the move to an overall "enterprise computing strategy." Their affect will be felt in the systems we will design in 1991 and beyond.

The September 5 announcements, however, change little in the majority of the chapters of this book. Two new CPI services were announced, the Print Interface and the Resource Recovery Interface, along with several products which implement them in selected environments. Additional details were released on how the various database management systems will implement the distributed relational data strategy, although products which provide these features will not be available until late 1991 and beyond. A few new language product announcements were also made, filling some of the holes in the chart of SAA lanaguage availability on SAA systems. And the role of the VSE operating system was expanded so that it becomes almost (but not officially) a participant in SAA. New "SAA applications," particularly SystemView (an AD/Cycle-like approach to providing a broad range of systems management products), will become important in the future.

Product announcements and statements of direction on other SAA topics will be forthcoming from IBM every few months. Each will fill in a little more of the puzzle, each will make the picture a little clearer. And through it all, *SAA: A Guide to IBM's Systems Application Architecture* will continue to serve as a source for increasing your understanding of SAA and all it implies. In time, this book will need to be revised and go to press as a "second edition." For now, IBM's announcements will serve as a continually expanding supplement!

The introduction of SAA by IBM has already had, and will continue to have, a profound effect on the computer industry. While some industry gurus debate the validity of SAA as a standard and its relation to other industry and international standards, this book is not intended to pass judgment on those issues. My two purposes in writing *SAA: A Guide to Implementing IBM's Systems Application Architecture* are to provide a framework for understanding SAA as it exists today and as it is likely to evolve tomorrow, and to provide a guidebook for those of us who have to live with and implement SAA.

A Reader's Guide

In any book of this scope, there will be portions that may be of more interest to one group of readers than another. Without attempting to limit your perusal of the contents, I suggest the sections listed below for the indicated audience:

Senior Management: Ch. 1 (all), 3.1, 6.6, 8.2, 8.3, 8.5, 9.2, 16.2, 17.4.

Information Systems Management: Ch. 1, 2, 3, 6, 8, 9, 10, 12.2, 12.3, 12.4, 14, 15.2, 16, 17.2, 17.3, 17.4.

Application Design Staff: Ch. 1, 3, 4, 6, 7, 9, 10, 11, 12, 15.3, 15.4, 16, 17.

Application Programming Staff: Ch. 1, 4, 10, 11.4, 12.4, 12.6, 15.3, 15.4, 16, 17.

Technical Specialists: Ch. 1, 2, 5, 7, 10, 13, 15, 17.

Application Users: Ch. 1, 6, 16.

Acknowledgments

All book acknowledgments begin (or end) with a disclaimer: "the ultimate responsibility for the contents of this book lies with the author." This is certainly true. Equally true is the statement that "the completion of this work would not have been possible without the contribution of countless others," all of whom deserve acknowledgment here:

To Rick Jensen, Mary Maher, Dick Osterman, and especially Al Atherton, who formed my informal "IBM advisory committee;" and to the many others at IBM who commented on portions of my manuscript.

To Bob Koteen and Jill Williams of IBM who provided access to numerous IBM people and publications, and to their managers for allowing them to spend time in these pursuits.

To Milt Hess of AMS, whose ideas on application architecture helped me to clarify my own (and who read every word at least twice).

To the "first SAA implementation team" at AMS who learned along with me what that means, particularly Todd Ashworth, Stuart Hoffman, Paul Hudecek, Mark Schroeder, and especially Robert Lindsay for his detailed discussions of the technology underlying SAA.

To my many friends and associates who rendered advice, support, and critical reviews of my work: John Baker, Donna Deeley, Sue Hanley, Bill Inmon, Trish Newton, Mark Raiffa, Steve Ranney, Marie Taylor, Tim Taylor, and Ed Ward (AMS); and Ben Shneiderman (Univ. of Maryland).

To Fred Forman, Pat Gross, and Charles Rossotti for their support throughout the writing of this book, and for creating an atmosphere at AMS that fosters the cooperative exploration of new ideas; and to Ivan Selin, for starting the several chains of events that led me to my current position and to authoring this book.

To my wife, Louise, and children, Rebecca and Joshua, for learning to do without me on so many nights and weekends. And of course, to my parents, for sending me to summer school to learn about computers and for other things too numerous to mention.

J.M.G., Washington, D.C.

Introduction

On March 17, 1987, IBM made a strategic announcement whose impact is only now beginning to be understood. Systems Application Architecture, SAA, is the IBM blueprint for future software development - not only for IBM itself, but for any organization using or interacting with IBM computers. While the cynics will say that SAA is simply a necessary competitive response by IBM, it is clearly a broader strategy. It is an attempt by the world's largest computer manufacturer to bring order to the chaotic world of computer software and software development.

Not since the introduction of the System/360 computer series in 1964 has there been such a coordinated effort from IBM to change the face of the computing landscape. The difference this time is that IBM is attacking the software environment rather than hardware. In the three years since the first announcements, IBM has displayed the broad scope of the SAA plan.

A grand scheme for standardizing applications software, SAA addresses software development, use, and maintenance across IBM's major computer hardware and operating systems. It lays out strategies for improving the quality of computer systems as seen by all who come in contact with them, whether as software engineers or as users of their wares. It is intended to improve the productivity of those same practitioners and users by standardizing software internals and externals. And, it is intended to be universally applicable, whether you are dealing with the smallest application on a single personal computer or the largest using all the facilities of multiple interconnected computing behemoths.

This book addresses questions that are being asked in every organization - corporate and governmental, large and small, software developer and software user - about how to respond to SAA. SAA is more than a series of rules to be followed by software developers, more than a specification of how applications should look and feel to computer users, more than a definition of allowable software constructs and architecture. SAA defines a strategy for delivering computing power that will affect every aspect of the organization, from its day-to-day functioning to its basic structure.

Systems Application Architecture provides us with the outline of a plan for twenty-first century computing. While there are other such strategies under development at other computer manufacturers and in industry consortia, none will have as great an impact on as large a body of computer users and developers. The issues dealt with in this book provide just a glimpse of the future that implies.

Part I: What is SAA?

Today, IBM announces IBM Systems Application Architecture, a collection of selected software interfaces, conventions and protocols that will be published in 1987. IBM Systems Application Architecture will be the framework for development of consistent applications across the future offerings of the major IBM computing environments -- System/370, System/3X and Personal Computer.

"IBM Systems Application Architecture,"
IBM Programming Announcement 287-088, March 17, 1987

This announcement is not about a specific product, but rather a pervasive software architecture that underlies the commitment to provide, in an evolutionary way, cross-systems consistency across a broad spectrum of hardware, architecture, and operating systems environments. It is a software-based approach to present the breadth of IBM's product line to its customers as a family of software systems - a family that will provide enterprise-wide solutions to business computing problems.

"Introduction to Systems Application Architecture," E.F. Wheeler and A.G. Ganek,
IBM Systems Journal, Vol. 27, No. 3, 1988

1. A Common Strategy

Ay madam, it is common.
Wm. Shakespeare, Hamlet, Act I, Scene 2

The branch banking officer in Ellicott City looks at her computer screen. The display is somewhat like her desk, with a clock, a calculator, a telephone, an "in box," an "out box," and several folders and papers (see Figure I.1). Using a hand-held pointing device (a "mouse"), she selects the in box to begin her day's work.

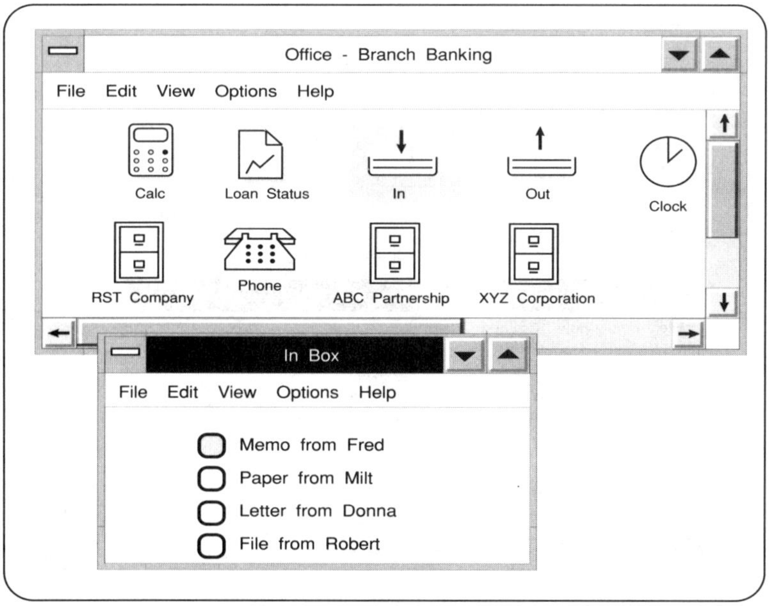

Figure I.1 The Computer User's "Desktop"

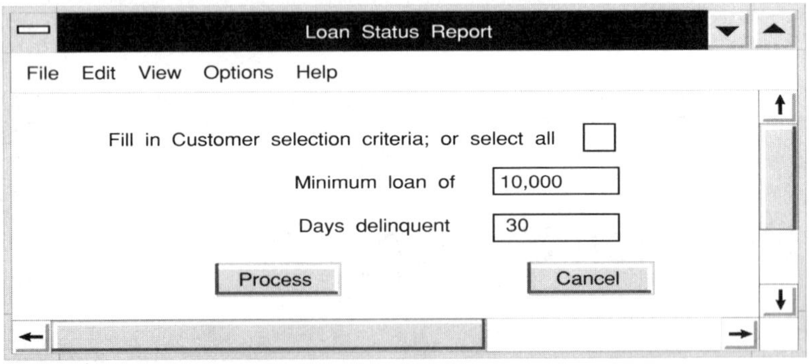

Figure I.2 Database Query Selection Window

The display shows several items in the in box. After selecting and reading the memo from her boss in Baltimore, she realizes that her latest management summary needs to be updated with outstanding loan balances for her key customers. Selecting the "report" labeled "Loan Status," she is presented with a screen asking which loans she wants to update (Figure I.2). She fills in the smallest balance she is interested in and is presented with a list of all customers whose loans exceed that amount.

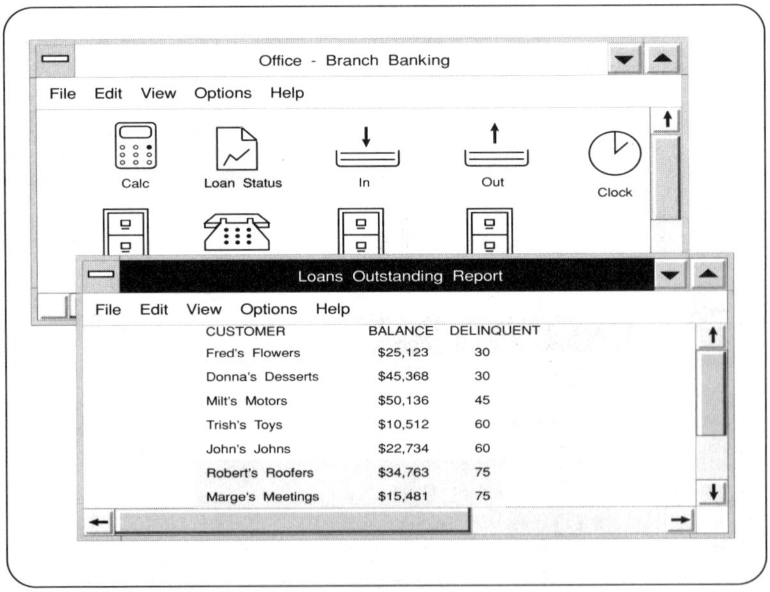

Figure I.3 Direct Movement of Information

Using the mouse, she highlights the information on the screen that she wants to present to her boss (see Figure I.3) and points to a memo pad. She then adds a brief message and "moves" the memo to her out box, knowing it will automatically appear in her boss's in box.

This scenario is an example of the computer environment that you can create today using software which implements IBM's Systems Application Architecture. The appearance of the screen and the way in which the user interacts with the computer are the visible parts of the SAA influence. But SAA is also present in an "invisible" way:

- The applications running on the banking officer's personal computer are operating in concert with applications running on a 3090 mainframe computer hundreds of miles away (to retrieve the loan data she needs).

- She is using a PS/2 on a Token Ring Network while her boss's non-programmable terminal is directly connected to an AS/400.

- All the machines, mainframe, mini-, and personal, are connected via a complex nationwide network.

- Both she and her boss communicate with each other via the same totally familiar, intuitive mechanism (the in box/out box metaphor).

Systems Application Architecture is a set of standards, development approaches, and software interfaces that together define a strategy for system design and development. As shown in the example above, implementation of the SAA strategy will result in application software that is readily understandable to the computer user. System developers following SAA standards and using SAA compliant interfaces will be able to create applications that effectively use multiple hardware environments.

SAA is IBM's vision of how to create software that retains essential common elements regardless of the hardware platform it operates on or the specific functions it addresses. It forces us to re-think the way in which users will interface with computer applications. It encourages us to establish an "enterprise" view of computing. And, it gives us the underlying software, the "enabling" programs and the control programs, to do this.

1.1 Simple Concept, Difficult Implementation

SAA is really a simple concept: standardize the interface between users and applications, between programmers and computers, and among programs that communicate with each other. In so doing, you will reduce the complexity of software and of its use.

The SAA concepts and definitions are described in a large number of IBM manuals (see References section), 20 at last count. These constitute the SAA "bible." The concepts and the definitions would not be much good, however, without software that implemented them. This is where IBM's products for system control (operating systems), communication (teleprocessing monitors, etc.), and application enabling (language compilers, database managers, etc.) come in. Specific products "deliver" the SAA standard definition in each IBM operating environment. Figure I.4 gives two examples of how the SAA concepts, definitions, and delivery mechanisms relate. [IBM has a single order number for a library of the 20 SAA manuals (SBOF-1240, as listed in the References).]

	Example 1: Languages	**Example 2**: User interface
SAA Concept	Common language definitions across all operating environments	Create consistent windowed application look
SAA Definition	Common Programming Interface COBOL Reference	Advanced Common User Access Design Guide
SAA Delivery Mechanism	COBOL/2 Compiler; COBOL/400 Compiler; VS COBOL II Compiler	Presentation Manager in OS/2 EE

Figure I.4 Example of SAA Concept, Definition, and Delivery Mechanisms

As you will see in later sections of this book, implementing such a straightforward, obviously useful concept was and is a massive undertaking for IBM. The number of applications enabling and system control software products that have to be modified is in the hundreds. The number of people involved is in the thousands. Once they have done their work, you still have to do yours to implement SAA in your organization.

1.2 The Four Components of SAA

There are four primary components in the SAA strategy. Three of these address the user, programming, and communications interfaces of systems. The fourth is the applications that follow and use the first three.

- User interface (Common User Access)

  CUA is a set of standards for designing what users see and how they interact with systems. Several IBM products provide facilities for implementing CUA-conforming applications.

- Developer tools and strategies (Common Programming Interface)

  CPI defines the languages and system interfaces that programmers should use. Multiple IBM and other vendor products implement the CPI. AD/Cycle is a set of software development tools that will assist in developing applications which use the CPI.

- Communications support for systems operating on diverse hardware (Common Communications Support)

CCS describes the components of a communications model for developing distributed and cooperative applications running on different hardware environments. Various IBM and other vendor products implement CCS.

Applications that follow the SAA standards and use SAA standard software interfaces are called "SAA Applications" and are the fourth component of the SAA strategy. IBM's first common application offering is OfficeVision. Independent software vendors and user organizations are also being encouraged to develop applications that use a consistent architecture based on the components of SAA.

[CUA, CPI, and CCS are a few of the many abbreviations you will see in this book. See the Abbreviations Glossary for a compendium.]

1.3 Common User Understanding

1.3.1 The Need for a Consistent Interface

One of the factors that has made the Macintosh computer successful is that the way in which users interact with the machine is common across many applications. The familiar action bar, pull-down menus, use of the mouse, and pop-up messages are all part of a widely followed standard for creating easy-to-use software.

Once you have mastered the essentials of this environment, you have also learned to use basic functions of every software application you will ever come across. Whether you are trying to open or save a file of data, change the type font for a printer, or get further information about how some function is provided ("help"), you can invoke these capabilities in exactly the same way regardless of the specific piece of software you are using.

This level of common functioning has generally been missing from software developed for IBM computers, mainframe as well as mini- and personal computers. Although the reasons for this are many, users and developers alike have suffered. In the past, the software industry has had a very low level of receptivity to standards (COBOL and UNIX notwithstanding). However, the success of the Macintosh has shown the significant leverage that adherence to user interface standards can provide.

```
File Spreadsheet Document Graph Comm Print Settings Quit
```

Figure I.5 Lotus Command Line

Some software vendors have already made attempts at standardizing the user view of their products. For example, millions of personal computer users are familiar with the "Lotus command line," a way of displaying the available software functions in a row across the top of the screen (Figure I.5). Each can be accessed by typing its first letter or by moving a highlighted cursor to the appropriate word and pressing "enter" on the keyboard. This level of interface standardization rarely extends even to the complete line of software from a single vendor (Lotus being a rare exception), let alone multiple vendors.

At the next level of interaction, however, even Lotus's standards sometimes break down. All of Lotus's products provide a "help" screen when the user presses the "F1" key (in the PC-compatible environment at least), but require different keystrokes to print a document. [After nine years of software development for PC-DOS, "help" and "F1" have become almost synonymous. WordPerfect,. the number one word processing package, may be the single exception to this rule - it uses "F3".]

An example cited in Hartson and Hix's article on "Human-Computer Interface Development" makes the same point by quoting from a user manual for a multi-function office product:

> *The comma key on the minikeypad is the HELP key for forms. While in the ABC-Style Editor and Calendar Management, use PF2 for HELP; use "H" for HELP while in the Desk Calculator; use the "GOLD" key plus an "H" key while using the XYZ-Style Editor.... By the way, if you need help creating a document, it is better to be in the Word Processing Menu when you press HELP rather than in the main menu... It is a good idea to remember the location and purpose of each key mentioned above.*

With four possible ways of getting help, it is no wonder that users are confused.

Worse still, some vendors pride themselves on providing software which is cosmetically different from others of similar function in order to distinguish themselves in a crowded market (most often with the claim that their "user interface" is somehow better than the others). Unfortunately, this often means that the hapless user has to re-learn basic command sequences in order to use two different but related applications.

1.3.2 The SAA Solution: Common User Access

SAA attempts to remedy the absence of a standard user interface by defining, in great detail, how an application should present itself to a computer user and how that user should be able to interact with the application. This component of the SAA strategy is called Common User Access, CUA.

CUA is described in two publicly available "interface design guides." They discuss the principles of human-computer interaction and how these are translated into a set of specific rules for presentation of information and interaction with computer functions. They distinguish interface features for different types of applications as well as for different terminal and workstation hardware. In sum, they provide the rules to follow in creating consistent, easy-to-use application software for IBM computers.

The specifics of CUA can be debated *ad infinitum* (why does a control button have to be a rounded rectangle?). The important point is that IBM's Common User Access is written down, publicly available, and supported by systems software that provides help in adhering to its rules.

Improved user understanding of computer applications is the primary goal of SAA Common User Access. At IBM's May 16, 1989, SAA press conference at its New York headquarters, over a dozen independent software vendors (ISVs) showed versions of their software that comply with CUA. Even though the applications ranged from spreadsheets to accounting systems to development tools, the overall impression was that they all "looked" the same. As consultants and members of the press toured the demonstration area, they saw that these applications not only looked the same, but that they had many functions in common and that almost every user interaction was performed in the same way. They saw CUA in action.

1.4 Common Developer Understanding

One of the hardest jobs in computer practice is maintaining and enhancing existing software. This is such a difficult task because the only effective way to understand how a system works is to laboriously study the program code (documentation is almost always nonexistent, incomplete, or out of date). And the reason this is so hard is that very few systems have programs that exploit uniform structures and interfaces that would be commonly understood.

Just as in the case of a common user interface, there have been attempts at creating a common structure and form for computer programs. They have either been at a very high level, such as the various techniques for creating "modular" programs, or they have been so specific that they are only applicable to single organizations or even single application systems (each perhaps encompassing multiple functions). Even "structured programming," which is now widely and generally followed (e.g. creating self-contained blocks of code, often nested within other blocks, having only a single entry and exit), has not done enough to make the large systems of programs we currently develop accessible to anyone besides the original programmers.

SAA directly addresses the ability of application developers and maintainers to create and enhance complex systems of programs by defining a Common Programming Interface and by promoting "object-oriented" development.

1.4.1 The SAA Common Programming Interface

The SAA Common Programming Interface (CPI) is a collection of programming languages and application interfaces to system control and application enabling software. Portions of the CPI are standard definitions of programming languages (COBOL, FORTRAN, C, RPG, PL/I, REXX) which IBM intends to maintain on all of the hardware and operating systems defined to be part of SAA. Other components, like the Presentation Interface and the Communications Interface, represent new systems software that IBM is providing as part of the SAA strategy. Still others, such as the Database Interface and the Query Interface, are special purpose language constructs which can be used in conjunction with other programs. The CPI defines syntax and semantics for all these languages and interfaces; numerous IBM system control and application enabling products implement ("deliver") them on a wide range of hardware.

By using the software products that deliver the CPI, that is, the language compilers and interface routines, programmers will more easily be able to create applications with common form and structure. The SAA CPI does *not* address "high level" methodology issues, however, such as rules for creating modular programs or establishing object hierarchies. It remains with the information systems organization to deal with these issues directly.

The CPI is a necessary step toward creation of common developer understanding of program structure and purpose. Definitions in the SAA CPI will create a common body of knowledge which developers can learn once and use repeatedly in different situations. It is this "reuse" that is key to improving productivity in software development.

1.4.2 Object-Oriented Environment

Object-oriented programming has received much publicity in the past several years as a new software development paradigm. The basic concept of object-oriented programming is to create "objects," i.e., programs which surround ("encapsulate") data and provide the only access point to that data. These programming objects provide the interfaces (called "methods") for accessing the data, e.g. adding values, changing, deleting, etc. Objects are grouped into object hierarchies, with subsidiary objects "inheriting" the methods of the higher level objects. In an object-oriented system, objects send messages to other objects (with some help from the operating system or environment), which then respond when their work is complete. [Chapter 10 includes a primer on object-oriented concepts.]

Key benefits of object orientation are:

- significant gains in programmer productivity and software quality through software reuse;

- improved maintainability due to procedure and data encapsulation (sometimes called "information hiding").

IBM is not the first to jump on the object-oriented bandwagon ("OOB"), but its movement in this direction will be very important. By providing a large number of common "programming objects," for example in the form of OS/2 Presentation Manager routines and Repository Manager/MVS Object Services, IBM is giving programmers an opportunity to learn and use these techniques. While this will not magically turn everyone to an object-oriented approach, it will help to make programs more understandable and programmers more productive.

1.4.3 Relationship of CPI and CUA

The language compilers and operating system interface routines that implement ("deliver") the CPI are used to develop applications that conform to Common User Access. For example, the Presentation Interface and the Dialog Interface define subroutine calls ("call interfaces") that allow you to implement CUA-conforming applications. In OS/2, the Presentation Manager and the Dialog Manager are the software products which implement the Presentation and Dialog elements of the CPI, respectively. These two "enabling software" products can be used to implement applications which follow the rules of CUA, as defined in the CUA specification manuals. Figure I.6 depicts these relationships.

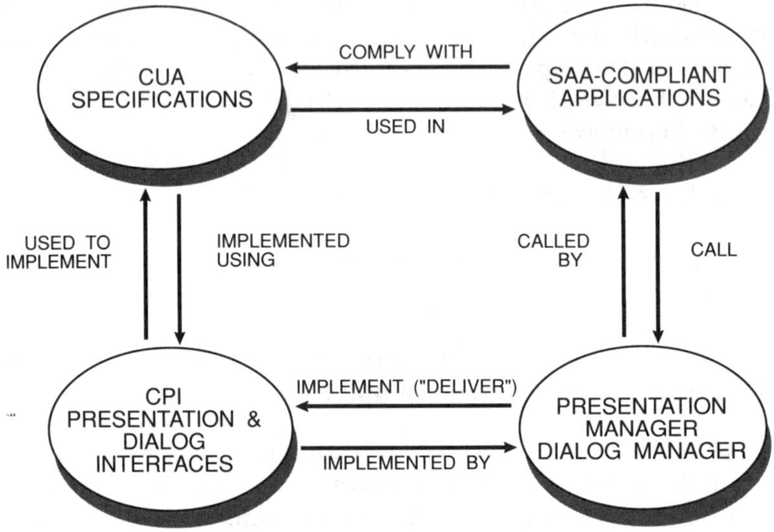

Figure I.6 Relationship Between CUA and CPI

1.5 Distributed Computing Strategy

SAA advances the idea of partitioning applications among multiple computers on a network to make more effective use of those computers. Systems that distribute display, functions, and databases among more than one computer are generically called "distributed systems." Different forms of distributed systems are often given different names: cooperative processing, distributed processing, client-server architecture, distributed database. Much of IBM's literature on SAA refers to "cooperative processing." Under any of its guises, distributed systems are clearly key to SAA and, more broadly, to the enterprise computing strategy.

The idea that not all of an application and its data need reside on a single computer has been around for a long time. In fact, most modern mainframe computer "systems" already engage in a form of distributed processing, albeit within the confines of the central computer room. When a channel "computer" executes an input/output program that is coordinated with the main program running on the central processor, these two computer programs form a "distributed processing system." Admittedly, application users and programmers do not usually pay any attention to this level of processing (nor do they necessarily realize that it is happening), but that is just the point. The highest form of distributed processing should be transparent. The applications should appear to users to be totally local to their workstations. For the most part, they should appear that way to the programmers who program them as well.

1.5.1 Variations on a Theme

In the three years since SAA was introduced, much has been written about distributed and cooperative processing; much of it is wrong. Many writers have portrayed cooperative processing as a more complex topic than it needs to be. IBM is trying to draw a distinction between the terms "cooperative processing" and "distributed processing," a distinction that is often lost.

An application can be considered a distributed processing application if it has the following characteristics:

- It involves two or more programs.
- It involves two or more computers.
- The programs running on the different computers know of and expect interaction with their "cooperating" counterparts.

This definition does not say anything specific about databases, user interfaces, processing functions, or any other aspects of what the programs do. It is a general definition of an application system designed to be distributed across multiple computers. The goal of distributing systems in this way is to maximize the effective use of human and computer resources in the broadest sense.

IBM has tried to draw a distinction between the general term "distributed processing" and a more specific use of "cooperative processing." In the special issue of the IBM Systems Journal on SAA (see References), "cooperative processing" was defined in the lead article by Earl Wheeler and Alan Ganek:

> *In cooperative processing, intelligent workstations are used in conjunction with host systems in an integrated way to provide the end user with the advantages of both personal and host-based computing. Cooperative processing allows the user to have a single, seamless view of the function of an application, whereas, in fact, the implementation is split between the workstations and the host.*

"Introduction to Systems Application Architecture," E.F. Wheeler and A.G. Ganek, IBM Systems Journal, Vol. 27, No. 3, 1988.

In another article in the same issue, other authors took a broader position:

Cooperative processing applications are those for which portions of the application or its services are executed in more than one processor. The designer's objective should be to use each processor for the operation it performs best.

"Designing SAA applications and user interfaces," W.P. Dunfee et al, Ibid.

This definition is actually closer to the definition of *distributed processing* given by Wheeler and Ganek, i.e., "distribution of functions across multiple host systems as well as intelligent workstations." More recent IBM literature has been following the Wheeler and Ganek definitions, using the term "cooperative processing" to refer specifically to distributed processing between workstations and hosts.

Until the definition debate is settled, the terms cooperative processing and distributed processing will be used more or less interchangeably. In this book, other authors' use is followed in quotations and references.

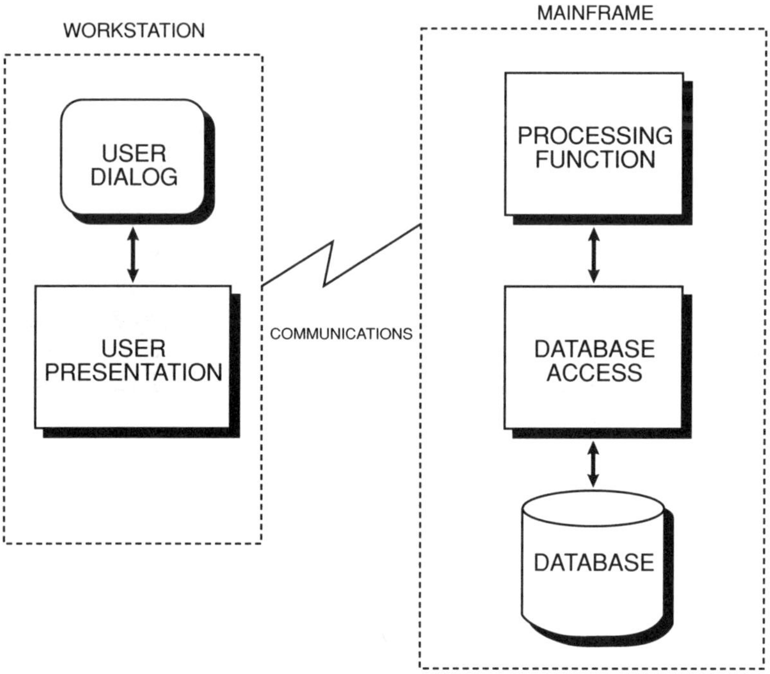

Figure I.7 Distributed User Interface

An example of cooperative processing in its simplest form involves a mainframe computer and a programmable workstation. An airline crew scheduling application, for example, is divided into three parts: access to a large database of crew and flight information, complex mathematical processing to develop a master schedule, and user presentation functions to display a particular crew schedule. The first two functions would be performed on a large mainframe (perhaps with vector processing capabilities) with the user presentation programs executing on each user's programmable workstation. Figure I.7 shows such a situation.

In this case, the system was split to use the power of two different types of processors, a large mainframe and graphical workstations. Other examples of cooperative processing may be created for a variety of other reasons, e.g. security of data, response time to users, sharing of expensive resources.

The distributed nature of an application system may be totally transparent to both user and programmer, or it may exhibit different degrees of transparency to each. A workstation user may have to access a mainframe database specifically (by including the location of the database in the request), but may not have to be concerned with different underlying access mechanisms. A programmer may be able to issue "remote procedure calls" without worrying about where or how the remote procedure is actually executed, or may have to set up a programming dialog explicitly with a similarly configured program on the cooperating system.

Regardless of the degree of transparency or the number of computers involved, distributed and cooperative processing brings together the resources of different computers to provide more effective computer systems. SAA recognizes the need to provide a robust set of communications capabilities to do this and defines them as its Common Communications Support component.

1.5.2 Common Communications Support in SAA

Common Communications Support (CCS) defines the protocols for implementing cooperative processing applications. It also deals with more mundane tasks of all types of teleprocessing and deals with communications between and among computers, peripherals, and programs.

CCS defines the protocols necessary for sending information

- from a processor to a printer;
- from a word processing program on one type of computer to a different word processing program on another;
- from a user interface program on a workstation to a program on a mainframe, mini-computer, or other workstation;
- from one computer to another across a network.

It defines high level protocols for applications to talk to each other and low level protocols for the bit streams sent between two hardware devices. The software that implements CCS allows you to implement all types of teleprocessing applications in creating a cooperative processing environment.

CCS does not define a complete communications model (as the Open Systems Interconnection Model of the International Standards Organization attempts to do). It includes a diverse set of components based largely on IBM's existing Systems Network Architecture (various ISO protocols have been added as well). Its protocols and standards do, however, fall within a *consistent* model of the communications process, illustrating different levels of communication between devices, networks, systems, and applications, and how they interact.

1.5.3 Relation of CCS and CPI

As with other elements of the SAA strategy, Common Communications Support consists of concepts and definitions, but needs also to be studied in terms of the products that implement them. CCS is delivered by a wide variety of IBM products. Some of these are used directly in developing cooperative processing applications. Some are used by other IBM products so that their use is hidden from the application programmer.

For example, VM/CMS includes a set of subroutine calls which can be used by application programmers to develop cooperating programs. These subroutines implement LU6.2 "program-to-program" communication defined in CCS. In doing so, these subroutines also implement the Communications Interface of the CPI (sometimes abbreviated as CPIC). An application would be using these subroutines indirectly by issuing an SQL statement for a database on a remote system. The Remote Relational Access Support facility in SQL/DS creates the same type of program-to-program communication to fulfill the SQL request. Figure I.8 shows these relationships among components of SAA and software which uses them.

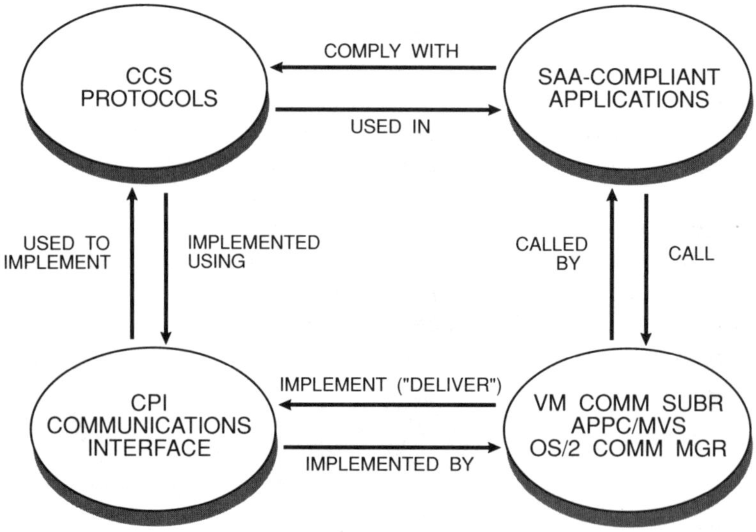

Figure I.8 Relationship Between CCS and CPI

1.6 Enterprise Computing Strategy

With the introduction of SAA, IBM hopes to convince organizations to develop an "enterprise computing strategy" that will encompass all computing resources in the organization. This strategy will define a role for all hardware platforms, whether at the personal, departmental, or organizational level. It will encourage the development of "enterprise models," overall descriptions of the data and function of the organization. In turn, this will foster more effective use of computing resources by expanding the concept of application systems to span hardware and software environments, utilizing those most appropriate to the tasks at hand.

1.6.1 Enterprise Applications

The creation of an enterprise computing strategy (rather than a departmental or other sub-unit strategy) requires cooperation among systems at all levels. It is not so much that the same application programs will actually run on separate computers at the personal, departmental, and organizational level, but rather that compatible, cooperating components of a system will operate at each level. These applications, following CUA and using CPI and CCS, will be the "SAA Applications." Some will be developed by IBM, some by independent software vendors, and some by organizations for their own use.

For example, a large corporation or government agency requires a hierarchy of accounting systems to function effectively (see Figure I.9). At the organization-wide level, managers need to know overall financial performance and have the ability to find out, if necessary, more detailed information. At the individual project level, managers need to know who was working on what for how long and at what cost. Different systems may be required to provide each manager with the specific information needed, but those systems must be able to communicate with each other if auditability and accountability are to be maintained.

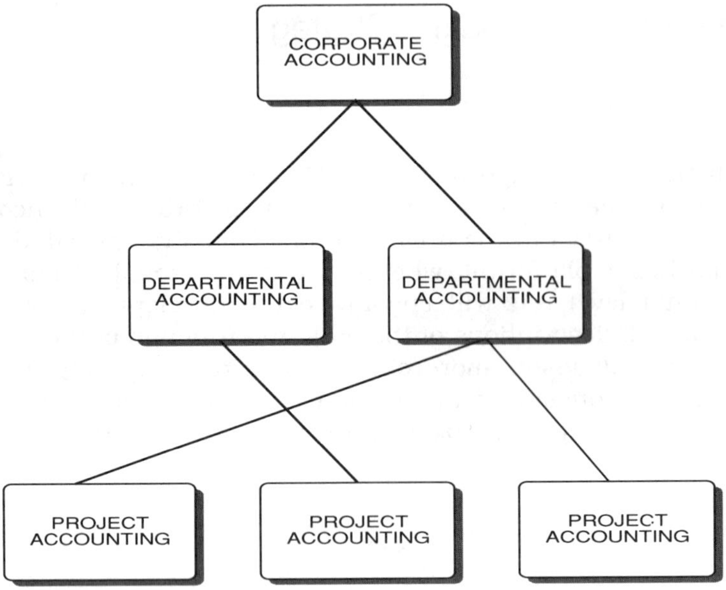

Figure I.9 Multiple Coordinated Applications

1.6.2 Enterprise Data

In the same example, there are some types of information that must be maintained centrally but used throughout the enterprise. Charts of accounts, tables of organization, and personnel information are generally controlled by central departments but must be used consistently in all systems, whether developed for the personal use of a project manager or for the corporate accounting department.

The enterprise computing strategy will define which kinds of data are central to the operation of the organization and which are local. Enterprise data models, at various levels of scope and detail, will be created as a key step in developing this strategy. SAA Applications will provide access to data described in the model, based on users' needs. Regardless of where or how data may be stored, SAA Applications will provide appropriate access. This too is part of the enterprise computing strategy.

1.6.3 An Approach to Application Portability

Cooperative processing is concerned with application systems that are split among different computers. Another aspect of the SAA strategy, however, is the ability to operate the *same* application system on different hardware platforms without reprogramming. No longer a major theme in the SAA literature, application portability is enhanced by the SAA strategy and the IBM software products that implement it.

For those parts of the CPI available in all the SAA environments, applications will be source code compatible regardless of the platform they may have been developed for originally. Application programmers are already getting a taste of this capability when they use the COBOL/2 compiler on the PS/2. Their programs will also compile using VS COBOL II under MVS and VM, although they may still need minor changes to operate consistently. Not only does this signal future operational portability, but also the creation of "cross system" development environments. [Chapter 15 discusses this topic in more detail.]

1.7 Implementation

A set of standards that is not followed is useless. IBM is working toward the day when all of its software conforms to the SAA CPI and allows developers to implement distributed applications that follow CUA. In the meantime, some IBM system control and enabling software follows the SAA definitions and some does not. In the following chapters, several tables show the state of implementation as of mid-1990. Each announcement of a new release of software brings IBM closer to its goal of institutionalizing SAA into all it does.

1.7.1 SAA Evolution

The four basic components of SAA were outlined in March 1987. Details were sketchy and many constituent parts were ignored. SAA interfaces have generally not been announced until some of the software to implement them was in progress within IBM (with availability typically no more than two years away). As Figure I.10 shows, new interfaces have been added on a regular basis. This announcement strategy has caused some people to believe that IBM purposely wants to exclude certain environments from SAA and to phase them out. Other people believe that the strategy is to provide every possible interface on every IBM hardware and software operating environment, but that even IBM cannot be everything at once. So far, IBM seems to be taking a very pragmatic view that "what ought to be common should be common." The question is: what ought to be common?

IBM Announcement	Number	Date
Systems Application Architecture	287-088	3/17/87
Communications CPI	287-471	10/20/87
RPG CPI	288-336	6/21/88
Distributed Data Management in CCS	288-336	6/21/88
OSI Protocols in CCS	288-490	9/20/88
Distributed Relational Data CPI	288-545	10/4/88
Expanded Role for the PWS	289-219	5/16/89
New CUA Models (CUA 1989)	289-219	5/16/89
Object Interchange Architectures in CCS	289-219	5/16/89
PL/I CPI	289-456	9/19/89
Repository CPI	289-456	9/19/89
Distributed Relational Data Architectures	290-363	6/26/90

Figure I.10 SAA Announcements

1.7.2 Major SAA Software Announcements

Along with the announcement of SAA interfaces comes the announcement of software products which provide or use those interfaces. In some cases, this software may be completely new (as in the case of Repository Manager), while in others it may be enhanced versions of existing product lines (e.g. CICS and IMS/DC). As time goes on, and as IBM receives feedback from users and independent software developers, priorities are re-assessed and more IBM products are added to the list of SAA enabling and system control products. As new hardware is announced (such as the AS/400), its compatibility with SAA is also discussed. Figure I.11 lists some of the major software and hardware announcements since SAA was introduced.

IBM Announcement	Number	Date
CICS/MVS, IMS/VS DC Participation	287-471	10/20/87
OS/2 Extended Edition	287-100	4/2/87
OS/400	288-336	6/21/88
CICS for VSE Subset	288-456	9/13/88
OfficeVision	289-200	5/16/89
AD/Cycle	289-456	9/19/89

Figure I.11 Additions to SAA Environments and Applications

1.8 The SAA Logo

There have been several versions of the diagram IBM uses to portray SAA. The diagram in Figure I.12 is used on the cover of the manuals in

IBM's SAA Library. It shows the four elements of SAA surrounding the system software which implements them.

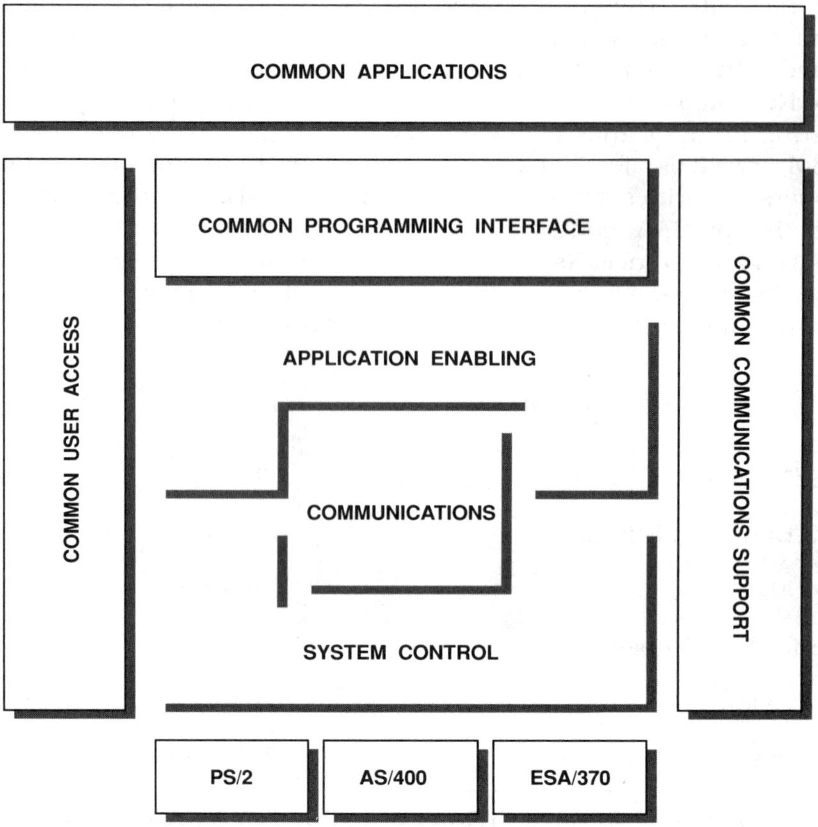

Figure I.12 Systems Application Architecture

The three interface definitions included in SAA (CUA, CPI, and CCS) "surround" the system software:

- "system control" programs (computer operating systems and related programs);

- "application enabling" software (database managers, language compilers, etc.); and

- communications systems (teleprocessing monitors and access methods).

These three types of software provide the foundation for all applications. They will "deliver" the three SAA interface definitions to the application software developer. Due to their interlocking nature, application enabling and system control are shown surrounding a communications tier. Together, these three can be thought of as the "systems tiers" shown in the earlier architecture diagrams.

Common Applications ("SAA Applications")are shown across the top of the diagram to indicate that these applications use software that follows the SAA interface definitions.

The entire structure is shown above boxes representing the three major IBM hardware environments, PS/2, AS/400, and ESA/370. The SAA strategy is that all common elements will be available on all three supported hardware lines.

1.8.1 The "New" SAA Logo

In one of IBM's newer publications, *SAA Applications, A Value Guide*, CPI is shown extending across the entire width of the diagram, as shown in Figure I.13. This portrayal also is on the cover and elsewhere in the IBM Systems Journal describing SAA. In other IBM publications, only Common Applications extend across everything; CPI is narrower and CUA and CCS extend up past its sides, as seen in Figure I.12.

My preference in the "logo wars" is Figure I.13. It is a more appropriate representation of SAA since it is the CPI which "delivers" the capabilities defined in CUA and CCS. Regardless of which you prefer, the general concept is the same. Sooner or later, IBM will have to create a "common logo" to enhance our common understanding.

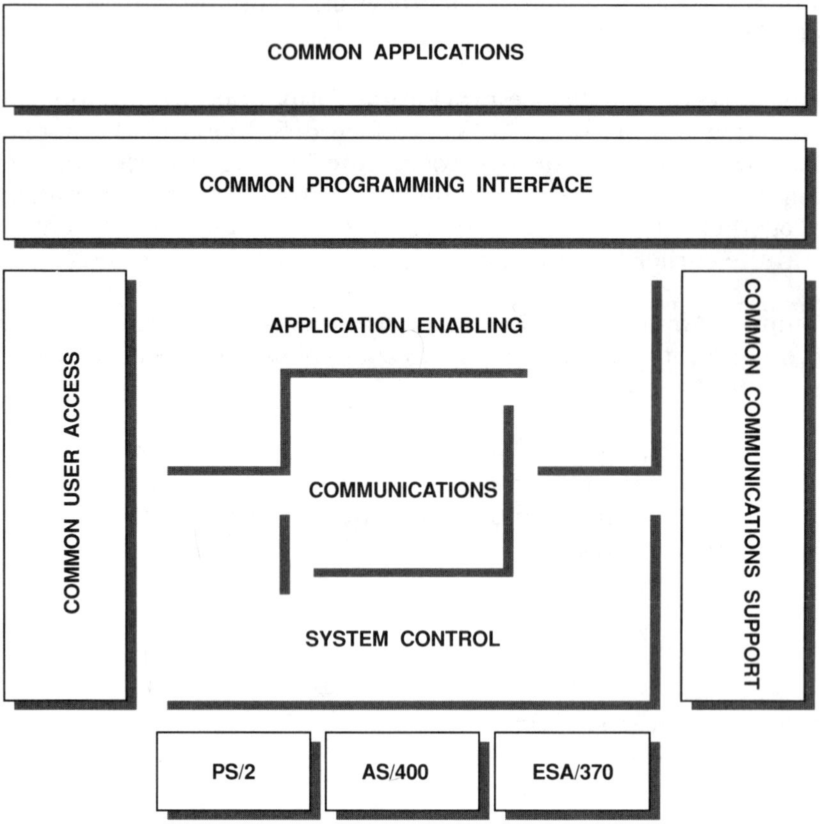

Figure I.13 Systems Application Architecture

1.8.2 Adding Color

Insiders at IBM sometimes refer to the various components of SAA by color, as in "she's in charge of marketing the Red layer." According to Michael Killen, in his book *IBM: The Making of the Common View*, this usage dates back to 1983 when IBM first designated Green, Yellow, Red, and Blue Teams "to help manage 370 software development." In some

SAA publications, the SAA logo and other markings are shown in similar colors:

- CPI and Applications Enabling in green
- CCS and Communications in yellow
- Common Applications in red
- System control and enabling in blue
- CUA in purple
- Hardware environments in black

Whether there is any significance to this use of the spectrum is an open question. [One reviewer of my manuscript speculated on the symbolism in this color scheme: green representing money, red -- anger, blue -- despair, etc. "Color science" may yield some answers yet.]

1.9 The Impact of the Common Strategy

Two points stand out in assessing the impact of SAA: the focus on common user and developer environments, and the strategic importance of treating computing as an enterprise-wide resource.

With the common language definitions and operating system interfaces that IBM is supplying as part of SAA, application developers will be able to focus on the business functions and usability of their software. With the commitment from IBM to deliver common interfaces across the SAA-defined operating environments, developers will be able to run their software on large machines and small, whichever makes the most sense. Implementation of common applications will nurture a common understanding among computer users of how applications work and a common understanding among developers of how applications have been developed. Having a common strategy for software development and use will free us from the time-consuming drudgery of making the same decisions over again every time we develop computer systems, and from learning how to use them again every time we try a new application.

The emphasis in SAA on "enterprise computing" will also signal the increased importance in maintaining a strategic computing plan for the entire organization. Whether the IS function is handled primarily by a central group or is dispersed throughout the organization, common goals and strategies then will be required. With the focus on the workstation (advanced function personal computer) as the window into the enterprise computing network, the domain of the IS organization will be significantly expanded.

Whether these factors will result in the next computer revolution that some are predicting is questionable. But it will certainly result in our taking major steps up the evolutionary scale.

2. Operating Environments

All [environments] are created equal, but some are more equal than others.

With apologies to George Orwell

2.1 SAA Operating Systems

SAA defines common programming and user environments across the major IBM hardware platforms and software operating systems. Operating system environments designated as "SAA environments" are strategic to IBM with the implication that IBM will maintain and enhance them far into the future. As new components are added to the SAA CPI, IBM will provide mechanisms and products that make them available in the SAA environments. Although many parts of the CPI may be available today in other environments (not designated as SAA environments), IBM has been careful not to lock itself into future compatibility.

Figure I.14 lists the major types of computers manufactured by IBM and the operating systems available for them. In general, the newer operating systems are the strategic environments, i.e., OS/2 Extended Edition, OS/400, VM/SP, VM/XA, and MVS/ESA. Older operating systems, such as PC-DOS and VSE, support some components of SAA, but are not designated as "SAA environments." AIX (IBM's version of

UNIX) occupies a separate place in the universe of operating systems, mimicking some aspects of SAA, duplicating others, and ignoring still others.

Operating Systems Hardware	SAA Strategic	Not SAA Strategic
PC, PC-XT	[None]	PC-DOS
PC-AT	OS/2 EE [*]	PC-DOS OS/2 SE [*,S]
PC-AT/370	OS/2 EE [*]	PC-DOS/370 OS/2 SE [*,S]
PS/2 (286-based)	OS/2 EE [*]	PC-DOS OS/2 SE [*,S]
PS/2 (386/486-based)	OS/2 EE	PC-DOS OS/2 SE [*,S] AIX [X]
RT, RS/6000	[None]	AIX [X]
System/36, /38	[None]	OS for S/36,38
AS/400	OS/400	[None]
ESA/370	MVS TSO VM/CMS CICS/MVS [IMS/ESA TM]	CICS/VSE [P] AIX [X]

[*] = OS/2 currently operates on 286-, 386-, and 486-based machines.
[P] = CICS/VSE "participates" as a host-environment via LU6.2; see Section 2.2.
[S] = OS/2 Standard Edition does not provide database and communications facilities.
[X] = AIX is positioned as a parallel environment with some duplication of SAA, some bridges, some differences; see Section 2.3.
[IMS/ESA TM] = New version of IMS/VS DC (see following text).

Figure I.14 SAA Operating Environments

[With Release 3.1 of IMS/ESA, the data communications component was renamed "Transaction Manager" (TM). In this release, the IMS Database Manager is a prerequisite to the use of the Transaction Manager. However, "this product packaging provides a view of the IMS/ESA product structure of the future," i.e., that they will eventually be separately operable. The abbreviations IMS/ESA TM and IMS/TM are used to refer generically to the data communications portion of IMS. The abbreviations IMS/VS DC is used in referring to certain SAA documents which mention this product specifically.]

2.2 Role of "Participating Environments"

The issue of whether an operating system is a full-fledged "SAA environment" or only a partial participant is one of intentions, IBM's intentions, that is. The first version of "Systems Application Architecture: An Overview," listed the SAA environments as:

- *System/370 (TSO/E under MVS/XA, and CMS under VM)*
- *System/3X*
- *Personal Computer (Operating System/2)*

The latest version has expanded and restated the list:

- *TSO/E in Enterprise Systems Architecture/370*
- *CMS in VM/System Product or VM/Extended Architecture*
- *Operating System/400*
- *Operating System/2 Extended Edition*
- *CICS/MVS in Enterprise Systems Architecture/370*

- *IMS/VS Data Communications in Enterprise Systems Architecture/370*

The next version of this manual will probably change IMS/VS DC to IMS/ESA TM, according to IBM's latest terminology for ESA systems.

CICS and IMS/TM are "in"; VSE for System/370, PC-DOS, and OS/2 Standard Edition are not.

2.2.1 CICS and IMS Data Communications in SAA

The initial announcement regarding the role of CICS/MVS and IMS/VS DC (*Programming Announcement 287-471*) seemed clear, but actually served to confuse SAA watchers regarding IBM's intentions. It stated that these operating systems would "participate in Systems Application Architecture as host environments" and that parts of the CPI (C, COBOL, Application Generator, Database, and Communications) would be implemented for them. Since this left out several languages and service interfaces, it was assumed that CICS and IMS were not full-fledged SAA environments like the others.

As the concept of SAA evolved to focus on the workstation as the user interface for all host environments, it became clear that the CPI components listed for CICS/MVS and IMS/VS DC (or IMS/ESA TM) would indeed permit *full* participation in SAA. IBM's primary emphasis is on using mainframe environments such as CICS and IMS/TM as "host" environments for cooperative processing applications. In such applications, some or all of the application function and database access would take place on the host. User interface functions (following Common User Access guidelines, of course) would be provided via programmable workstations (PS/2s) networked with the host via the Common Communications Support protocols. The issue then becomes what environments IBM wants to support in each role in the future.

The net result is that CICS/MVS and IMS/ESA TM are now listed right along with all the other strategic "SAA environments."

[Note that only the data communications portion of IMS is discussed here. With Release 3.1, IMS is separated into Database Manager (DM) and Transaction Manager (TM) (formerly Data Communications, DC) products. IMS Database Manager is not included in the SAA definition.]

2.2.2 VSE's Relationship to SAA

There are more licenses for VSE in use on System/370 machines than there are VM and MVS combined. In spite of this, its inherent limitations as an operating system do not make it an ideal candidate for future complex programming systems and enabling software. Thus the dilemma: how to allow VSE users to bring some of their applications into the SAA fold without committing to bring all of SAA to VSE. The answer, of course, is straightforward -- bring some of the SAA CPI to VSE products.

Programming Announcement 288-456 regarding upgrades to CICS/VSE shows that IBM is taking the pragmatic approach:

> *IBM is identifying a subset of defined SAA programming interfaces for the CICS operating environment under VSE which will provide application portability with CICS/MVS, and the ability to write Common User Access (CUA) conforming applications that use the OS/2 Extended Edition as a front end. It is IBM's intention that the Communications Interface will be implemented by CICS in the VSE environment...*
>
> *Further, IBM is identifying a subset of SAA communication protocols for VSE which will allow the CICS environment under VSE to participate with networks of SAA systems.*

Some components of the Common Programming Interface are also available under VSE. Specifically, upgraded language compilers will allow the use of the appropriate SAA CPI. The Database CPI will be implemented in SQL/DS and applications written using the Application Generator CPI will be executable under VSE.

Contrary to some initial reports, SAA does not sound the death knell for VSE. It provides a path for integration of VSE systems into larger networks and for use of advanced workstation capabilities with VSE systems. What is missing is the long term commitment from IBM to make VSE strategic to its SAA planning. And it has so far shown no signs of doing so. This will not stop the ardent supporters of VSE from continuing their lobbying efforts, and, who knows, they may some day be successful in convincing IBM to bring VSE into the fold.

2.2.3 A Non-participant: PC-DOS

PC-DOS (and the generic MS-DOS) is the operating system used on millions of IBM and IBM-compatible personal computers. It has been called a "first generation" PC operating system, considered by many to be in its waning years. In spite of various attempts to add to its capabilities, it does not provide the flexible, expandable environment necessary to carry the SAA banner into the twenty-first century.

With the addition of Windows Release 3, a sophisticated add-on to the operating system, PC-DOS will remain a viable platform for many types of applications. Many of these applications will function as part of an SAA enterprise network and will themselves comply with the standards set by the SAA strategy. This approach will extend the useful life of DOS and will, for many vendors, mean a dual support burden (OS/2 and DOS with Windows) for a long time.

This still does not make DOS an SAA environment. Its history as the first PC operating system, implemented to support the limited (by today's standards) processing capabilities of the Intel 8088, provides the reasons why this is so.

2.3 Relationship of AIX to SAA

UNIX is a high capability operating system that has been implemented on a wide range of computers of all sizes. It traces its roots as far back as the Multiplexed Time-Sharing and Computing Service (Multics) project at MIT, Bell Labs, and General Electric in the mid-1960s. Multics was being developed to operate on large scale GE hardware (which subsequently became Honeywell's when they bought GE's computer business) in competition with IBM's 360 Model 67. The project was taking too long for some members of the Bell Labs team so they decided to develop a scaled down version to run on mini-computers (at that time, the Digital PDP-7). The operating system they developed was called UNIX ("one of" whatever Multics was "many of"). Obviously, UNIX today is much more mature than OS/2 and provides a rich environment for application development.

AIX is IBM's version of UNIX. It is "the IBM strategic software platform that addresses the fast growing, open-standard UNIX market opportunity" (*AIX Family Definition Overview*). IBM is not attempting to subsume UNIX under SAA. Even though IBM markets AIX for PS/2 (models using the 80386 and 80486 CPU), RS/6000, and 370 lines of computers, it is not designated as an SAA environment. IBM is, however, specifically addressing SAA-to-UNIX connectivity, which it has dubbed "interoperability." IBM is also expanding its line of UNIX applications. For example, its Computer Integrated Manufacturing (CIM) systems are implemented under AIX, with only partial availability in SAA environments. Other applications will similarly be released for both SAA and AIX environments.

The question of SAA - AIX interoperability has been raised from the very beginning. IBM has always indicated that it will provide some way for UNIX-based systems to work in tandem with SAA systems, and more recent announcements and public statements have made good on this promise.

AIX systems will be able to participate in enterprise networking through the implementation of Common Communications Support protocols under AIX. With the implementation of the CUA-compatible AIXwindows graphical user interface, the AIX workstation can have software with the same look and feel as that available in SAA environments. With the planned implementation of X Window System client software in SAA environments, AIX systems will be able to act as the workstation component in cooperative processing applications. Future versions of AIX programming languages (C, COBOL, and FORTRAN) will be compatible with the corresponding SAA CPI definitions. IBM is building bridges and duplicating facilities across AIX and SAA to ensure a high degree of interoperability.

There are standardization issues other than SAA that also affect AIX. The UNIX operating system world suffers from some level of incompatible interfaces across implementations on different machines (although not nearly as badly as one would experience crossing IBM operating systems prior to SAA). There are several standards groups working on a "common architecture" for UNIX, all of which include some degree of compatibility with SAA standards. AIX already complies with most of these and the IBM Statement of Direction says that the others will be followed in the future. The impact of this on AIX's future development is not entirely clear. It may mean that IBM has to implement to other organizations' standards in future releases.

3. Common User Access

A foolish consistency is the hobgoblin of little minds...
Ralph Waldo Emerson, Essay on Self-Reliance

People aren't trying to use *computers, they are trying to get their jobs done.*
From Human Interface Guidelines: The Apple Desktop Interface

3.1 Goals of CUA

In the past, the combination of hardware and software limitations, along with the absence of any commonly used principles of human-computer interface design, resulted in computer applications that looked choatic and disorganized, were difficult to understand, provided insufficient feedback, behaved in unexpected ways, and that were generally unfriendly. Users had to learn to work in that environment and to translate between the world as shown on the computer screen and their "real" world. Not only were computer users unhappy, they were losing critical productivity.

Common User Access is the specification of what the computer user should see and be able to do in interacting with application software. It defines the "user interface," how the person communicates with the computer and *vice versa*. Far from being a "foolish consistency," the SAA CUA cultivates consistency in an area where current inconsistency is creating needless confusion among countless computer users and developers. Its goal is to help people get their jobs done more rapidly and with fewer errors.

The objective of CUA is to make computers more usable by:

- providing an easily understandable, "familiar," "intuitive" environment; and by

- establishing consistency across applications to maximize the transfer of users' knowledge of computer interaction.

It does this by setting standards for:

- *Presentation: what the users see*

- *Interaction: how users interact with the components*

- *Actions: how similar actions are implemented in the same way*

- *Process sequence: how users and the computer communicate with each other.*

CUA Advanced Interface Design Guide

IBM's CUA designers performed experiments, sought advice, and studied the literature on human-computer interface design (the CUA design guides provide five pages of references, surely a first for IBM manuals!). The general principles they enumerated, rooted in the field of human-computer interaction, guided the development of specific features of CUA and the definition of the different CUA models. While most public attention has been focused on the presentation aspects of CUA, this is only one component of the user interface. CUA deals with all of the factors which together comprise the user interface, from how users form conceptual models of their environment, to how they physically interact with hardware, to how the they control the software they are using. It is this total view that makes CUA so powerful a concept.

3.1.1 Familiar, Intuitive Environment

To be most productive in working with the computer, people have to see things that have an obvious interpretation and be able to take actions in an obvious way.

First-time computer users sometimes express a fear of working with screen and keyboard. Some users are afraid to touch the keys or the pointing device because they know "from experience" that the machine often acts in strange and mysterious ways. Who hasn't seen someone press a key labelled "pause" and then be surprised that the machine doesn't? Or someone afraid to press the "break" key because they didn't want to damage the machine? (One trainee was perceptive enough to ask why anyone would want a key which "breaks" the machine in the first place, to which I responded that it is a great frustration reliever, and it only causes a "temporary" break.)

Even when a computer application is supposed to automate tasks they currently perform, novices usually perceive significant differences between their usual working activities and interacting with a computer workstation. Anyone who has looked at a printed form from a company or a governmental agency and then looked at the supposedly corresponding computer screen could tell you why users are puzzled (see Figure I.15). Most printed forms have a graphical logo, or at least an organization name and address, in a different size and style of type than the form body. Areas of the form are separated from each other by one or more lines, often using different levels of shading to enhance readability (even IRS forms have these characteristics). Upper and lower case print is used in the obvious places. How many computer screens have you seen that look anything at all like their printed counterparts?

CUA advocates the creation of visual metaphors that will make it easier for users to understand what to do and how to do it. In the case of data entry applications, for example, on-line screens should copy existing paper forms (applications should be "WYSIWYG" or "what you see is what you get"). [If you have ever done your income taxes using a spreadsheet and then switched to a program that creates on-screen duplicates of IRS forms, you know the impact that this can have on your ability to learn and use the software.] By encouraging the use of the graphical capabilities of programmable workstations, CUA-conforming applications will present a much more familiar environment to the application user.

If you want to discard something, what could be simpler than "picking it up" (by selecting a picture representing the object) and "dropping" it in the trash (dragging it over the picture of the waste basket and letting go)? Pictures of familiar objects (such as documents, file folders, and trash cans) and sequences of actions that are similar to real world actions are easy to understand, "intuitive," and contribute to a high productivity environment.

```
ACTION SCAN  MODE N   USER FREDTUSER  PASS          STAT K

VENDOR CODE         BMC1990
VENDOR NAME         BUSINESS MACHINES CORP INTL
VENDOR ADDRESS      999 WHEELERS FARM ROAD
VENDOR CITY/ST      FORDMILL, CT                  ZIP  13245

PO NUMB 9012345  PO DATE 900901  SHIP DATE 900930  TERMS 1

ITEM
NUMB   DESCRIPTION                       QUANT   AMOUNT

A7140  PERSONAL COMPUTER-HEAVY DUTY        1     5500.00
A2347  MONITOR-COLOR 14 INCH               1      945.00
B5219  KEYBOARD WITH FUNC KEY ON LEFT      1       99.00
B6291  PRINTER - FAST W/ COLOR             1     1455.00
K3947  TRACKBALL                           1      123.00

       TOTALS                              5     8122.00
```

OLSEN BROTHERS CORPORATION
THE OLD MILL
MAYNARD, MA 02199

Purchase Order To:

Business Machines Corp Intl
999 Wheelers Farm Road
Fordmill, CT 13245

PO Number	PO Date	Ship Date	Terms
90-123-45	9/01/90	9/30/90	COD

Item	Description	Quant	Amount
A7140	Personal Computer - Heavy Duty	1	5500.00
A2347	Monitor - color 14 inch	1	945.00
B5219	Keyboard with func keys on left	1	99.00
B6291	Printer - fast w/ color	1	1455.00
K3947	Trackball	1	123.00
	TOTALS	5	8122.00

Figure I.15 Screens and Printed Forms

[By the way, unless you work for the CIA, anything you put in the waste basket should stay there until you explicitly empty it, something the user interface designers of the Macintosh Desktop remembered; the OfficeVision designers also remembered, but they explicitly provide a shredder.]

CUA standards also direct developers to create computer environments in which user actions have a more intuitive meaning. Selecting "escape" should exit you from what you are doing; pressing "enter" should accept and process the screen you have been working on. By doing what a person might expect, regardless of the specific application being used, the developer will further the feeling of "intuitive" operation. By so doing, the computer will become a familiar environment.

3.1.2 Consistent Environment

The goal is to provide a consistent interface for users of many machines, so that users can take advantage of the unique features of each machine within the context of a familiar and approachable interface.

Human Interface Guidelines: The Apple Desktop Interface

CUA encourages consistency in several ways. It defines the user interface for a wide variety of possible applications, for a large number of possible actions, and in a variety of hardware and software environments.

CUA encourages consistency:

- within a single application;
- across multiple applications;
- across multiple hardware platforms.

Even within a single application, a user is likely to have access to many different screens (in some cases, hundreds). The information presented on those screens can have a common appearance by following a consistent set of rules and by drawing upon a consistent set of "screen objects."

If the user is being presented with several data entry fields, they should be lined up the same way on each screen (the entry portion should begin in the same vertical column) as should the literals which define them (left justified with enough space after the shortest so that the data entry fields still line up for the longest). If the user has to select from one of several actions, the actions and the selection boxes should be in the same format and use the same graphical element (box or circle or oval) regardless of the screen on which they occur.

All of the "within application" consistency rules should also be "across application" rules; why do one application differently than any other? In addition, routine commands and actions, e.g. print, save, exit, help, should be implemented the same way in each. As dramatically demonstrated by Apple's Macintosh computer line, a computer interface that is consistent across multiple applications will be easily learned and widely accepted.

To the extent allowed by hardware limitations, users of different hardware and operating systems should see a similar type of consistency. Many elements of the interface can be provided in common to the user of a non-programmable terminal (NPT) connected to a host computer, of a stand-alone personal computer, or of a personal computer used as a "programmable workstation" (PWS) in concert with software on a host computer.

3.2 The Development of CUA

CUA did not spring whole from the mind of a single designer. The principles on which it relies have been developed over many years in the labs at universities and commercial organizations (Xerox, Apple, Microsoft, IBM, and others). But the Common User Access definition itself is uniquely IBM's.

3.2.1 The First CUA Definition

In spite of differences in the hardware capabilities of NPTs and PWSs or in the needs of different kinds of applications, the first version of CUA (defined by the now obsolete IBM manual *Common User Access Panel Design and User Interaction*) attempted to establish a common denominator for the user interface. This approach essentially ignored differences in application function and delivery media. The reason for this is fairly evident. IBM wanted to promote the use of its PS/2 personal computers in the role of front end processors to host-based applications, but it could not ignore the millions of NPTs (mostly in the form of IBM 3270 terminals) then in the field. This version of CUA was introduced in 1987 and is sometimes referred to as "CUA 1987" or CUA 1."

This attempt at establishing user interface standards often led to a "*least* common denominator" definition. It made little use of the advanced capabilities of today's personal computers while attempting to force fit certain features onto host terminals. Furthermore, it showed a much greater concern with office automation applications than with the data entry and database applications found on mainframes. IBM's first SAA application was to be OfficeVision, and that project team undoubtedly worked closely with the CUA designers.

3.2.2 The Second CUA Definition

In May 1989, IBM announced a new version of CUA, called "CUA 1989" or "CUA 2," which corrected many of these problems. This version of CUA established a more advanced kind of interaction for a user at a PWS, and distinguished various types of user interface models for different types of applications. As evidenced by the participation of over a dozen third-party application vendors (most from the mainframe world) in that same announcement, IBM had significantly expanded its sources for advice and counsel on the CUA definition.

Figure I.16 depicts the usage of the four interface models of CUA 1989, i.e., Entry, Text, Graphical, and Workplace. They all have a common ancestry, but are optimized to both hardware and application. The specific differences are explained later in this chapter.

Workstation Application Type	NPT	PWS
Data entry intensive	ENTRY	ENTRY
Decision intensive	TEXT	GRAPHICAL
Database intensive	TEXT	GRAPHICAL
Office automation	n.a.	WORKPLACE
NPT = Non-programmable terminal (e.g. 3270) PWS = Programmable workstation (e.g. PS/2)		

Figure I.16 Common User Access Models

Although the goals of CUA include cross-application and cross-hardware consistency, software developers will have to address themselves to this more diverse CUA specification and deal with the implications of the different models (Chapter 11 discusses these issues). There are many trade-offs among consistency, effective performance on diverse tasks, and use of unique hardware capabilities. The CUA designers are trying to strike an appropriate balance.

3.2.3 Future CUA Definition

CUA 1989 represents a significant maturation of the CUA definition. It was developed over a period of two years with direct input from developers and users trying to work with the first CUA definition. While it is a significant improvement over CUA 1987, it is clearly not a final statement of how users and computer should interact (will there ever be such a thing?).

In the *CUA Advanced Interface Design Guide* published in June 1989, IBM highlights the expected evolution of CUA and notes the following areas for the future:

- *a tailorable mouse interface (user definition of what the buttons do)*
- *a tailorable keyboard interface*
- *alternative input (e.g. "touch")*
- *further definition of interfaces for database applications*
- *context menus (menus associated with specific objects on the screen)*

CUA will expand in these areas and others. It defines rules that are applicable to a broad range of applications, but not broad enough. Database application developers, for example, need a significant expansion in areas of selection, scrolling, and user notification to accommodate their unique needs. There will have to be a more or less continuous evolution as software developers feed back problems and suggestions borne of actual use of the CUA standard.

[An example of just such continuing evolution is the revised screen look of OS/2 Release 1.2. Icons and other screen formats are more advanced than the ones in the CUA 1989 manuals, including three-dimensional highlights and shading. Keeping software and documentation synchronized will continue to be a problem as CUA evolves.]

The CUA designers note the expected evolution of hardware, particularly larger screens. Once you use applications in a multi-window environment, you will immediately see the benefits that a larger screen will provide (many UNIX-based computers already come with 17-inch or larger monitors capable of displaying 1024 by 1280 pixels). The trick for CUA designers will be to anticipate the capabilities that users will need to work effectively with a larger screen and make the CUA definition robust enough to support them.

IBM has also shown a willingness to learn from other organizations. Although developed independently, the CUA definition and the Apple Macintosh "desktop interface" show an obvious similarity. IBM has also licensed technology from NeXt (the "NextStep" user interface is now available as an option under AIX) and Metaphor (used in the IBM Data Interpretation System). In the announcement of its Data Interpretation System, IBM stated its intent:

> *Many of the design principles used by common user access (CUA) were also used in the design of the IBM Data Interpretation System. There are similarities between the user interfaces of these systems including graphical interface with windows, pointing device support, and colors. There are differences in presentation and implementation.* These differences will diminish as CUA extensions and the IBM Data Interpretation System evolve over time.
>
> *Programming Announcement 289-215 [emphasis added]*

In general, IBM is very up front about the future evolution of CUA:

> *CUA will evolve as technology expands and as users from different backgrounds begin to use personal computers for more and more tasks.*
>
> *Advanced CUA Interface Design Guide*

Applications developed to the CUA 1989 standard will meet the goals of CUA, but software developers should anticipate many expansions in "CUA 3" and beyond.

3.3 CUA Advanced Interface

The advanced CUA interface defines a competitive user interface that can be developed with today's technology. It is specifically designed to use the facilities of OS/2 and its Presentation Manager (available in both OS/2 Standard Edition and Extended Edition).

The *CUA Advanced Interface Design Guide* presents the concepts of good user interface design as well as the specific constructs that constitute the Graphical and Workplace Models. The Graphical Model develops a basic "windowed" user presentation. The Workplace Model extends this to include a "desktop" and the interactions among the facilities (applications) that exist on it.

3.3.1 Graphical Model

The CUA Graphical Model defines a multiple "window" user interface with "pull-down" menus and "pop-up" dialog boxes. It defines actions that can be selected using a pointing device (typically a "mouse") or a keyboard. It is the most flexible of the CUA models for a single application. Applications designed using the Graphical Model can be incorporated in a system using the Workplace Model for interacting with other applications.

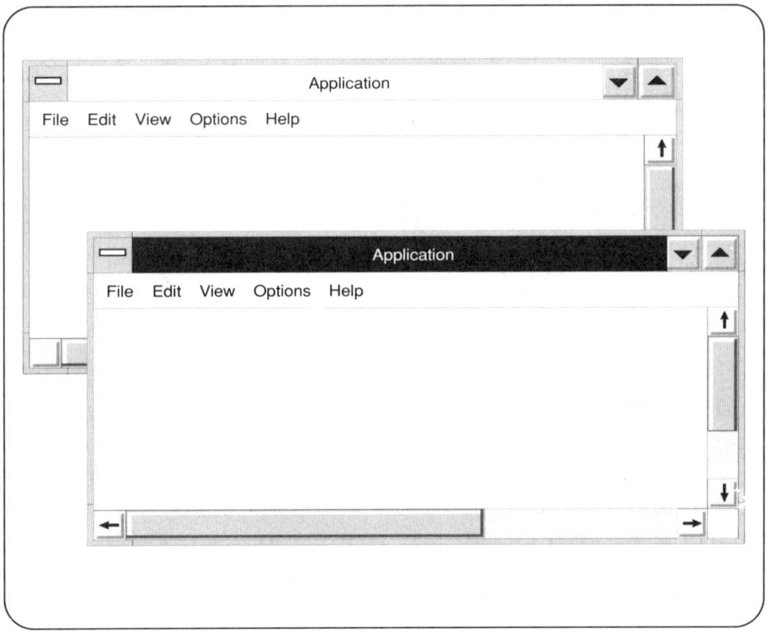

Figure I.17 CUA Screen Layout

The Graphical Model definition focuses on the presentation of windows and their components (scroll bars, list boxes, etc.), and on the manipulation of user "objects" in those windows in an "object-action" sequence. The windows shown in Figure I.17 and earlier in Figure I.2 are examples of the use of the Graphical Model. Both windows shown in Figure I.1 follow the Graphical Model, although the "desktop" itself uses the cross-application facilities of the Workplace Model.

The CUA Graphical Model specifies window construction, placement, and usage. It defines four different types of windows (illustrated in Figures I.18, 19, and 20):

- The primary window of the application displays the user objects and actions.

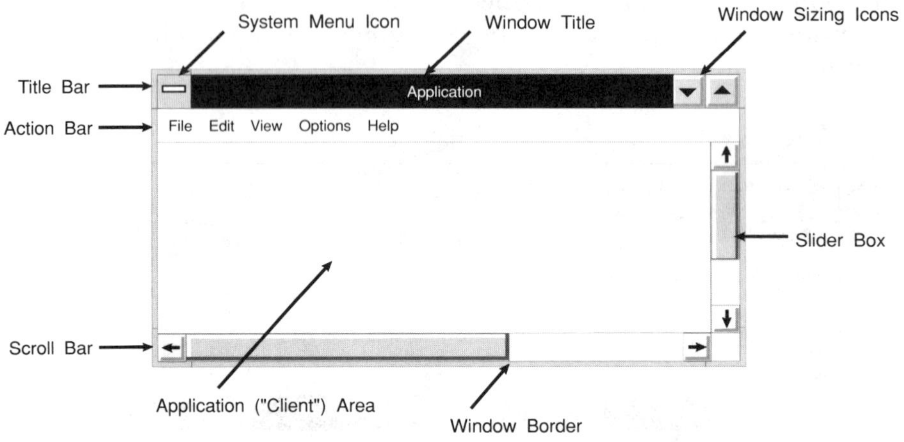

Figure I.18 CUA Primary/Secondary Window Layout

- Secondary windows are always associated with primary windows. They may be created by the application when necessary to allow the user to perform some secondary function while maintaining the information on the primary window. Multiple secondary windows can be open at the same time. A user request for "help" with an object or action on the primary window will "pop-up" a secondary window. A secondary window might also be used to allow an accounting clerk to look up an account code while filling in an accounting transaction on the primary window.

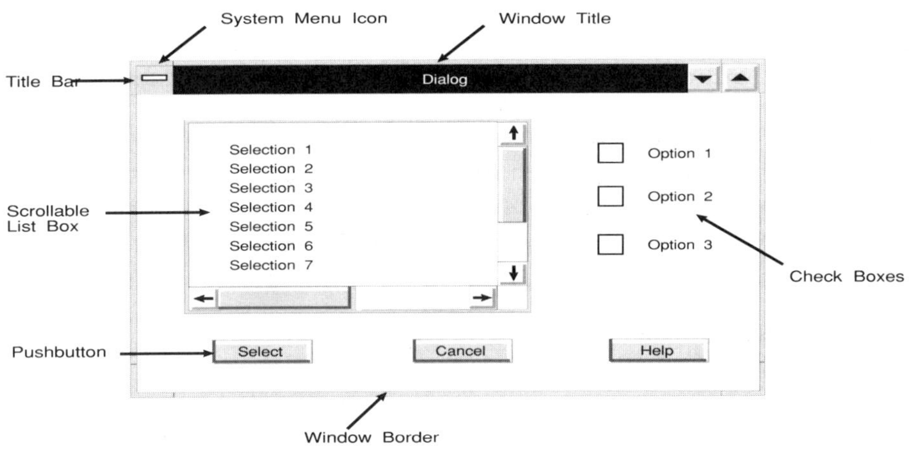

Figure I.19 Typical Dialog Box

■ Dialog boxes are a special type of secondary window that requires a user response. They are used when information is needed by the application to complete a function in a primary or secondary window. A dialog box does not contain scroll bars nor can it be re-sized. It may contain an internal scrollable area called a "list box." This type of window may be used for selecting fonts for a text object, displaying a progress indicator, asking for search criteria against a document displayed in an associated window, etc.

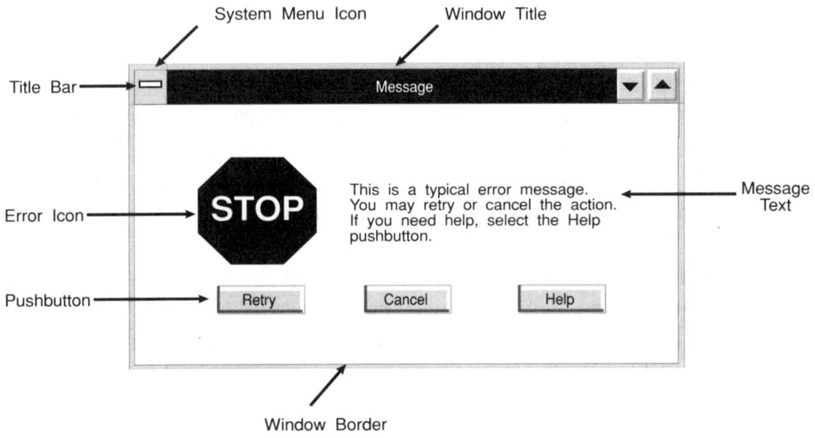

Figure I.20 Typical Message Box

- Message boxes are used to display errors, warnings, and other messages. They may request the user to select an action via a pushbutton but cannot contain other user selectable elements.

The CUA Graphical Model specifies a variety of possible window components in addition to the standard ones shown. For example, the examples above show pushbutton, check boxes, and list boxes. These are members of a class of standard user interface constructs defined as follows:

- "pushbuttons" (selecting any button in the set causes the indicated action to be performed)

- "scrollable list box" (one or more items can be selected for processing)

- "radio buttons" (selecting one button in a set causes any other to be deselected)

- "check boxes" (select as many as you want in the set)

- and "spin buttons" (select the associated arrows to "spin" to the desired value)

CUA specifies each control's graphical form, allowable actions and responses (e.g. when the mouse is positioned over a check box and the user pushes the left mouse button, the application should fill the check box with an "x"), and suggested usage.

The Graphical Model recommends a "mouse" pointing device. To increase usability, it also requires a parallelism between mouse and keyboard so that actions can be initiated from either. The "point and shoot" capability of the mouse, while applicable in many situations, may be slower or more awkward than pressing a key in others.

The CUA definition provides obvious possibilities for creativity on the part of the programmer (using spin buttons to select dollar and cents amounts instead of typing them in). It also prescribes and proscribes many specific constructs. How well application designers and programmers follow its guidelines will be a significant factor in how successful CUA is in establishing "common" user access across a wide variety of applications.

3.3.2 Workplace Model

The Workplace Model adds cross-application capabilities to the Graphical Model. It describes a user interface which appears "familiar" by representing electronic objects (applications, databases, files, physical devices) by icons which resemble physical objects. Objects have certain properties and relationships to other objects (defined in system control tables) which make it easier for users to manipulate them and otherwise do their work.

The rules and standards of the Workplace Model deal with presentation and user interaction among multiple applications, in contrast to Graphical Model rules which deal with the objects of a single application. In the Workplace Model, selecting a document icon and dragging it over an out-basket icon will send the output of a word processor as an electronic mail message. "Dragging" a file icon from one disk to another will copy it. You take the obvious action, the system does the rest.

To provide this kind of capability, the application developer uses two new types of windows defined by the Workplace Model:

- The *workplace window* displays the icons for applications, files, and devices accessible via the workplace model application (Figure I.1 shows a workplace window).

- An *object handler* window is the window you see when a user opens an object (by doubling clicking on its icon) in the workplace window. A *list handler* window is a special type of object window used when the object contains other objects, e.g. an in box (as also seen in Figure I.1).

The Workplace Model also defines the way in which data on a window from one application can be selected for use in another application by "direct manipulation." The scenario at the beginning of Chapter 1 contains an example of this process:

Using the mouse, she highlights the information on the screen that she wants to present to her boss (see Figure I.3) and points to a memo pad. She then adds a brief message and "moves" the memo to her out box, knowing it will automatically appear in her boss's in box.

OfficeVision is an example of an application which uses the CUA Workplace Model. Various software vendors have modified their applications to work in conjunction with the OfficeVision desktop interface by using the additional APIs provided with that product. Their applications then appear as icons in the OfficeVision workplace window and are able to exchange data with other objects in that window. IBM has not as yet addressed the implementation of similar APIs in Presentation Manager to make it easier to implement Workplace Model applications outside of the OfficeVision framework.

3.4 CUA Basic Interface

CUA 1989 defines two interface models for use with non-programmable terminals. They are based on the user interface model in CUA 1987 and have many of the same elements of the "advanced" CUA models intended for use with programmable terminals. These two models are defined in the *CUA Basic Interface Guide.*

The Text Model for NPTs is a subset of the Graphical Model for PWSs. It provides some of the elements of a windowing environment in the obviously restricted processing environment of a host-connected dumb terminal. The Entry Model is new to CUA 1989 and was developed to satisfy the need for high volume data entry work performed on NPTs. It is a standardized version of typical data entry application screen elements seen today on millions of 3270s.

3.4.1 Text Model

The Text Model (formally called the "text subset of the graphical model") brings to the NPT many of the same constructs used in the Graphical Model on the PWS. Referring to Figure I.21, you see a full screen panel (equivalent to the primary window of a Graphical Model application) with action bar and pull-down menu. You also see a function key area, a "more" indicator (instead of a scroll bar), and a command line interface. Figure I.22 shows another Text Model window with a "pop-up" being used to gather more information from the user. These similarities to Graphical Model constructs not only provide similar functions, but make it easier for users to move from one hardware environment to another and to migrate from NPT to PWS terminals.

```
   File  Edit  View  Options  Help
-------------- +-----------------+ -------------------------
               | 1 1. All        |
               |   2. Some...    |
               |                 |
 Make text chan| _ 1. By subject |
               |   2. By date    |          More:     +
-------------- |   3. By name    | -------------------------
 January 24, 19|   4. By other...|
               +-----------------+
 MEMO TO:      P.W. Bonham
 FROM:         D.C. Smith
 SUBJECT:      Printer Update

 Patricia,

 I have just received the latest prototype of the printer adapter
 and its new specifications.  This is a big improvement over the
 previous version.  I think it will allow us to deliver a more
 attractive product - one that fits in well with the rest of the
 new product line.

 Command ===>
 F1=Help  F3=Exit  F7=Bkwd  F8=Fwd  F9=Retrieve   F10=Actions  F12=Cancel
```

Figure I.21 CUA Text Model Showing Pull-down Menu

The Text Model also requires the "object-action" orientation of the Graphical Model. Since use of the mouse is not supported, users select objects by the use of a slash character (/) in selection fields. They then select actions from the action bar and its pull-downs (using the cursor movement keys and the enter key to get the pull-down, and then typing the number of the selected action). This preserves the similarity of processing sequence between the Text and Graphical Models.

The Text Model was originally provided so that developers would have a guide for implementing the key elements of CUA in the NPT environment. With the expanded emphasis in SAA on always using PWSs for user interface processing, the Text Model becomes a transitional interface for applications being ported from mainframe applications. The Dialog Manager under OS/2 provides facilities for implementing Text Model applications which were originally developed using ISPF in a mainframe environment.

```
   File  Edit  View  Options  Help
 ----------------------------------------------------------------------
                   +---------------------------------------------------+
                   |                                                   |
                   |                  Send a Message                   |
 Select one or mo  |                                                   |
 Then select an a  | Type the message. Then Enter to send it.          |
                   |                                                   |
   Name            |NOTE FROM:   A. C. Brown                           |
                   |                                                   |
   / Anderson, Ri  |This is a sample message.  Users would write their |
   _ Collins, Al   |own messages.                                      |
   _ Hanson, Char  |                                                   |
   _ Lopez, Crist  |                                                   |
   _ Warner, Roxa  |                                                   |
                   |                                                   |
                   | Enter  F1=Help  F12=Cancel                        |
                   +---------------------------------------------------+

 Command ===> ________________________________________
 F1=Help  F3=Exit  F10=Actions  F12=Cancel
```

Figure I.22 CUA Text Model Showing Pop-up

3.4.2 Entry Model

The Entry Model provides a basic standard for the user interface of NPT-based applications. Entry Model applications can be menu-driven or may include commands in the work area of the screen (or "panel" as it is called by CUA). Panels following the Entry Model rules will display many of the elements of the general CUA approach (selection fields, prompt fields, help panels, etc.), but will not have action bars and pull-downs. The model also allows an "action-object" orientation in place of the object-action approach in the Graphical and Text Models.

The Entry Model is intended for data-entry intensive applications typical of many operational mainframe systems in existence today. It provides an "entry level" into the world of CUA, both for new applications and for upgrading existing ones.

3.5 Implementing CUA-Conforming Applications

CUA-compliant applications can be implemented in a variety of ways. You could begin with the principles and rules specified in the CUA definition and write programs that specifically follow them. For non-programmable terminal applications following the CUA Entry Model, this is certainly feasible (and the most likely implementation approach). For workstation applications using the Graphical and Workplace Models, however, the enormity of this task would quickly become apparent. For these situations, higher level programming tools, ranging from subroutine libraries to application generators, are a necessity. Some of the higher level programming tools available from IBM and third parties can directly create multi-windowed applications following these models.

Presentation Manager and Dialog Manager are essentially libraries of routines that implement the Presentation and Dialog elements of the SAA Common Programming Interface, respectively. PM is used for implementing Graphical Model applications while DM is used for Text

Model applications. Presentation Manager and Dialog Manager routines perform such functions as displaying and sizing a window and displaying the contents of a list box or panel. There are over 500 calls available in PM, and over 80 calls and tags in DM, which in turn uses PM.

Using PM and DM, however, does not guarantee CUA compliance. The PM calls, for example, can be used to create a much broader class of windowed interfaces than are specified by CUA. Some of the higher level (application generation) products already on the market claim to have rules built in which guarantee conformance to CUA. IBM is taking the lead in this type of product with Easel, an application generator for Graphical Model applications. These implementation issues are discussed further in Chapter 11.

4. Common Programming Interface

When you're lying awake with a dismal headache, and repose is tabooed by anxiety,

I conceive you may use any language you choose to indulge in, without impropriety.

Sir Wm. Gilbert, Iolanthe, Act II

4.1 Languages

The SAA Common Programming Interface defines the programming languages that will be supported by IBM as part of SAA. The individual language standards specify the key words, operators, and syntax that can be used with uniform results wherever they are available in SAA-compatible IBM products.

Most of the compilers and translators that implement the SAA languages today do not exactly match the SAA CPI. Some provide more than the CPI and others less. This situation, of course, stems from IBM's desire to have a definition of each language that can be provided on multiple platforms within a reasonable time. The constructs in the CPIs are likely to increase over time to provide the maximum compatibility consistent with the particular language standard being followed. For example, the COBOL definition in the CPI does not allow nesting of the "OCCURS DEPENDING ON" construct (for creating variable length data structures). Although this is supported in the MVS COBOL compiler, it is not available in either OS/2 or OS/400 COBOL.

The CPI definition for each language is contained in a corresponding CPI Reference Manual. Each manual has a section showing differences between the CPI and various implementation of the language. IBM has been adding "SAA compatibility" switches to its compilers so you can see what parts of your program may be acceptable to the compiler but are not consistent with the CPI.

As noted elsewhere in this book, software implementing SAA is not yet available in all environments. Figure I.23 shows which languages exist on which platforms. All languages listed have been announced as being part of the SAA definition, although implementations have not yet been announced for all SAA environments.

Language	MVS TSO/E	VM/SP CMS	OS/400	OS/2 EE
C	C/370	C/370	C/400	C/2 V1.1
COBOL	COBOL II R3	COBOL II R3	COBOL /400	COBOL/2
FORTRAN	FORTRAN V2 R3	FORTRAN V2 R3	[NYA]	FORTRAN/2
PL/I	OS PL/I V2	OS PL/I V2	[NYA]	[NYA]
Procedures Language	TSO/E REXX	REXX VM/SP R3	[NYA]	Procedures Language 2/REXX
RPG	[NYA]	[NYA]	RPG/400	[NYA]
[NYA] = Not Yet Announced				

Figure I.23 SAA Languages

4.1.1 COBOL

The COBOL language has been around longer than many people now programming in it. There are literally hundreds of implementations as well as national and international standards. The SAA CPI for COBOL is based on the national standard Programming Language COBOL, X3.23 -- 1985 Intermediate Level.

The CPI implementing products for COBOL are VS COBOL II Release 3 for MVS and VM, COBOL/2 for OS/2, and COBOL/400 for OS/400. Each compiler implements the COBOL elements in the CPI. Each also implements a number of extensions specific to its environment. For example, VS COBOL II implements the "high level" ANSI standard and COBOL/400 contains constructs for System/36 and System/38 compatibility. VS COBOL II, COBOL/400, and COBOL/2 compilers all have "SAA compatibility" switches which will flag statements that are not in the current CPI.

4.1.2 FORTRAN

FORTRAN is the primary language of the scientific and engineering programming world. It is a toss-up as to whether there are more implementations of FORTRAN than of COBOL. There are also numerous national and international standards relating to this language.

The SAA CPI is based on ANSI Programming Language FORTRAN, 77 level.

4.1.3 C

C is a very powerful high level procedural language. Its roots, like the UNIX operating system for which it was implemented, go back to the Multics project and a PL/I derivative called EPL (Early Programming Language). When UNIX was first implemented as a scaled down Multics to run on the Digital PDP-7, its developers produced another PL/I derivative language called "B" (for Bell Labs). This language was revamped and called "C" when it was re-implemented on the PDP-11.

Given this history and as UNIX was ported to a large number of different computers, C became the language of choice for mini-computer programmers. C implementations quickly sprang up for the IBM PC under PC-DOS and also became the most widely used language of independent software developers. Almost all of the major application software packages for this environment are written in one of these C versions, some comprising several million lines of code.

In 1990, a definition of C finally made its way through the standardization process of the American National Standards Institute. The SAA C CPI is based on that ANSI standard. At the current time, OS/2 C and C/400 deliver the SAA CPI although IBM System/370 C "can be used to gain early experience with the C interface" (*SAA CPI C Reference*).

4.1.4 RPG

RPG is the most widely used language on the System/36, System/38, and AS/400 computers. As much as 85% of all programing on these machines is done in one of the RPG derivatives (RPG II, RPG III, and RPG/400). In spite of this, RPG was not included in the original SAA CPI announcement, presumably because IBM could not promise to deliver it in other environments in any reasonable time frame.

When the AS/400 computer series was introduced in 1988 (it had been widely rumored and IBM even referred to it as "System/3X" in the initial SAA announcement), RPG was added to the CPI. The AS/400 RPG implementation provided the basic CPI definition, although some constructs were left out (listed in Appendix A to the RPG CPI Reference Manual).

IBM has committed to deliver the RPG CPI in all SAA environments. As of this writing, only RPG/400 has been delivered.

4.1.5 PL/I

IBM developed PL/I (Programming Language/I) in its Hursley Research Laboratory after its definition by a joint IBM/SHARE study group. It was an attempt to come up with a "standard" programming language that could be used for a wide variety of applications. Some of its definers meant it to be the successor to both COBOL and FORTRAN, although it was developed under the SHARE FORTRAN project with a bit of ALGOL mixed in (some IBMers were calling it FORTRAN VI for a while). Unfortunately, PL/I barely established a beachhead in the United States and there are currently many more adherents in Europe and elsewhere in the world.

PL/I was added to the CPI in the September 1989, AD/Cycle announcement. While some people have continued to associate PL/I with AD/Cycle, this joint announcement was more a matter of convenience than one of special implication. Dates have not yet been announced for delivery of implementing software in the OS/2 and OS/400 environments.

4.1.6 Procedures Language

In addition to the languages used for writing programs, such as COBOL, FORTRAN, C, and RPG, every computer has another language used for controlling the execution of those programs. It is used to issue operating system commands, execute programs, perform file manipulation, and, in general, control the application flow from one program to another. The SAA CPI calls this language the Procedures Language, presumably because it is used to create "command procedures." The Procedures Language is also a "procedural" language in the sense used by computer scientists, as are the other CPI languages (except RPG which might be called "semi-procedural").

Languages for creating command procedures existed in all SAA computer environments long before the definition of the SAA CPI. Although similar in purpose, they had quite different structures and commands (as opposed to other languages such as COBOL and FORTRAN which existed in a very similar form in multiple environments). Job Control Language for mainframe computers operating in batch mode was basically the same in both MVS and VSE environments, but was fundamentally different from the procedures languages used with IBM's various time-sharing operating systems. Furthermore, the CLIST (Command List) language used on the TSO time-sharing system was quite different from the EXECs and REXX used on VM/CMS. On PC-DOS systems, Batch File Programming was a very primitive EXEC-like language.

IBM has made a major step forward in committing to create a common SAA Procedures Language on all SAA environments. That language is a subset of REXX and has already been delivered in TSO, VM, and OS/2. Although IBM batch processing environments are not mentioned in the SAA announcements, it is interesting to speculate on whether REXX, with some adjustments, might also be available as an alternative to JCL at some time in the future.

4.2 Application Generator

An application generator is software for producing software. It takes a specification of an application (in some "high level" language) and produces the working code for that application (in some lower level language). The high level language used in IBM's Cross System Product, CSP, is the basis for the Application Generator element of the CPI. CSP is "the SAA application generator" and is included in the AD/Cycle application development environment (see Chapter 7).

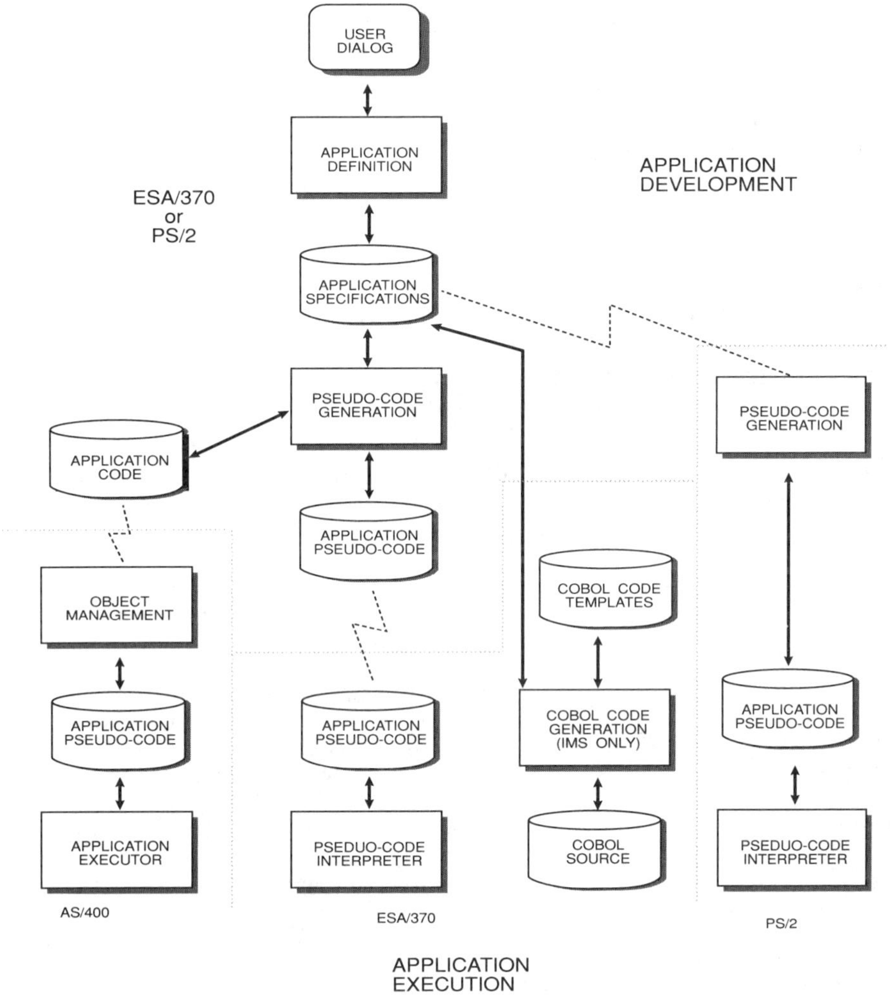

Figure I.24 Cross System Product

The CSP product consists of both a development system and an application execution system. CSP/AD, the development system, can produce code that will execute on any platform running CSP/AE, the execution system. The Application Generator element of the CPI defines the constructs in the CSP language that will be supported in the application execution (AE) systems available in each SAA environment. This distinction between the Application Generator CPI element, i.e., a specification of the semantics of a language, and the application generator product itself will allow IBM (and others) to deliver a variety of development tools, all producing application specifications which follow the CPI. Although an important distinction, this nuance is often lost in discussions of CSP and the CPI.

CSP/AD and CSP/AE are composed of several identifiable modules. In CSP/AD, the application specification is created via an interactive dialog module. The working code is produced in a machine-independent pseudo-code language (for System 370) or in directly executable code (for the AS/400). Version 3 Release 3 also generates COBOL, although only for IMS applications. Run-time environments are necessary to execute the CSP-generated modules.

The relationships among CSP components are shown in Figure I.24. Environmental differences are explained in the following sections. Figure I.25 lists the implementing products.

Environment	Application Development	Application Execution
OS/2 EE	EZ-PREP	EZ-RUN [X]
OS/400	[NYA]	OS/400 V1.1 [Y]
MVS	CSP/AD V3 R3 M2	CSP/AE V3 R3 M2
VM	CSP/AD V3 R3 M2	CSP/AE V3 R3 M2

[NYA] = Not Yet Announced.
[X] = Does not support OS/2 EE Database.
[Y] = Future support for OS/400 Database.

Figure I.25 Applications Generator Availability

4.2.1 Application Development

The application development component of CSP provides five major functions:

- application definition
- data definition
- screen and report format definition
- interactive testing
- code generation

The first three produce the application specification which is used to generate application code. The interactive testing facility allows you to test incomplete specifications and to detect specification errors.

Application specifications are stored in the Member Specification Library, MSL. The MSL definition is read by the code generators. This mechanism provides the "cross system" portability of applications.

The code generation component of CSP/AD operates differently in different environments. When generating for System 370 systems, it reads the application specifications from the MSL and produces a machine-independent pseudo-code (Application Load File, ALF). New features in Release 3.3 allow the direct generation of COBOL source code for IMS applications (but not for DB2). For AS/400 systems, CSP produces code packaged as OS/400 code objects. PS/2 programs are run interpretively after being partially generated using a PS/2-based pseudo-code generator.

The new export mechanism announced with Release 3.2.2 of CSP/AD in the 370 environments produces a "tag language" source file called External Source Format, ESF. This file contains all of the information about an application, its data, and its screens and reports. It can be used to drive application generator "back-ends" as well as other computer-aided software engineering (CASE) tools. A parallel import mechanism means that CASE design or "front end" tools can produce

ESF files which will, in turn, drive the CSP/AD generator, or any other CASE tool that reads ESF.

IBM is encouraging tool builders to use ESF (Synon, Index Technology, KnowledgeWare, and Bachman Information Systems have all announced interfaces). IBM is signalling that ESF will be incorporated as part of the Information Model in the AD/Cycle repository to complete the connection between the repository and CSP. IBM is, however, placing some restrictions on the use of ESF by requiring that certain tool builders (those planning on importing ESF into application generator tools that compete with CSP) secure a license from IBM.

As an SAA development tool, CSP is still lacking. It does not produce CUA-compliant screens nor can it be used to develop cooperative processing applications. Coordination of CSP and Easel might provide a more complete "SAA" development environment.

Complete CSP/AD is available in the MVS/TSO, VM/CMS, and PS/2 environments. The code generation function is separately available for the PS/2. With the announcement of AD/Cycle (IBM's SAA application development environment), the PS/2 is expected to become the focal point for future expansion of CSP/AD (as well as the workstation for SAA application users).

4.2.2 Application Execution

The CSP Application Execution system will exist in all SAA environments. In most cases, it executes applications interpretively using the pseudo-code produced by CSP/AD. This mode of operation sometimes results in performance problems in larger applications and has been the source of negative publicity about the product. The OS/400 version uses a higher performance compiled approach. IBM has indicated its support of CSP as a major part of the SAA application development strategy and will undoubtedly deal with other environments in future releases.

CSP/AE for the PS/2 requires that the code generation also be done on the workstation. Code is generated by the EZ-PREP product (considered part of the Application Development component of CSP) and executed by the EZ-RUN. Both products are available under PC-DOS. They have been converted to run as standard OS/2 EE applications, i.e., *not* in the DOS compatibility box.

OS/400 applications use compiled program "objects." A CSP object manager running on the AS/400 takes code generated by CSP/AD and packages it appropriately for execution. ALF is not used in the OS/400 CSP. So far, this is the only environment to use compiled, rather than interpreted code.

4.3 Support Services

In addition to the language definitions, the SAA CPI defines extensive support services. The support services are subroutine interfaces for the programmer to use in accessing operating system or application enabling system capabilities. Database inquiry, presentation services, and program-to-program communication are some of the support services interfaces defined in the CPI. Figure I.26 shows which services are currently available in each of the SAA environments. [A more detailed chart is updated regularly in "SAA Customer Briefs" available from IBM.]

Not all CPI support services will be provided in every SAA environment. The Presentation Interface and the Dialog Interface, in particular, have been specifically designated as interfaces available only under OS/2. This is a direct outgrowth of the strategy of using workstations as the user interface platform for *all* applications, regardless of where the remainder of the application resides. Other interfaces, such as Query and Repository, have not been announced for CICS and IMS/TM. IBM seems to be saying that the CPI will provide common definitions for support service interfaces, but that those interfaces will be provided (via enabling software) selectively.

Services	MVS TSO/E	VM/SP CMS	OS/400	OS/2 EE
Presentation	[GDDM]	[GDDM]	[NA]	OS/2 EE V1.1
Dialog	[ISPF V3.1]	[ISPF V3.1]	[NA]	OS/2 EE V1.2
Database	DB2 R3 V2	SQL/DS	SQL/400 V2 R1	OS/2 EE V1.0
Query	QMF V2 R3	QMF V2 R3	[NYA]	OS/2 EE V1.2
Communi-cations	[APPC]	VM/SP R6	[APPC]	[APPC]
Repository	Repository Manager /MVS	[NYA]	[NYA]	[NYA]

[NA] = Not Available.
[NYA] = Not Yet Announced.
[GDDM] = GDDM supports part of the CPI; see Section 4.3.1.
[ISPF V3.1] = ISPF implements part of the CPI; see Section 4.3.2.
[APPC] = APPC is compatible with CPIC.

Figure I.26 Implementing Software for Support Services CPI

4.3.1 Presentation Interface

The Presentation Interface provides subroutine calls which programmers can use to display information on a user's screen and receive and process input from the user and from other programs. It is the basic mechanism by which programmers implement applications that conform to the Graphical Model of CUA. There are over 500 functions defined in the Presentation Interface.

Presentation Interface functions include the manipulation of screen "windows," various window components such as scroll bars and sizing controls, user selection displays such as menus and "radio buttons," and type fonts and styles. It also provides the interface routines for creating event-driven programs that communicate with each other via a message passing mechanism. This same mechanism is used to receive "messages" from the user, for example when a key is pushed or the mouse is moved. The programming style used in PI applications is an example of an "object-oriented" approach.

Consistent with the strategy of using workstations as the user interface processor in cooperative processing networks, the PI is implemented by the OS/2 Presentation Manager. [Using the subroutines provided in PM does not in itself guarantee that you will conform to CUA, however.] The roots of the Presentation Interface and of the Presentation Manager can be found in the Graphic Data Display Manager on the System 370. GDDM implements parts of the PI, but is not intended as a strategic SAA product.

4.3.2 Dialog Interface

The Dialog Interface defines another programming interface for control of the user interface. It offers a higher level view than the Presentation Interface, providing a more limited capability for manipulating individual screen elements. It provides standard services to create "panels" (windows) and control the interactive dialog with the user. These services allow you to implement text-based windows which follow the CUA Text Model (subset of the Graphical Model).

The Dialog Interface element of the CPI has two components:

- subroutine calls which handle dialog management and which access the Presentation Manager; and

- Dialog Tag Language for defining panels and some dialog elements.

The subroutine calls are essentially those in the previously existing ISPF products. ISPF has been a mainstay of interactive programming under VM and MVS for many years. ISPF functions handle panel display, sequencing, and data transfer. The ISPF kernel interprets the panel definitions and controls the dialog among user, panels, and programs.

The Dialog Tag Language is new to IBM programming environments but is based on the ISO Standard Generalized Markup Language (SGML). SGML provides a standard for embedding formatting and control information in a text information stream. It is used in publishing applications (including IBM's Bookmaster system) and other situations where it is useful to specify these characteristics of the data stream independently of its information content. The ISPF panel description format was too limited to define screens in the graphical, windowed environment described by CUA, so the Dialog Tag Language was introduced.

The Dialog Interface is implemented by the Dialog Manager under OS/2. ISPF under VM and MVS implement some of the DI, but are not considered strategic SAA products. [Software to implement the Dialog Interface is not available under OS/400.]

4.3.3 Database Interface

The SAA Database Interface defines access mechanisms for relational databases. [The only database structures discussed in SAA are relational.] In a relational database, data are stored in "tables," groups of records having single or multiple field keys. Each table contains a single record type with all records at the same level (no implied hierarchy). Tables are independently defined with neither hierarchical nor network structure. You can create "virtual" hierarchies or networks of tables using "foreign keys," data fields in one record that are keys to another table. Ensuring that foreign keys are consistent with real keys is called "relational integrity." User access to relational databases is via "set" manipulation commands defined in the ANSI Structured Query Language, SQL.

SQL/DS was IBM's first database to provide relational structure. There are also many third party vendors supplying relational databases for IBM systems, ORACLE being foremost among them. The OS/400 and

OS/2 EE Data Base Managers also implement relational databases accessed via SQL.

The Database Interface element of the CPI is very close to the ANSI standard for SQL. IBM has indicated its intent to comply both with this standard and with the ISO SQL.

4.3.4 Query Interface

A query is an SQL program, i.e., a set of commands to access data in a relational database. The Query Interface defines procedural commands that cause queries to be run and the results to be displayed or printed. It is the procedure language for executing SQL programs. The Query Interface also allows query language commands to be called from the other programs written in one of the SAA languages. This is the query "callable interface."

The concept of a procedure language for executing queries is straightforward. There are only ten commands in the language, and two of these relate specifically to the callable interface. The query language allows you to add parameters to your SQL programs and to create nicely formatted output. It also provides import and export facilities to bring database information and the queries themselves into editable files. The query language is recursive to the extent that one of the query commands allows the execution of other query language programs.

Figure I.27 diagrams the relationship between the query language, queries (SQL programs), and the relational databases they access. The query language procedure RUNs an SQL program after SETting any variables occurring in that program. You can also RUN another query language program. Results can be PRINTed using a FORMat specified in a format description file. You can also PRINT query language programs using this command. Query programs can be RUN from C and COBOL programs after STARTing the query manager. Variables can be SET and interrogated (GET). Although the various files are stored in different formats, the IMPORT and EXPORT commands will produce editable (sequential text) files of SQL QUERYs, print FORMats, query language PROCedures, and database TABLEs.

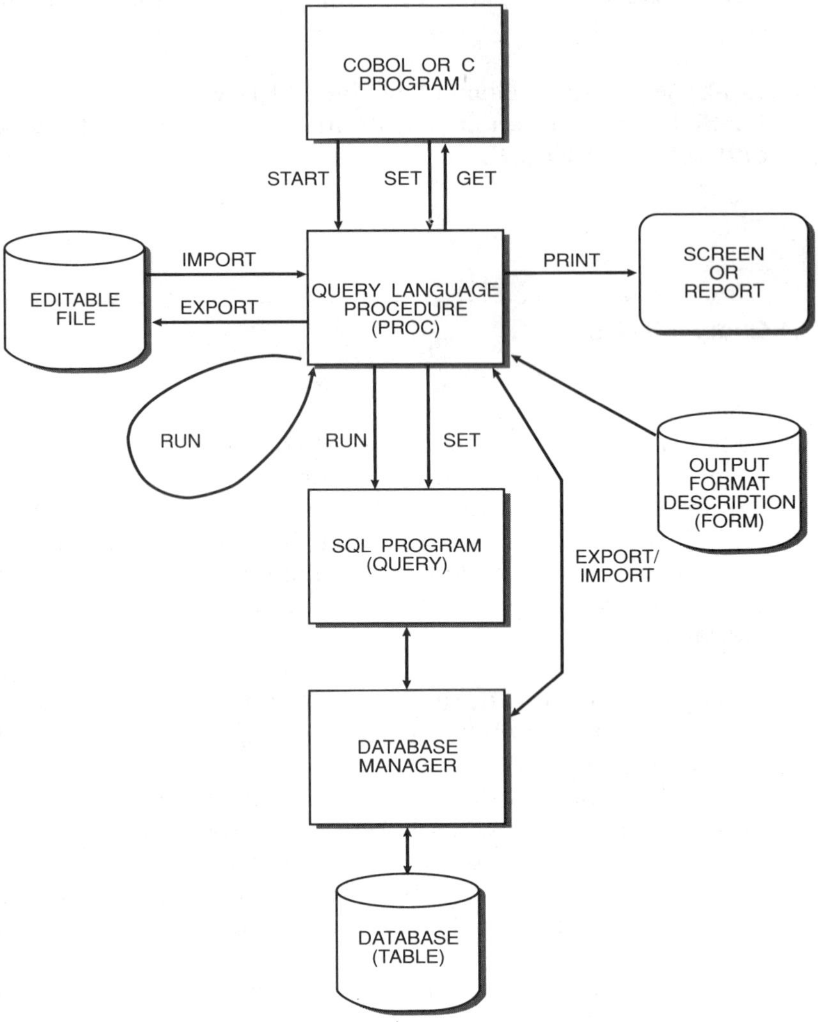

Figure I.27 Query Interface

The OS/2 EE Query Manager implements the SAA Query Interface. The QMF product on MVS/TSO and VM/CMS implements the Query Interface in those environments. [The OS/400 Query Manager is not yet available.] QMF implements the callable interface only through COBOL and C; OS/2 EE Query Manager implements it in COBOL, C, REXX, and Fortran.

4.3.5 Communications Interface

The Communications Interface element of the CPI (often abbreviated CPIC) defines a specific type of inter-program communication in which programs hold a synchronized "conversation" with each other as peers. The programs are implemented to know and expect this type of conversation to take place (they use the call interface specified by CPIC). This type of peer-to-peer communications takes place over a logical connection set up following the SNA Logical Unit 6.2 (LU6.2) protocol. An earlier subroutine call interface, Advanced Program to Program Communications (APPC), also uses LU6.2 and is the basis for CPIC. Programs written to CPIC can coexist with programs written to APPC.

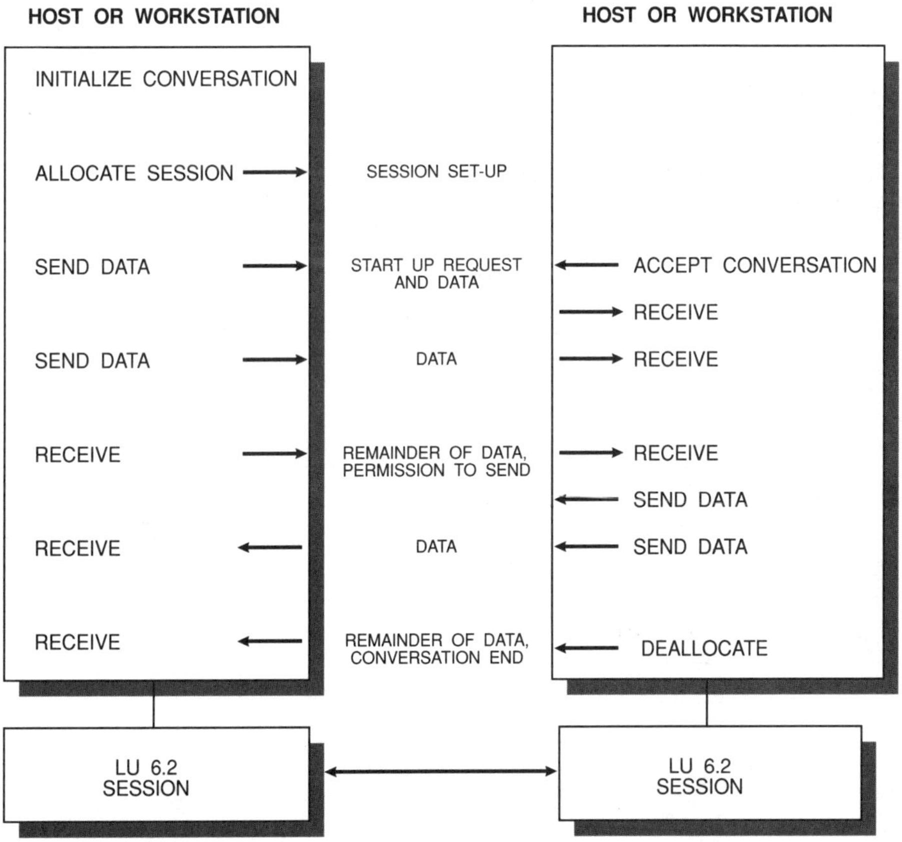

Figure I.28 Programs Using the CPI Communications Interface

Peer-to-peer communications can be contrasted with other communications protocols, e.g. remote file transfer protocols, or mainframe-to-terminal protocols where one program is clearly in control of the session. LU6.2 communication opens up a much more sophisticated type of program-to-program communication across the SAA environments.

Figure I.28 shows two programs interacting using the CPIC call interface. One program initiates the conversation and the other program "accepts" the conversation. From then on, data transfer takes place by a series of "send" and "receive" calls until the conversation is terminated by the originating program.

LU6.2 implementing software is available in all SAA environments. However, the subroutine set defined in CPIC is currently available only under VM/CMS. Figure I.29 shows software implementing either APPC or CPIC. [Note that this chart refers to software for implementing LU6.2 communications. The LU6.2 Session Services protocol itself is a component of SAA Common Communications Support.

LU 6.2 API Operating Environment	APPC	CPIC
MVS TSO	VTAM	[NYA]
VM CMS	VTAM	CPIC
OS/400	OS/400	[NYA]
OS/2 EE	OS/2 EE V1.1	[NYA]
IMS/TM	Subset	[NYA]
CICS	VTAM	[NYA]
[NYA] = Not yet available		

Figure I.29 Communications Interface Availability

4.3.5.1 Hidden Communications in Enabling Software

It is not always necessary to use the CPIC or APPC subroutines directly in order to establish this type of communication. While you may want to use these calls in your programs to control all aspects of the conversation, there are many situations where you can achieve similar results without doing all the work.

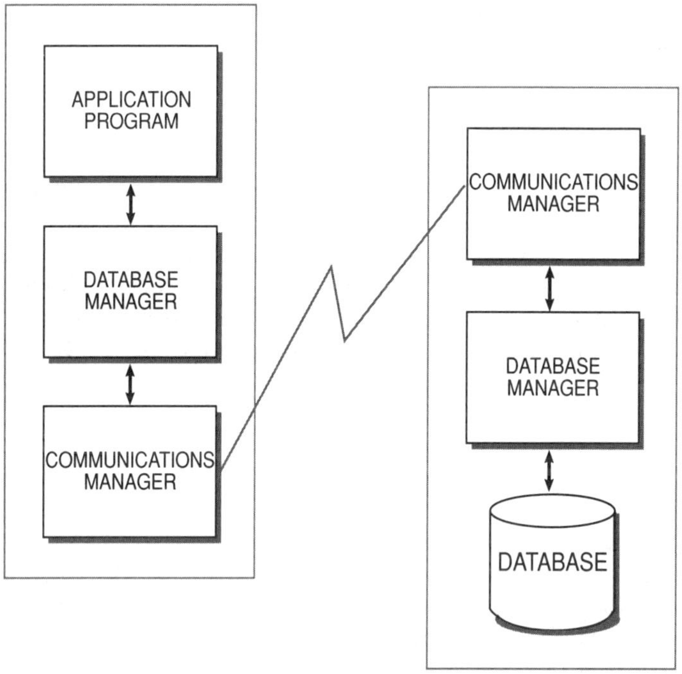

Figure I.30 Use of Communications By Enabling Software

The distributed processing mechanisms being developed as part of enabling software for other CPI services use LU6.2 as their underlying communications mechanism. Distributed data interfaces in SQL/DS and OS/2 Database Manager, for example, use LU6.2 communications to accomplish their tasks, but hide its use from the application programmer. The diagram in Figure I.30 portrays this concept as it is implemented in OS/2. An application program makes a database access request to the Database Manager. In turn, the DBM uses the Communications Manager to retrieve the data from a remote system.

Using service facilities such as these is often simpler than using CPIC or LU6.2 directly.

[Most enabling products that use LU6.2 for creating distributed interfaces currently use APPC subroutines. APPC communications programs are compatible with CPIC programs.]

4.3.6 Repository Interface

With the announcement of AD/Cycle, IBM's SAA application development environment, a Repository Interface was added to the CPI. The Repository Interface defines the call interface that can be used to put data into or retrieve data from a data repository via an entity-relationship model of data access. The initial implementing software is Repository Manager/MVS (versions in other environments are promised) which provides a development data repository implemented in DB2. Chapter 7 describes this software in detail.

The Repository Interface provides a way of gaining access to data via "encapsulating programs," i.e., gatekeepers which check access rights, edit your data, and perform various other functions (defined by you) before giving you access to the data. This is effectively an implementation of an "object-oriented database" and will have many potential uses (see Chapter 10 for a primer on object orientation). In addition to being the focus of application design and development data in AD/Cycle, it is also used in IBM's Computer Integrated Manufacturing systems and is intended to be used in a new network definition program (*Programming Announcement 289-479*). As the capabilities of object-oriented databases become more widely understood, the Repository Interface will be expanded to include object-oriented interface elements.

4.4 Other Application Support Services

There are several other application services provided in one or more of the SAA operating environments that deserve mention here. They are not implementations of parts of the CPI, but they provide services at a similar level. They are indicative of the types of services that programmers might want added to the CPI in furtherance of the idea of common programming interfaces.

4.4.1 Help

CUA specifies the incorporation of user "help" facilities into the user interface of all applications. Users should be able to get help information regarding:

- use of the application ("tutorial" help),
- the application screen they are using ("extended" help),
- the actions they are performing ("command" help),
- the special keys called for ("keys" help),
- the specific fields on the screen ("contextual" help),
- how to use the help system itself ("help" for help), and
- cross-references to other help information ("reference phrase" and "index" help).

The Help Manager provides the programmer with system services for implementing these various types of help facilities. Help Manager functions can be invoked in programs via direct subroutine calls. Help panels are defined using the Dialog Tag Language (see above). Specific tags identify the panel as a "help panel." They assign a name to the help panel, and that name is then used in the application to specify where it should be invoked. ["When" it should be invoked is up to the user, of course, and the way in which he or she requests help.] Help panels appear as pop-up windows near the window they are associated with. Figure I.31 shows a typical help panel.

The Help Manager was introduced with Release 1.2 of OS/2 in both standard and extended editions. IBM has not committed to implementing a full Help Manager in other SAA environments (the CUA models calling for help are specifically targeted at the PWS environment).

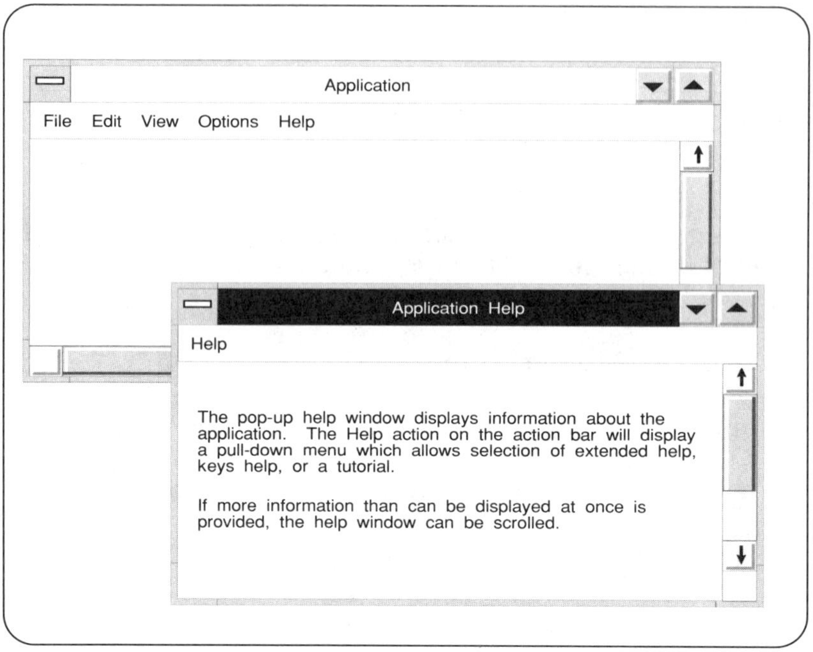

Figure I.31 Pop-up Help Window

4.4.2 Application Manager

In the announcement of OS/2 Standard Edition Version 1.2 (*Programming Announcement 289-218*), one of the "highlights" of the release is listed as:

> *User interface enhancements through the Desktop Manager using iconic representation and direct manipulation for files and programs*

The Desktop Manager is the first step at providing overall applications management and high level interaction. It allows applications to be invoked by selecting its icon (double clicking the mouse button) or by selecting a file which is designated as needing that application (not unlike the Macintosh desktop interface). It also allows interaction among files and devices, for example, copying a file by moving its icon over a disk icon.

Applications management will become an increasingly important function of the operating system, particularly as applications move more and more into the distributed and cooperative processing arena. OfficeVision provides an indication of the type of application management that is necessary in the enterprise systems environment.

The OfficeVision desktop implements the CUA Workplace Model. It provides "iconized" application and file management capabilities both for local and distributed applications. Users of OfficeVision can invoke application functions in a common way, regardless of where the underlying application is operating. They have access both to local and remote data, sometimes without having to know which is which. In short, OfficeVision attempts to provide a "single system view" to applications across the enterprise. [Chapter 12 discusses the implementation of the single system view strategy.]

The current OS/2 Desktop Manager provides only a minimum number of application management functions. Whether some of these will be migrated from OfficeVision to future versions of OS/2 remains to be seen.

4.5 Distributed Data

A major component of IBM's strategy for enterprise-wide computing is to provide users with transparent access to data regardless of its location. Although not itself a separate component of SAA, the implementation of this strategy is embodied in products which implement the Database Interface and Common Communications Support. Hidden behind names like Distributed Data Management (DDM), Remote Data Services (RDS), and Remote Relational Access Support (RRAS), IBM is trying to bring together a set of diverse components into a common approach to distributed data among applications and operating environments.

Distributed data can be stored in either files or relational databases. Distributed file management deals with access to files and their contents. Distributed relational data deals with access requests from relational database management systems on the various SAA platforms. Current IBM products implement only a small fraction of a fully integrated distributed data access strategy.

4.5.1 Distributed Relational Data

The eventual aim of the distributed relational data strategy is to provide the ability to issue SQL statements on any SAA platform without regard to where individual tables are actually stored. This strategy will be implemented using the Distributed Relational Data Architecture introduced in June 1990. At the current time, only a few parts of this overall strategy are available in delivered software. There are so many restrictions that IBM refers to different level capabilities separately, as shown in Figure I.32 and discussed below. [Note that while ECF and AS/400 PC Support do not implement specific SAA interfaces, they provide some of the capabilities discussed in this section.]

Services	MVS TSO/E	VM CMS	OS/400	OS/2 EE
Remote Request	ECF [*]	ECF [*]	AS/400 PC Support [*]	Via ECF and AS/400 PC Support [*]
Remote Unit of Work	DB2 V2 R2	RRAS SQL/DS	[NYA]	OS/2 EE 1.2
Distributed Unit of Work	DB2 V2 R2 (read only)	[NYA]	[NYA]	[NYA]
Distributed Request	[NYA]	[NYA]	[NYA]	[NYA]
[*] = See text note [NYA] = Not Yet Available				

Figure I.32 Distributed Data Services

In a remote request, a program is requesting access to a single remote database per SQL statement. Each statement is independent of every other (i.e., each statement is an independent "unit of work," implying a "commit point" or synchronization point). Remote unit of work allows multiple SQL statements to be performed in a single unit of work accessing single remote databases. Distributed unit of work expands this capability further to include multiple databases at one or more nodes on the network. Various database releases implement this part of the distributed data architecture. Distributed request is the broadest capability in that multiple databases could be accessed in any SQL statement and multiple SQL statements could be contained in a unit of work. No IBM products currently implement this level of distributed function.

One other set of restrictions needs to be considered at the current time. Implementation of remote and distributed unit of work is limited to "like-to-like" database access. RRAS only allows SQL/DS systems to access SQL/DS systems; OS/2 EE systems can only access OS/2 EE systems. Products implementing remote request, e.g. Enhanced Connectivity Facility and AS/400 PC Support, allow workstation access to remote host databases. "Cross system" distributed relational data access capabilities are being added one step at a time.

4.5.1.1 Implementation in DB2 and SQL/DS

DB2 Version 2 Release 2 includes initial remote unit of work and distributed unit of work support. SQL/DS currently provides only remote unit of work. The limitations in this support are significant. Communication is only among "like" systems: between DB2 and DB2 or between SQL/DS and SQL/DS; relational databases running on OS/400, OS/2 EE systems cannot be accessed at all. There are also some differences depending on whether you are trying to *read* remotely or *write* remotely. You can read data from any number of DB2 systems within a single SQL unit of work. However, you can only write to a single DB2 system, and that system must be local if you are using IMS/TM or CICS, but can be remote if you are using TSO or batch. Got that? If not, see Figure I.33.

Distributed Data Function Requester/Server	Read	Write
MVS Batch to Any MVS	Multiple local or remote [2]	Single local or remote [1]
MVS CICS or IMS/TM to Any MVS	Multiple local or remote [2]	Single local only
VM to VM	Single local or remote [1]	Single local or remote [1]
[1] = Remote Unit of Work	[2] = Distributed Unit of Work	

Figure I.33 DB2 and SQL/DS Distributed Data Access Restrictions

4.5.1.2 Implementation in OS/2 EE Database Manager

The situation with OS/2 EE Database Manager is somewhat clearer. The Remote Data Services features of Release 1.2 of OS/2 EE allows applications to access databases on the same or other OS/2 EE DBMs. Access to DB2, SQL/DS, and OS/400 Database Manager is not yet provided, although near-term announcement of "cross system" distributed data access is expected.

This release implements the remote unit of work capability allowing only a single database to be accessed within a commit point. Multiple databases can be accessed from separate SQL units of work within the same program. Distributed access functions the same for both reading and writing.

Figure I.34 summarizes the distributed data capabilities provided by the OS/2 EE Release 1.2 Database Manager and the DOS requestor feature.

Distributed Data Function Requester/Server	Read	Write
OS/2 EE to OS/2 EE	Single local or remote [*]	Single local or remote [*]
DOS to OS/2 EE	Single remote [*]	Single remote [*]
[*] = Remote Unit of Work		

Figure I.34 OS/2 EE DBM Distributed Data Access Restrictions

4.5.2 Distributed File Management

Just as there is a distributed relational data strategy, there is a parallel strategy for access to flat files. This strategy ranges from the simplest transfer of files from one machine to another to direct access of individual records in different files on different machines. Some aspect of distributed file management is in use in most organizations today.

Host-PC file transfers and file movement across a LAN via a file server represent one level of distributed file management. Programmers must have a mechanism for effecting the transfer, and system administrators must have procedures for dealing with data integrity. IBM products which assist in implementing this capability include AS/400 PC Support and the MVS and VM Enhanced Connectivity Facility (ECF).

Distributed file management also provides access to records within files. Existing record oriented language instructions (e.g. OPEN, READ, WRITE, CLOSE) will be used to access both local and remote files. The distributed file management capability provides a directory of where files are located and uses communication facilities to retrieve them as if they were local.

This function was introduced to SAA with the announcement of OS/400. OS/400 implements the Distributed Data Management architecture first announced in 1986 for the System 36 and System 38. IBM added DDM to the SAA Communications Support and stated its intention to add this capability to the other SAA operating environments. At this time, DDM is used primarily with IBM mid-range computers, System 36, 38, and AS/400, although it also allows retrieval of data from CICS/MVS systems. When DDM products are implemented in other SAA platforms, this architecture should see wide applicability in distributed applications.

5. Common Communications Support

What we've got here is a failure to communicate.
Donn Pearce, "Cool Hand Luke"

Communications is the heart of the cooperative processing strategy. Standard, easy to use, reliable communications mechanisms are required for effective use of enterprise-wide computing resources. SAA Common Communications Support (CCS) defines the architectures, protocols, and strategies that will be implemented across the SAA platforms. While much of this world will be hidden from view for the typical application system developer, it is important to have at least a broad understanding of system-to-system communications mechanisms.

At first glance, Common Communications Support looks like a hodgepodge of standards designed to fit existing IBM products. It does take more of a product-oriented approach than other components of SAA (versus the standards-oriented approach of CUA, for example) and is largely based on IBM's other major architectural strategy, Systems Network Architecture. The various CCS components are grouped according to the level of communications they deal with, i.e session, network transmission, data link, etc. Additionally, components have been added to facilitate implementation of the international standard Open Systems Interconnection communications model. Together, they provide a common strategy for transparent communications among cooperating applications across an enterprise network.

[One of the purposes of the layered communications model is to isolate programs at higher levels from the details of what is going on at the lower levels. Similarly, "higher level" readers only need to become familiar with some of the terminology and can skim the following sections of this chapter, returning to those few that directly affect their SAA implementation.]

5.1 Multi-layer Data Communications Model

It's all in the packaging.

Advertising axiom

As in the case of a general software architecture, communications architects have divided their world into "layers." These range from the "physical" layer of wires to the "application" layer. The first deals with the capability to transmit and receive electrical signals; the last tries to hide the entire communications process from the application programmer by providing higher level services. Each layer in between specifies the way in which information will be packaged and interpreted by different devices attached to a network.

There are two widely referred to models of communications, the International Standards Organization (ISO) Open Systems Interconnection (OSI) model, and IBM's Systems Network Architecture (SNA) model. When SAA Common Communications Support was defined, there appeared to be yet another layered communication architecture entering the picture. CCS only treats some of the SNA layers, combining and splitting others. It also now includes OSI as a parallel architecture. If for no reason other than to increase common understanding, it is worthwhile to review these architectures side by side.

5.1.1 OSI vs. SNA vs. SAA

In 1974, IBM introduced the Systems Network Architecture. SNA was to provide an overriding structure to the increasingly complex world of computer networks. It was to categorize the myriad communication protocols in use and yet to be defined, and clarify the interfaces among them. In 1977, the International Standards Organization proposed the Open Systems Interconnection Seven Layer Reference Model of communications protocols, similar in most respects to the SNA approach. In 1987, SAA Common Communications Support presented its "layered" architecture. Figure I.35 attempts to line up the layers in each model.

At the lowest level, both SNA and OSI provide guidance for physical interconnection of devices. These are hardware standards and, therefore, are not dealt with in SAA CCS which is a software architecture.

The next level deals with the control data necessary to transmit information across a physical link. It specifies the bits that have to be added at the front and back of a message so that it can be shipped around a network, across a telecommunications line, or on a public network. Data link protocols are often implemented by hardware or in a combination of hardware and software.

Several commonly referred to communications architectures are actually only data link protocols. For example Synchronous Data Link Control (SDLC) is a data link control layer protocol, as is the token-ring network protocol (although the term token-ring is often used to refer also to a physical ring architecture as well). The recently introduced Integrated Services Digital Network (ISDN) also contains a standard for data link control (as well as separate standards for physical and network layers). Older network architectures, e.g. the Xerox Network System (XNS) commonly used on Ethernet networks, include data link protocols but actually overlap several of the OSI/SNA layers.

At the next layer, the architectures start to diverge. OSI distinguishes a network layer which controls routing of traffic on the network, and a transport layer which deals with transmission of data and error recovery. In SNA, a single path control layer is defined for these functions. In CCS, this layer is called the network layer.

Both OSI and CCS define a session services layer. This layer defines the way in which two programs on different nodes in the network coordinate the transfer of data. SNA splits this layer into transmission control and data flow control. LU6.2 is a session services protocol.

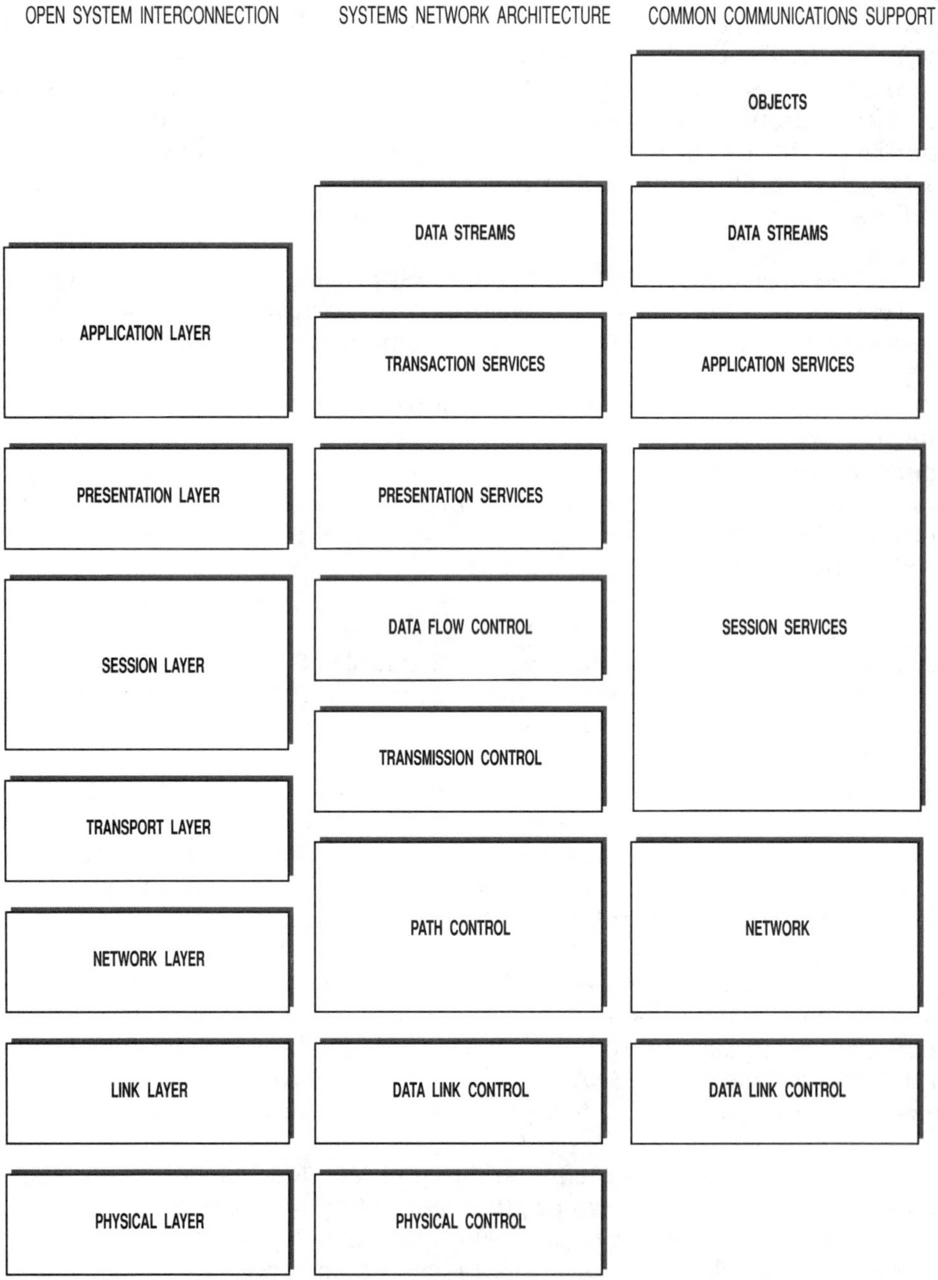

Figure I.35 The OSI, SNA, and SAA Communications Models

Moving up in the "protocol stack," both SNA and OSI architectures define presentation services. Presentation services programs coordinate the translation of different data and coding structures on different types of computers and workstations. Presentation protocols specify how these streams should be encoded so that they can be commonly interpreted. These protocols and programs are concerned with data syntax, their patterns and representation, not semantics or meaning. ASCII to EBCDIC translation and data re-formatting programs may be presentation layer services. Translation of character sets across different languages ("code page translation") is also a presentation layer service. By inclusion of certain OSI protocols, CCS provides some presentation layer services for the OSI communications environment. SNA presentation layer services are not included.

Application services (called "transaction services" in SNA) are programs which communicate directly with the user, such as file transfer and electronic mail. Some functions considered application services by OSI are off the chart for SNA (they are considered part of the application itself and not part of the communications architecture). CCS has a similar application services layer.

CCS and SNA also define high level "data streams," the contents and control information of a message in a specified format. Data streams are defined for messages between programs and non-programmable workstations, printers, or other programs. CCS further includes the definition of "objects" as components of a Document Content Architecture data stream.

For the most part, application programmers deal only at the session layer and above. LU6.2 is a session layer protocol. Document Interchange Architecture is an application services layer component. 3270 Data Stream and Document Content Architecture are data streams.

5.1.2 Using the Layered Model

The purpose of the layered model is to delineate different communications functions and separate the programs that have to deal with them. This allows different types of activities to go on at different levels, without regard to functions that may be taking place at lower levels, or even how they may change over time.

Creating this type of model requires the construction of messages that have "header data" targeted for programs at each level. Figure I.36 shows the construction of a communications message. Each level in the "protocol stack" has added its headers to the user data. Each header is typically one to four bytes. While this may seem excessive, remember that even simple telecommunications systems using character mode terminals on asynchronous communications lines had their "ACK" characters and start and stop bits. Trying to route full screens or documents around a wide area network obviously requires somewhat more control information.

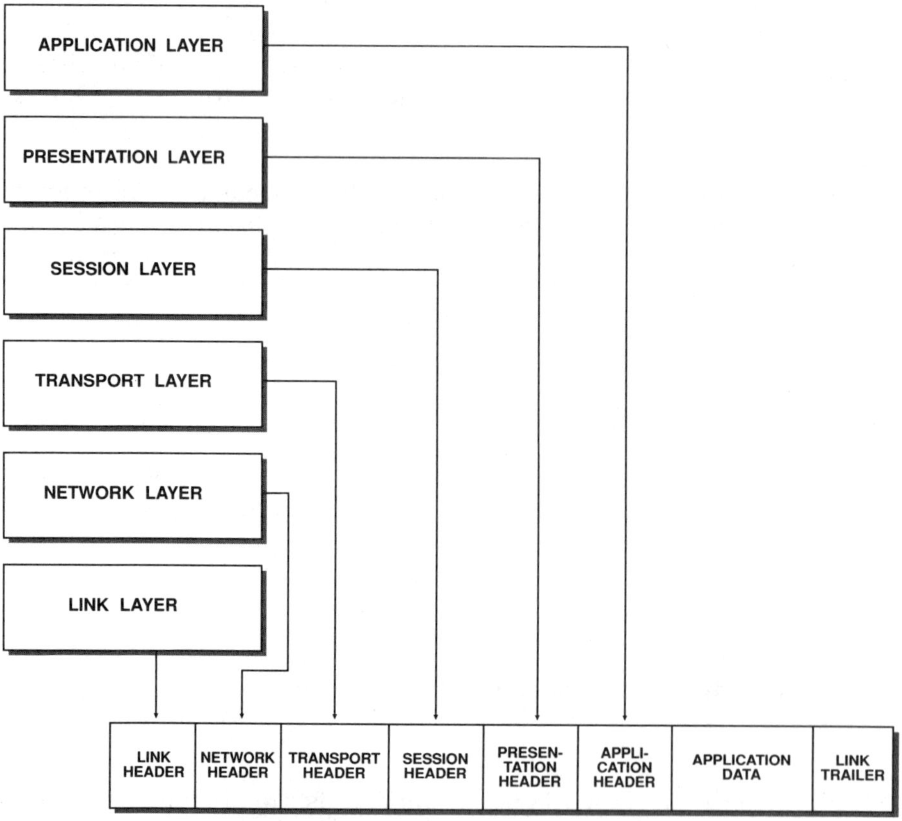

Figure I.36 Layered Communications Message

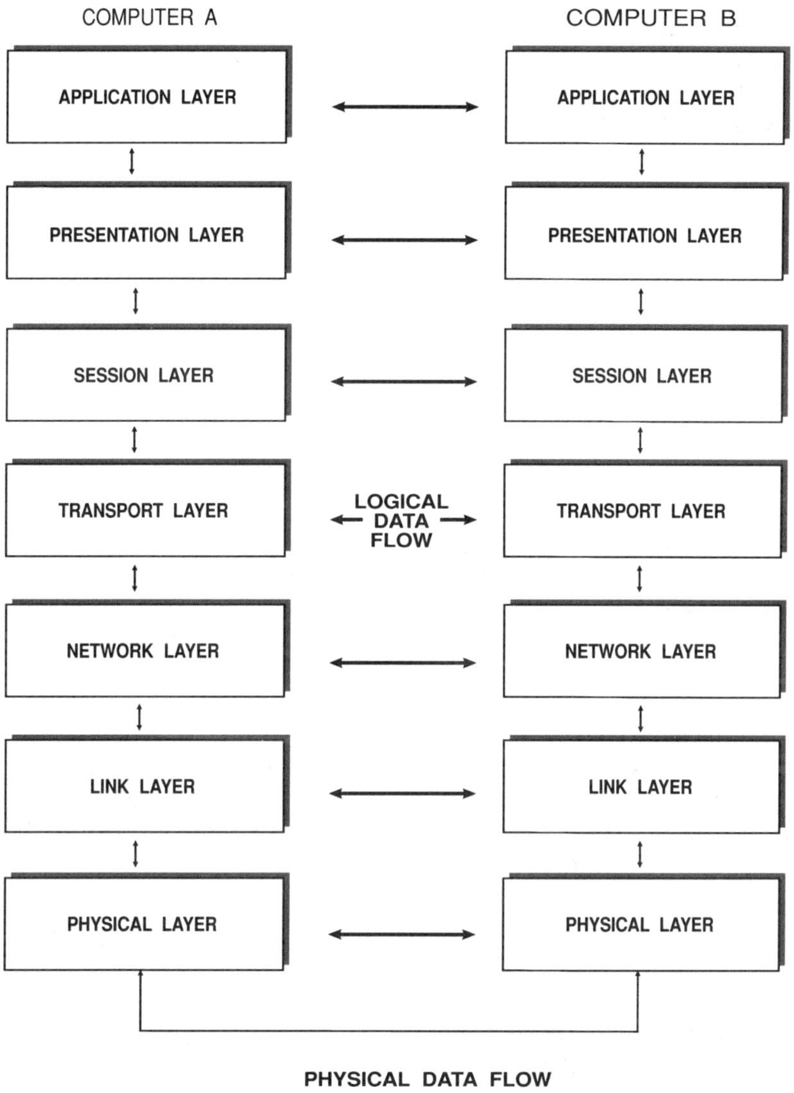

Figure I.37 Using the Layered Communications Model

Programs on different computers wishing to communicate establish "logical" connections at the same level. A network control program on one machine establishes connection with a similar network control layer program on another machine via the header information in the message specifically targeted to it. This "logical connection" is indicated in Figure

I.37 as the logical data path. The physical data path goes down the protocol stack on one machine with the program at each level adding its header information, and up the protocol stack on the other with each program stripping away the appropriate header as it is interpreted. Programs on the same computer deal only with programs in the next higher or lower layers. Programs on different computers logically deal only with programs on the same level.

5.2 Data Link Controls

Data link control protocols are the basic mechanisms for putting data onto communications networks. They allow for control of the rate at which data flows onto a communications line, for the detection of and recovery from errors, and for distinguishing between control information and data.

Data link controls are typically implemented in a combination of hardware and software, often via programmable read-only memory (PROM) programs executed by a special processor chip. From among the many data link controls in use, CCS includes three, although there are indications that others may be added.

5.2.1 Local Area Network Data Link Protocols

5.2.1.1 Token-Ring

The token-ring control architecture is the only local area network data link protocol included in SAA Common Communications Support. It is used in local area networks whose stations are electrically connected in a ring. Token ring was a relatively late entrant into the local area network market and does not yet enjoy the popularity of other network protocols.

["Token-ring" is used to refer both to a physical layer topology and the protocol to send information over it. This dual use is often a source of confusion. Furthermore, you can use SDLC and TCP/IP protocols on top of a token-ring protocol on token-ring networks. Maybe someday the priesthood of networking will specify their products in terms of the OSI protocol layers they map to.]

[While we are on the topic of token-ring networks, don't assume that the stations need be physically in a ring. Clever use of wiring control stations called multistation access units (MAUs) allows workstations to be in any physical configuration you want. Typically, all offices on a floor are wired into a central wiring closet where the MAUs are located. When a workstation or other device is powered up, circuitry in the MAU connects it into an appropriate place on the ring.]

5.2.1.2 Other Networks

Ethernet is currently the most popular physical networking approach for local area networks. It was developed at Xerox's Palo Alto Research center by some of the same people who had worked on the Department of Defense Arpanet, the granddaddy of wide-area networks. Support for Ethernet networks is now available in both OS/2 EE and MVS, and is widely available for UNIX systems, including AIX. This means that part of the enterprise network can use Ethernet and part token-ring, with appropriate hardware and software bridges between them. Application programmers accessing higher level protocols, such as the LU6.2 session layer protocol, should not even know the difference. Ethernet is not, however, an element of SAA CCS.

IBM has also introduced TCP/IP support on top of token-ring networks (the TCP/IP message is encapsulated by the token-ring control headers) under AIX (IBM's brand of UNIX). This will make it easier to connect UNIX systems onto SAA networks. Full support of TCP/IP across SAA platforms cannot be too far behind. For example, TCP/IP Connectivity Utilities for the AS/400 were announced in September 1989 and delivered in January 1990.

IBM is increasingly recognizing the need to provide support for a variety of network types and protocols. While token-ring continues to grow in popularity, thousands of networks of other types exist, and the key to transparent distributed processing and wide-area networks is interconnectivity. While IBM is now supporting the major network protocols on many of its product lines, it has not made the strategic statement implied by including them in CCS.

5.2.2 Synchronous Data Link Control (SDLC)

Synchronous Data Link Control is most widely used on networks of IBM mainframe computers. Many thousands of 3270-type terminals are connected to controllers which communicate with System/370s using SDLC. It is now and will continue to be a major component of SAA networking.

SDLC is used for controlling the transmission of data streams from one point to another, from one "link station" to another on a wide area network. Link station refers to the portion of a computer (both hardware and software), controller, or terminal that attaches to a communications line and controls the transmission. SDLC communication can be sent over point-to-point direct communications lines, switched point-to-point, and non-switched multi-point. The communications line itself can range from telephone lines to high-speed optical lines to satellite links. This range of options makes SDLC a very versatile data link protocol.

SDLC transmissions are organized into "frames" consisting of data and control information. The details of SDLC transmission frames are available in numerous manuals and texts for those who are interested. Briefly, headers and trailers defined by the SDLC protocol are placed around a message passed down from a higher level communication protocol, just as was generally discussed above. Receiving stations interpret this information, determine if the message is intended for the station receiving it, deal with any errors, and acknowledge receipt of the message. The SDLC protocol thus provides a synchronized communications mechanism where sender and receiver are synchronized by the receipt acknowledgment. The remaining message is then available to be processed by higher level protocol routines.

[The word "synchronous" in SDLC actually refers to the method of synchronizing physical transmission via a clock signal, as opposed to the use of start and stop bits for each character as used in "asynchronous" transmission.]

SDLC is supported on all SAA platforms, via the OS/400 operating system, OS/2 EE Communications Manager, and the Network Control Program on System/370 operating systems.

5.2.3 X.25 Packet Switched Networks

X.25, the international standard protocol for packet-switched networks, is part of CCS. Using this data link protocol, gateways into public packet-switched networks, such as Telenet and Compuserv, can be supported under an SAA standard networking scheme. [Within the IBM Systems Network Architecture scheme, X.25 is considered part of the data link control layer. The X.25 protocol for OSI, however, includes network, link, and physical layer information.]

Packet-switched networks were created to share expensive long-distance high-speed communications lines among many users. "Packets" of data are sent by the sending device over a dedicated line to a packet switching node (special purpose computer). The packet switching nodes are connected via a series of shared communications lines. The packet is routed to the receiving station via a series of switching nodes and communications lines. Since there are typically several paths from one user to another, various schemes have been developed for "least cost" routing (these are not data link layer protocols). Users get the benefit of high-speed, reliable transmission, but pay only for the amount of data they send over the network.

X.25 is supported on all SAA platforms, via the OS/400 operating system, OS/2 EE Communications Manager, and the Network Control Program Packet Switching Interface on System/370 operating systems.

5.3 Network

Network control is the third level (counting from the bottom) in the OSI seven-level communications architecture. The primary function of network layer protocols is routing among nodes in a network.

CCS includes Type 2.1 Node architecture for SNA networks and two network protocols for OSI networks. IBM currently supports OSI Connectionless-Mode Network Services for local area networks and Connection-Oriented Network Services for X.25 networks via the OSI/Communications Subsystem for System/370 operating systems.

5.3.1 SNA Type 2.1 Node Architecture

SNA defines four "node types" to indicate the different network routing capabilities in specific devices. Only one of these, type 2.1, is available across the SAA operating environments. Other node types define higher (type 4 and 5) or lower (type 2.0) levels of capabilities at the network node.

Type 2.1 nodes are defined as "peripheral nodes," i.e., they provide end user access to the network rather than acting as network routing and control points. As opposed to type 2.0, type 2.1 nodes support direct connections to other 2.1 nodes without going through a network control point (useful in establishing routing for program-to-program communication).

Type 2.1 node protocol is supported on all SAA platforms, via the OS/400 operating system, OS/2 EE Communications Managers, and the Network Control Program/Virtual Telecommunications Access Method on System/370 operating systems.

5.4 Session Services

CCS Session Services encompasses both SNA and OSI protocols. SNA Logical Unit Type 6.2 (LU6.2) has received the most attention since it is key to the idea of program-to-program communication on a peer basis. OSI protocols which provide similar functions have been added to CCS and are currently implemented in the OSI/Communications Subsystem for the System/370.

5.4.1 Program-to-Program Communications

Program-to-program communication is a relatively new idea in teleprocessing. It stems from the desire to use programmable workstations as more than just terminal emulators when communicating with host-based systems.

Initial efforts at mainframe-workstation communication were "program-to-device." Many mainframes have had the ability to communicate with "dumb terminals" over telephone lines for a long time (using asynchronous communication, "async"). In the first PC-to-mainframe links, the mainframe thought it was talking with simple (dumb) remote terminals. These were character-by-character transmissions; all that could be sent was a simple stream of characters. The transmission began with a special "start of transmission" character (actually SOH for Start of Header) and ended with an "end of transmission" character. [Special characters are defined in the first group of characters in the ASCII character set.] Life was simple, but speeds were slow, error recovery was essentially nonexistent, and users were dissatisfied.

With the introduction of "screen-at-a-time" terminals (the 3270 series is by far the predominant type), life got more complicated. The 3270 Data Stream defined not only the individual characters, but where on the screen they should be placed (their position in a buffer which maps the screen), what color and other screen emphasis should be added, and other display-oriented information. It was still program-to-device communication, but at least the device wasn't quite so dumb (although it still wasn't programmable).

More interesting possibilities opened up when you substituted a personal computer for the 3270 device at the user end of the communication line . Not only was it possible to emulate the 3270, but also to write programs which sent messages back to the programs operating on the mainframe. Admittedly, this wasn't the purpose IBM designers had in mind when they created the 3270 Data Stream, but it was available and it worked.

The LU6.2 protocol was introduced to Systems Network Architecture to provide explicitly for communicating on a program-to-program basis. It is also a mainstay of SAA Common Communications Support.

5.4.1.1 Implementation and the CPI

The CPI Communications Interface provides the programming interface to use LU6.2 communications sessions. CPIC as an implemented software product is currently only available under VM/CMS. Advanced Program-to-Program Communications (APPC) also provides a programming interface to use LU6.2 and is implemented on the other SAA operating systems. Programs written using CPIC can communicate with programs written using APPC.

5.5 Application Services

Application services are utility programs which perform commonly used functions in network communications and management. The service programs included in CCS provide document transfer, message transfer, and network management services. Different programs are used in SNA and OSI networks. Since each application service defines an architecture for network traffic, programs other than IBM products can be constructed to conform to these components of CCS.

5.5.1 Document Interchange Architecture

Document Interchange Architecture (DIA) provides services to applications which must pass complex "documents" to each other. The DIA service programs provide distribution, library, and file transfer services. DIA invokes SNA Distribution Service for distribution of documents across the network.

DIA defines the control information for exchanging documents among different applications. The "documents" handled by DIA can be any file containing any type of information as long as the header and trailer are understood by DIA (uses its defined prefix, command sequence, and suffix around the data to be transmitted). DIA is used in IBM's (and other vendors') office systems and other products for inter-system communication.

DIA is currently implemented in several IBM products, including the OS/400 operating system and the Distributed Office Support System (DISOSS) under CICS. DISOSS is used by OfficeVision/MVS to connect to OfficeVision/2 LAN Server.

5.5.2 SNA Distribution Services

SNA Distribution Services (SNA/DS) specifies the components of a system for the movement and delivery of files, documents, or any other message across an SNA network. Using SNA/DS, the receiving user is not in direct communication with the sending user, but instead deals with a "distribution service unit," a node that is part of the SNA/DS distribution system. [DSUs may be established in any computer on the network as long as it is running programs which implement the SNA/DS architecture. Do not confuse the abbreviation DSU as used here to mean the "Data Service Unit" (similar purpose to a modem) of a digital communication circuit.] DSUs are logically connected to each other using LU6.2 connections. Since the receiving user need not even be attached to the DSU when something is sent to it, SNA/DS can provide a "store-and-forward" capability.

SNA/DS services are currently available in the OS/400 operating system and as the NetView Distribution Manager under CICS and TSO. SNA/DS is used in IBM office products such as DISOSS and OfficeVision.

5.5.3 SNA Management Services

The SNA Management Services (SNA/MS) architecture defines the messages that can be sent by different computers and devices on a network to help control the management of the network. Products like NetView initiate and interpret these messages to provide a user-level control center for problem management, performance and accounting management, and configuration and change management.

Not all components of the SNA/MS architecture are implemented on all IBM systems. In addition, some parts of the architecture are implemented on non-IBM systems that can connect to SNA networks. Problem management is currently the only function that is included in SAA. It is provided in VTAM and NetView on System/370 systems, as part of OS/400 communications support, and as a function of the OS/2 Communications Manager.

5.5.4 Distributed Data Management Architecture

Distributed Data Management (DDM) is IBM's architecture for implementing distributed data applications. Level 2 of the architecture dealt with file and record oriented data. Level 3, introduced in June 1990, adds IBM's strategies for implementing distributed relational data applications. DDM deals with the protocols for sharing data in sequential, direct, and stream data files, and in relational databases.

DDM specifies a set of verbs for opening and closing files, reading and writing data, locking data entries, and dealing with file directories.

Since DDM verbs can be used to access both local and remote data, products implement a "local data management interface" (LDMI) to determine whether the request can be satisfied locally. If not, it is passed on to a DDM process running on the local machine (called the "source" of the request). This process in turn establishes communications (typically via APPC) to a DDM process running on the "target" machine. This DDM process issues requests to the local data management system to fulfill the request and send it back to the source machine.

IBM products which implement DDM for non-relational data are currently available under OS/400 and CICS (operating as a target only). Products using DDM for relational data will be forthcoming.

[DDM should not be confused with the broader discussion of "distributed data" in the database sections of this book and of various IBM publications. This unfortunate historically based naming conflict is surprisingly unusual in SAA, given the number of different products and systems involved.]

5.5.5 Distributed Relational Data Architecture

In June 1990, the Distributed Relational Data Architecture (DRDA) was announced as a new application services protocol in CCS. DRDA specifies the commands and data to implement an SQL interface over a distributed database. DRDA uses LU6.2, Level 3 of DDM, Formatted Data Object Content Architecture (FD:OCA), and the Character Data Representation Architecture (CDRA).

5.5.6 OSI Application Layer Service

OSI application services included in CCS are:

- File Transfer, Access, and Management (FTAM) standard, to simplify transfer of files across systems regardless of data encoding, file access method or physical organization;

- X.400 Message Handling System, for creating electronic mail networks; and

- Association Control Service Element standard, for defining standard ways for applications to transfer information.

FTAM is implemented in the OSI/File Services products for System/370. X.400 is also implemented in a series of products for the System/370 operating systems. Association Control Service Element capabilities are included in the OSI/Communications Subsystem for these operating systems.

5.6 Data Streams

Some applications deal with streams of data elements, rather than relations, records, or files. Applications can communicate with each other more easily using common data stream formats. Two applications do not have to specifically know about each other's requirements if they are both using the same data stream format.

Data stream architectures specify control information for data streams to be passed between two applications or between an application and a device such as a printer or a workstation. Four data streams are defined in CCS:

- Mixed Objects: Document Content Architecture (application to application)

- Revisable-Form-Text: Document Content Architecture (application to application)

- 3270 Data Stream (application to workstation, application to application)
- Intelligent Printer Data Stream (application to printer)

Each data stream has unique characteristics that are required for its intended type of data transfer. The Document Content Architectures, for example, do not provide device specific information; 3270 Data Streams and IPDS do. The appropriate data stream can be constructed by an application and then sent to another application or device via a lower level communication service.

5.6.1 Document Content Architectures

Document Content Architectures (DCAs), first introduced in 1981, describe a standard protocol for applications to follow in exchanging certain types of data. DCAs specify control information for transmitting data which follows a document model, i.e., documents consist of pages which consist of objects of various types. DCAs can be used among applications operating on the same system or across a network (in which case the document data streams will be encapsulated in DIA headers and sent over LU6.2 connections via SDLC or token-ring data links).

The OSI model also includes a document content architecture, Office Document Architecture, as a Layer 7 protocol. While there are many similarities to IBM's MO:DCA, the OSI protocol is not currently included in SAA.

5.6.1.1 Mixed Object

Mixed Object: Document Content Architecture (MO:DCA) provides a generic capability for interpreting the component parts of a document. It is a relatively new DCA specification intended to expand upon the capabilities of earlier components.

The structure of the MO:DCA data stream can be thought of as a hierarchy of logical elements, from document to chapter to page to objects on a page. The objects on the page can be text, graphics (line drawings), or images. [The specification of the internal data in each object is defined in the Object Content Architecture for that type of object.] The function of the MO:DCA architecture is to specify the headers, trailers, and other control information for all aspects of the document structure.

In March 1990, additional specifications were added to MO:DCA to allow it to deal with "revisable form" documents in addition to its current capability to deal with "presentation form" documents. "Revisable form" implies that the document data stream contains enough information to continue working on it before it is printed on a specific device. These revisable documents can consist of text, images, and graphics. The MO:DCA specification, therefore, now includes a superset of the specification for Revisable Form Text:DCA and could be used as the data stream carrier for all components of all documents, regardless of form or content. The corresponding CCS element has not yet been updated by IBM to include this change.

Parts of the MO:DCA architecture are implemented in various IBM office applications such as ImagePlus and OfficeVision.

5.6.1.2 Revisable Form Text

Revisable Form Text:Document Content Architecture (RFT:DCA) includes text and formatting information so that documents can be passed to another application for further processing or assembled from components developed by several applications. RFT:DCA only deals with textual elements.

RFT:DCA is used by IBM's DisplayWrite word processing products and in OfficeVision on the AS/400.

5.6.2 3270 Data Stream

The 3270 Data Stream format was created for transmitting data from an application program to a 3270-type non-programmable workstation. In recent years, it has also been widely used to transmit data to personal computers operating in 3270 emulation mode and as an application-to-application protocol. This latter use will eventually be replaced by APPC type communication.

The logic behind the 3270 Data Stream format has to do with the hardware design of 3270-type devices. For screen display purposes, the workstation contains a buffer holding exactly the number of characters which can appear. Each character in the hardware buffer can be directly addressed so that specific characters on the screen can be changed.

3270 Data Streams specify either formatted strings of characters to appear on the screen or an unformatted data buffer (preferred for application-to-application communication). Header information and 3270 commands are included in the data stream specification.

3270 Data Streams are implemented in all SAA environments and many non-IBM environments. CICS, TSO, GDDM, IMS/TM, OS/400, and the OS/2 Communications Manager all provide this capability.

5.6.3 Intelligent Printer Data Stream

The Intelligent Printer Data Stream (IPDS) is used to send data from an application to a printer. It is primarily used in sending full pages from IBM host machines (AS/400, System/370) to laser printers. It provides for loadable fonts, stored overlays including graphics and bar codes, and printer device control. A wide variety of printers can interpret this data stream.

IPDS encapsulates objects using the same Object Content Architecture as Document Content Architecture. Pages can, therefore, contain text, images, and graphics. Using this approach, objects can be shipped from application to application and then directly to a printer without modification.

5.6.4 Character Data Representation Architecture

As part of the June 1990, announcement of architectures for distributed relational data, IBM announced the Character Data Representation Architecture (CDRA), a new data stream architecture for graphic characters. It is intended to ensure the unambiguous interpretation of data sent between the SAA database management systems. CDRA defines conversion mappings, character sets, and code pages for SAA platforms.

5.7 Objects

IBM has defined an Information Interchange Architecture for office products. It includes DIA, DCA, and at the highest level, "objects." [This use of the term "object" should be distinguished from its use in discussing "user objects" and "programming objects."] Object Content Architectures (OCAs) define the presentation formatting codes for different types of data that may be contained in office documents. Applications such as GDDM, DisplayWrite, PROFS, ImagePlus, and DISOSS create objects which follow the specified form and can then be interpreted by any other application which is prepared to process OCA.

The different object architectures defined as part of CCS are:

- Presentation Text Object Content Architecture specifies text string location, orientation, and content;

■ Image Object Content Architecture defines such parameters as size, resolution, compression algorithm, and image data elements;

■ Graphics Object Content Architecture defines drawing primitives (line, arc, areas) and attributes (color, pattern, line width, etc.);

■ Font Object Content Architecture specifies character shape, position, and overall font descriptive information; and

■ Field-formated Object Content Architecture provides for the specification of data types and data structures along with the actual data field to facilitate interpretation across SAA systems.

The Object Content Architectures define the objects that will be "carried" in a data stream, such as Document Content Architecture or the Intelligent Printer Data Stream.

In its March 1990, announcements, IBM added several new objects in this architecture by creating the Object Method Architecture for Revisable Form Documents and Business Graphics. A separate object method defines the style and format of each element of a document. These revisable form objects are not currently included in CCS.

5.8 CCS Summary

CCS includes those protocols and architectures from SNA and OSI that IBM intends to implement across all SAA platforms. Figure I.38 groups the CCS components by communication layer.

Protocol Type	CCS Component
Data Link Control	Token-Ring Synchronous Data Link Control X.25 Packet-Switched Data Network
Network	Type 2.1 Node OSI Connectionless Network Services OSI Connection-Oriented Network Services
Session Services	LU 6.2 OSI Session Layer
Application Services	Document Interchange Architecture SNA/Distribution Services SNA/Management Services Distributed Data Management Distributed Relational Data Architecture File Transfer, Access, and Management X.400 Message Handling Association Control Service Element
Data Streams	Mixed Object:DCA Revisable-Form-Text:DCA 3270 Data Stream Intelligent Printer Data Stream Character Data Representation Architecture
Objects	Presentation Text Object Image Object Graphics Object Font Object Field-formatted Object

Figure I.38 Summary of CCS Components

6. OfficeVision: SAA Application Software

My Oberon! what visions have I seen!
Wm. Shakespeare, A Midsummer Night's Dream, Act IV, Scene 1

On May 16, 1989, IBM announced its OfficeVision family of products. OfficeVision is a complete office environment, providing multiple office applications and a coordinating "workplace," all available in a wide variety of configurations over a wide variety of platforms.

OfficeVision's importance to IBM is as a way to "capture the desktop" of millions of office workers and from there to cement firmly the idea of cooperative processing *a la mode* IBM. For our purposes, OfficeVision's importance is as a major application system designed to take advantage of SAA.

6.1 General Capabilities

OfficeVision competes in the marketplace with Digital's All-In-One, Data General's Comprehensive Electronic Office, and Wang's Office, among others. It provides functions comparable to or exceeding the others in areas of electronic mail, calendar management, data storage and retrieval, help and tutorial functions, and overall application integration. IBM also supplies decision support software, some created jointly with independent software vendors, such as Metaphor's Data Interpretation System. With the addition of third party products, such as Lotus's 1-2-3/G or Microsoft's Excel, OfficeVision supplies a complete range of office software in highly integrated fashion.

	OS/2 LAN	OS/400	MVS	VM
Services				
Mail	R1	R1	[*]	[*]
Library	R2	R1	[*]	[*]
Contextual Search	R2	[NYA]	[NYA]	[NYA]
Calendar	R2	[*]	[*]	[*]
Address Book	R1	[*]	R2	[*]
Functions				
Folders	[SOD]	R1	[NYA]	[NYA]
Correspondence Editor [*]		R2	[*]	[*]
Decision Support	R2	[*]	R1	R1
Executive Support	[NYA]	[SOD]	[SOD]	R1
Facsimile	[NYA]	R1	R2	R1

[*] = Interim support provided by existing IBM products.
[NYA] = Not yet announced.
[SOD] = Statement of Direction issued without specific product announcement.

Figure I.39 OfficeVision Services and Functions

The OfficeVision family contains many components. Each operating environment has a basic "office feature" which includes certain "essential" office management services (by IBM's definition) and several optional functions. These major capabilities are listed in Figure I.39. Two major releases of the products were announced (at the same time) along with the availability of services and features in the different environments. The table shows which features will be available in Releases 1 and 2 for each of the SAA environments, as well as those cases where the capability is provided by some other IBM product on an interim basis. Due to a significant delay in delivering Release 2, IBM announced Release 1.1 to provide some features on a better schedule. Full availability of the OfficeVision/2 product is seen in the Release 2 deliveries.

6.2 An SAA Software Family

OfficeVision is an evolving family of products designed to work together in a wide array of cooperative processing environments. The current implementations are often based on previously existing IBM products, such as PROFS and AS/400 Office. The OfficeVision strategy shows how IBM is addressing migration to full SAA compliance within its own product line. It is an SAA application developed by the developer of SAA, and is a good case study of what following SAA really means.

OfficeVision conforms to many of the SAA standards. The "desktop interface" for workstation users follows the Common User Access Workplace Model. New office applications use the Common Programming Interface. The facilities of Common Communications Support are used to provide cooperative processing.

There are other aspects of OfficeVision that do not yet conform to SAA. NPT access to host facilities uses the formats of the underlying products, e.g. PROFS. In some cases, new PWS-based user interfaces have been implemented following the CUA Graphical Model. In others, the application appears in its older format even though it is invoked from the OfficeVision desktop. Some of the mainframe software, having been developed prior to the definition of SAA, is not implemented to the SAA CPI. Some types of cooperative processing use older communications protocols (remember that CPIC is only implemented in one environment at the current time).

OfficeVision is touted as an SAA product family, yet some parts do not follow SAA. All that this shows is that following SAA is not an all-or-nothing proposition. You can achieve the benefits of SAA by establishing an overall application architecture which allows you to evolve to full SAA compliance over a period of time.

And that is what IBM is doing.

6.2.1 OfficeVision Application Architecture

OfficeVision is an "architected" product family; there is an internal structure to the products which emphasizes commonality and extendibility. The internal program structure, at least of the OS/2 product, indicates that program functions have been grouped so that changes within a group can be made independently of changes in another group. This architecture is evident in the programming interfaces which accompany OfficeVision and which permit the integration of other office software.

Figure I.40 shows the architecture of OfficeVision/2 (for OS/2 EE LANs). In this product, IBM has built several levels of common function on top of the Common Programming Interface provided by SAA. These levels define the OfficeVision "application platform" which can be used by others in integrating applications into the OfficeVision workplace, or in developing their own office applications. [The application platform is included in Release 2.] The diagram shows four levels in the "application," each having at least a small interface with lower levels. Total isolation among architectural levels, while conceptually pleasing, is not likely in a real system. [This structure of the OfficeVision/2 product follows the tiered application architecture approach discussed in Chapter 10.]

The architectural tiers created in the OfficeVision/2 product are:

■ Extensions to the Common Programming Interface: routines that interface with the operating system to perform system-level operations, such as controlling task invocation and termination, manipulating queues, and managing memory. These routines are generally useful in programming complex PS/2 applications and could be, in a sense, additions to the SAA CPI. [These functions are listed under the System Resources Management heading in the OfficeVision/2 announcement (*Programming Announcement 289-201*).]

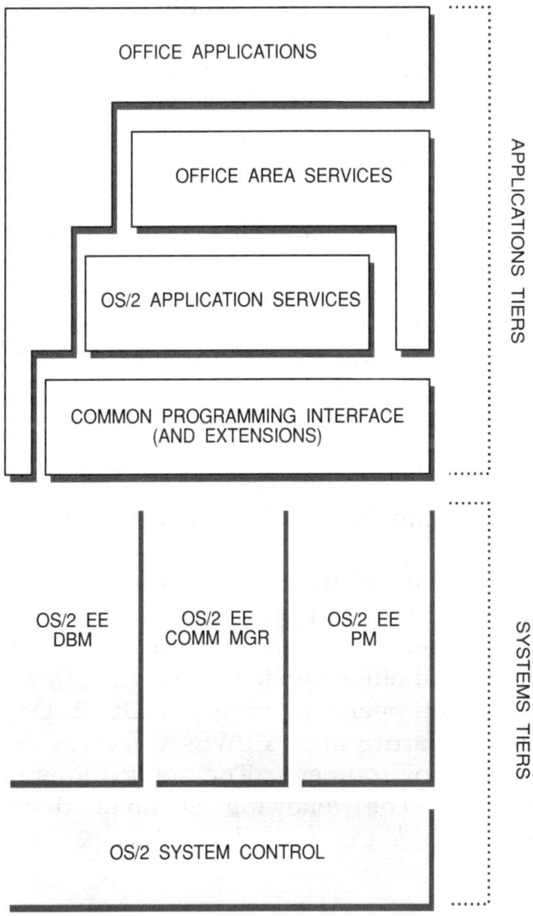

Figure I.40 OfficeVision/2 Architecture

- OS/2 Application Services: routines that perform common application functions of a general nature, such as directly accessing lines of text in a window, building and displaying error message windows, or converting dates and times to national language standards. These functions are more typically associated with applications than with the operating system (common application functions) and can be used across almost all types of applications. [Listed under the heading End-User Interface Implementation in the announcement.]

- Office Area Services: routines that handle functions common to the creation of office applications, such as retrieving the list of items in a mail in-basket, scheduling an event on a calendar, or translating a nickname into a network address. These are services which were created specifically to service office applications. [Announced as Office Application Invocation services.]

While certain functions are placed in certain architectural levels, any function (and the software which implements it) may migrate from a higher level to a lower level over time. That is to say, something created for a specific purpose may be found to have a more general purpose and should, therefore, be made available for that more general use. As an example, the items listed as Office Area Services could, with only slight generalization, be useful to other types of applications, e.g. Computer Integrated Manufacturing. They would then qualify as Common Application Services instead of just Functional Area Services. With even more generalization, they might even become part of the SAA CPI.

The overall architecture of the OfficeVision products is also evident at another level. The product in each environment is divided into an "office feature" (the desktop mechanism), a workstation connectivity feature, and the individual office applications. The office feature provides the user interface for each operating platform (OS/2, OS/400, MVS, and VM). The connectivity feature allows PWSs to act as user workstations regardless of the server environment. The applications provide the office functions themselves. The following sections discuss how these capabilities implement SAA Common User Access and the strategy of cooperative processing.

6.3 Cooperative Processing in OfficeVision

Office work is "cooperative work." I send you a status report; you send me a memo. We all schedule and attend a meeting. Several people sequentially review a document and add their comments. I have to do some of my work individually (preparing that report in the first place), but its purpose is for group consumption. OfficeVision supports cooperative work as a series of cooperative processing applications. Exactly how the cooperating group works and exactly how the cooperating applications are configured is up to you.

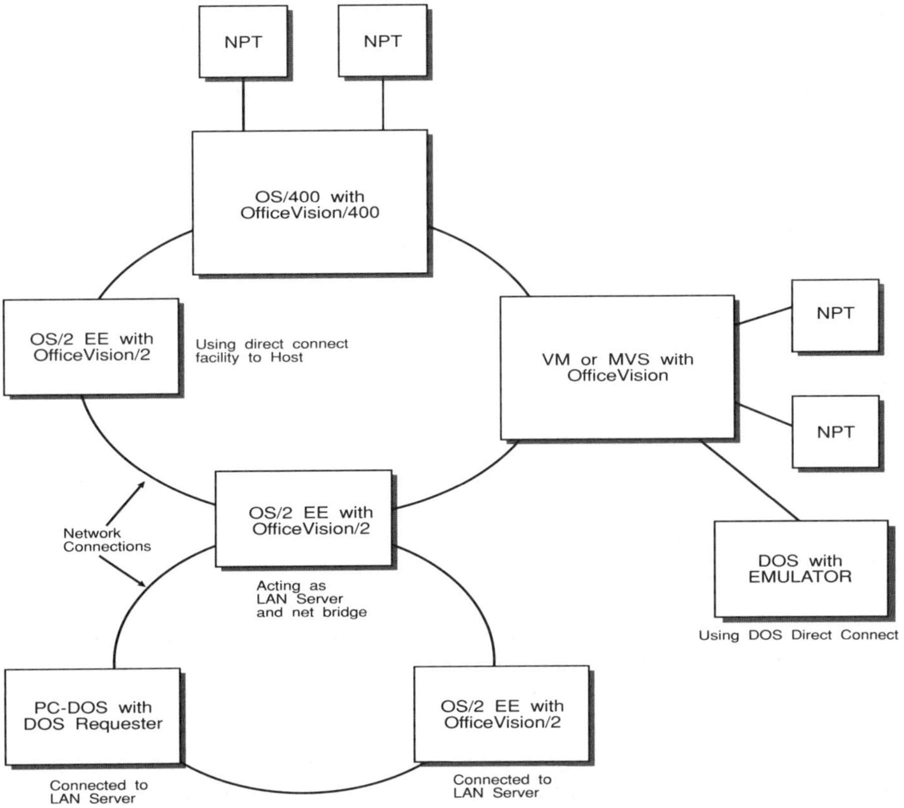

Figure I.41 Typical OfficeVision/2 Configuration

Figure I.41 is a schematic of a large scale OfficeVision network environment, perhaps the one suggested by the scenario in Chapter 1. OfficeVision users are physically connected via a network (for OS/2 and PC-DOS workstations) or to a host via a communications controller (for non-programmable terminals or PC-DOS workstations). They are logically connected either to the LAN server office software or to host office software via the "workstation connectivity feature." That is, some of the programs appearing on a PS/2 OfficeVision user's screen will be running locally, some on the LAN server, and some on a host. This distributed processing will be transparent because all will be invoked via the same user interface using the same steps. In this way, the PS/2 becomes a front end processor to any and all office software.

Even though some of the OfficeVision applications operate in stand-alone mode on individual platforms, the basic assumption is that the workstation, whether PWS or NPT, is attached to a "server." In this sense, a server is either a true LAN server or a host providing server-like functions. The server maintains the communications links among workstations and other servers. It also provides some of the processing functions. For example, regarding the calendar function in different situations:

- [Stand-alone] You may maintain your own calendar as a database application running on your individual PS/2.

- [Communications] Your calendar on your machine can be viewed by others using the Remote Data Services capabilities of the OS/2 DBM via network bridges and gateways.

- [Client-server application] A central calendar might be maintained on a database server machine. You would send a request to the meeting schedule application on the server and it would notify you when it had successfully scheduled the meeting.

Another capability of OfficeVision using the server approach is handling its own distribution. The OfficeVision software is installed on the LAN server and downloaded to the PWS. Capabilities will be available to automatically determine if the version of the software on a PWS is complete and up-to-date and to refresh it if necessary. This method of distributing application software uses the facilities of the server to ensure the integrity of software modules across the LAN. It anticipates a general "software distribution" capability which will become a necessity as distributed processing applications become more widely used.

6.4 Common User Access in OfficeVision

Not all components of the released OfficeVision product family follow CUA. But it comes about as close as you can get without throwing all your applications out and starting over. In the case of OS/2 applications, there were no existing applications so the new ones follow CUA. Existing host applications, for the most part, were left alone so that NPT users will see the applications they have been used to. Workstation users accessing host applications get a mixed bag, with some applications translated into a CUA format and others not. In either case, workstation users can invoke *all* applications, regardless of where they are or are coming from, via a CUA "workplace."

Workstation Host	PWS using OS/2 EE	PWS using DOS	NPT
OS/2 EE LAN	CUA Graphical and Workplace	"CUA-like"	n.a.
OS/400	[*]	Menu driven	Menu driven
MVS	[*]	Menu driven	Menu driven
VM	[*]	Menu driven	Menu driven

[*] = Mostly CUA Graphical and Workplace via OS/2 Office Feature; see text.

Figure I.42 Host-Workstation User Interfaces in OfficeVision

In general, OfficeVision applications get their CUA look from the use of PS/2s as front ends to all facilities. Whether your primary "office server" is another PS/2 on a local area network, or a host, the user interface function is based on implementing the CUA Workplace Model under OS/2 EE. NPT users today see whatever interface the existing applications provided. IBM has not specifically committed to making NPT access conform to the CUA Text Model or Entry Model, but it is reasonable to assume that they will. An additional step was taken for PC-DOS users with the inclusion of a "CUA-like" user interface based on third-party technology. This is available when the DOS machine is connected via a LAN. Figure I.42 summarizes the various interfaces available from different types of workstations communicating with the different host environments.

All host environments provide a "direct connect" capability with OS/2 workstations (environments indicated by [*] in Figure I.42). This OfficeVision feature (available in Release 2) allows workstation users to get some or all of their office functions by running mainframe applications. Under this mode of operation, the user may see a mixture of interface styles. Applications will all be invoked from the OfficeVision desktop, but the screens they will display may be in a non-CUA style.

Figure I.43 lists the interface styles for host office functions accessed on an OS/2 OfficeVision workstation using the direct connect capability. The host mail application data is always translated into a CUA window before being presented to the workstation user. Library and calendar functions (file manipulation) are, however, presented in whatever format the host would have presented them to a NPT. In this case, the workstation is effectively operating in "NPT emulator" mode. As new host-based address book functions are developed, corresponding cooperating OS/2 processes to create CUA-compliant screens are also being developed. The OS/400 address book feature does not yet have this capability. [There is also a "local" address book capability in OS/2 that provides a CUA interface.]

Host Facility	OS/2 EE LAN	OS/400	MVS	VM
Mail	CUA	CUA	CUA	CUA
Library	CUA	CUA	Old	Old
Calendar	CUA	Old	Old	Old
Address Book	CUA	Old	Old	n.a.

Figure I.43 User Interfaces Using OS/2 Directly Connected to Host OfficeVision

6.4.1 The OfficeVision Workplace

The "desktop view" presented in Figure I.1 at the beginning of this book is an example of OfficeVision running under OS/2. It follows the concept of the CUA Graphical Model with Workplace Model extensions. OfficeVision is *not* required to implement the Workplace Model, and in fact does not exactly conform to its current definition. [The OfficeVision Application Programming Interface does provide the one existing mechanism for programming in the style of the Workplace Model. Expected extensions to the Presentation Manager and Dialog Manager will allow Workplace Model programming without the OfficeVision API.]

Figure I.44 also shows the OfficeVision desktop window. With only one exception, the window structure is identical to that of a normal CUA-defined primary window. The OfficeVision "mini icon" appears next to the system menu icon. This icon not only appears on the main OfficeVision window, but in all windows of applications running under the OfficeVision application platform. It represents "all selected objects in the current window" and is used to copy objects directly from window to window. This is an example of "direct manipulation" of data.

The OfficeVision workplace window area is populated with icons. These small pictures represent applications or files linked to applications. For example, selecting the telephone would cause the OfficeVision telephone application to be invoked. Selecting the in basket would cause the mail application to be invoked. The file cabinet is a higher level representation of the file system which will contain multiple levels of files and directories, all represented by icons. Finally, user applications that have been integrated with OfficeVision also show as icons. In this example, a user report which is linked to a database application is shown. When the report icon is selected and the mouse button "double clicked," the underlying application is initiated with that report file as input. [This type of application management is also provided by the OS/2 Desktop Manager.]

OfficeVision represents a major step in the direction of simplifying user interaction with multiple coordinated applications. Its current release follows CUA in large measure and has added significantly to the development of the CUA models (the workplace model). In time, all of the components of OfficeVision will evolve to full CUA compliance. And that is probably the best strategy from both IBM's and its customers' points of view.

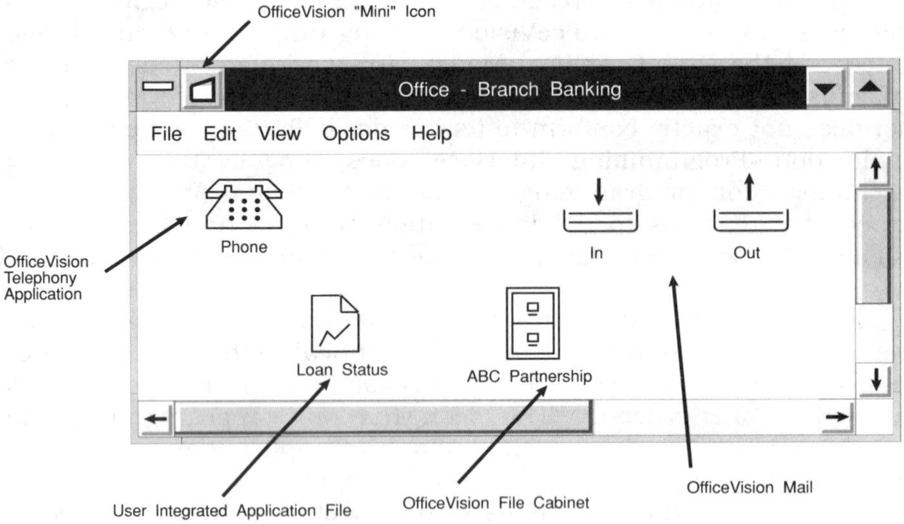

Figure I.44 OfficeVision Workplace Window

6.5 Integrating Other Applications

All members of the OfficeVision product family provide APIs that allow the integration of office functions with other applications, and that allow the integration of other applications under the office umbrella. The interfaces are specific to the OfficeVision family member.

On OS/2 workstations, OfficeVision provides for the inclusion of other applications on the OfficeVision "desktop." In its simplest form, this type of integration requires nothing more than responding to the application "registration" dialog supplied with the OS/2 Workstation feature of OfficeVision Release 2. This allows an application to be invoked by pointing to its icon and pressing the mouse button twice (or by invoking the "run" command from the pull-down menu). In its most complete form, you would include calls to OfficeVision APIs in your program. Additional APIs in the OS/2 environment facilitate the creation of CUA Workplace Model applications which have "drag and drop" and "direct manipulation" capabilities.

Applications and "application objects" (files created by a specific application) that appear in the OfficeVision workplace window have been "registered" with OfficeVision. When you point to an application icon and double click the mouse button, that application is started. An OS/2 file created by that application (such as a spreadsheet or document) may be saved so that it appears on the desktop or in a file drawer. When you point to such a file icon and double click, the associated application is started with that file as its input. This is similar to the facility popularized on the Macintosh and to a similar facility available in Microsoft Windows. The application being invoked can be any type of application, either a windowed Presentation Manager application or any other procedure (such as a REXX program). This allows existing applications as well as new ones to be started via OfficeVision.

Further integration can be achieved by calling OfficeVision Application Programming Interfaces (APIs) from your Presentation Manager program. For instance, you could directly interrogate the contents of an electronic mailbox and create a special icon to indicate the presence of a related message. You could also send something via electronic mail from within your application. Similar OfficeVision functions can also be called from your application in the OS/400, VM, and MVS environments using APIs provided by each member of the OfficeVision product line.

Office function integration obviously has to be designed into an application and specifically programmed. A number of independent software vendors are working with IBM to incorporate OfficeVision functions into their applications via the OfficeVision APIs in each of the SAA environments.

6.6 The (Possibly) Paperless Office

Is it really possible? Does the introduction of high quality, easy to use, familiar, intuitive, etc., software really mean that the paperless office may finally be on the horizon? Well, maybe. What is needed is continuing advances in electronic data interchange (EDI), imaging, high-speed communications, and mixed content databases.

Much of the paper coming into today's workplace is on standard forms. Remittance advices, purchase orders, insurance applications and claims forms, and income tax forms are all in well-defined formats. Many contain information that is computer generated and printed. Some of the forms themselves have been produced directly on computer printers (even personal income tax forms, using a $99 software package). The electronic transmission of this information would yield a corresponding reduction in paper flowing through the mails into offices. What is needed to make this happen are standards for electronic interchange of data (such as the EDI standards being developed by many companies) and simple, reliable communications. As organizations adopt the SAA Common Communications Support standards, they will find it simpler to pass information back and forth. With the acceptance of international standards and connection with public packet-switched networks (X.25) into CCS, the situation can only get better.

Some paper entering the office is not computer generated, for example, letters, handwritten forms, and personal checks. Computer imaging technology (scanners, high resolution displays, and laser printers) will stop this paper at the door, or at least at the scanner. Although still costly, this technology is growing in popularity, particularly in the insurance industry. IBM's initial imaging project was for a major insurance company, and other major computer companies, most notably Wang, are also joining the fray.

Improvements in communications will be necessary before image technology becomes widespread. Shipping image files around nationwide computer networks is going to require much higher transmission speeds than in common use. An 8 1/2 by 11 inch page scanned at 200 bits per inch yields an average 300 kilobyte file (although compression techniques can reduce this significantly). How long would it take to send a three-page document even in a highly compressed image format over a

9600-baud communication line? Answer: about a minute. Across a 16 megabit per second token-ring network? Answer: under a second. There is a world of difference in system usability in those two answers.

Database technology is also evolving to allow the incorporation of all types of data including images. It will be possible to reference an image of a typed or hand-written letter in much the same way that you can scan a customer name and address file. Operators can abstract information for direct input into other fields in the database, or in some cases, character recognition programs can do this work. Millions of checks which are processed manually every day (out of billions written) will be scanned with the resultant images run through character recognition programs or, in a few cases, displayed to operators who will interpret your illegible handwriting.

While there are still cultural and legal issues to be resolved (how do you "sign" an electronic document? is a scanned image of your signature worth anything in court, or does every piece of paper still have to be saved?), the combination of electronic data interchange, imaging technology, high-speed communications, and mixed content databases can reduce paper flow to zero in many industries and produce a truly paperless office. SAA will participate in this process via the introduction of Common Communications Support (including mixed content architecture documents and high-speed networking) and graphical user interfaces allowing easy image display.

7. AD/Cycle: The SAA Application Development Environment

Today, IBM introduces its Systems Application Architecture application development strategy. This strategy describes a framework that is designed to assist customers by improving the productivity, quality, and manageability of their efforts to develop applications. This framework will provide function across the application development life cycle through a staged set of IBM, user-written, and vendor-supplied tools... The set of offerings supporting this strategy will be known as the AD/Cycle framework.

"AD/Cycle - Application Development for the SAA Environments,"
IBM Programming Announcement 289-456

With the introduction of AD/Cycle, years of speculation about IBM's interest in computer-aided software engineering (CASE) were finally ended. IBM believed that automation of the development environment was an investment worth making and was prepared to back that belief up with strategic direction, products, and services.

What is AD/Cycle really? AD/Cycle is, like SAA, a framework. It specifies where and how different types of development tools fit into an overall application development environment (ADE). That ADE can be used to develop applications which are SAA compliant (or, at least it will be when all its parts are delivered). In a sense, it adds a "common developer interface" to SAA (Figure I.45).

In AD/Cycle, there are tools and services. Conceptually, the services (which include SAA standards such as CUA) make up an "application development platform." The tools use these services in performing their individual functions. Tools are classified according to the phase of the life cycle they are used for. Some are "cross life cycle," such as project management and documentation tools. Others are designed to assist in a particular part of the life cycle, such as database design or software testing. Figure I.46 reproduces the diagram from IBM's AD/Cycle Concepts that portrays these ideas.

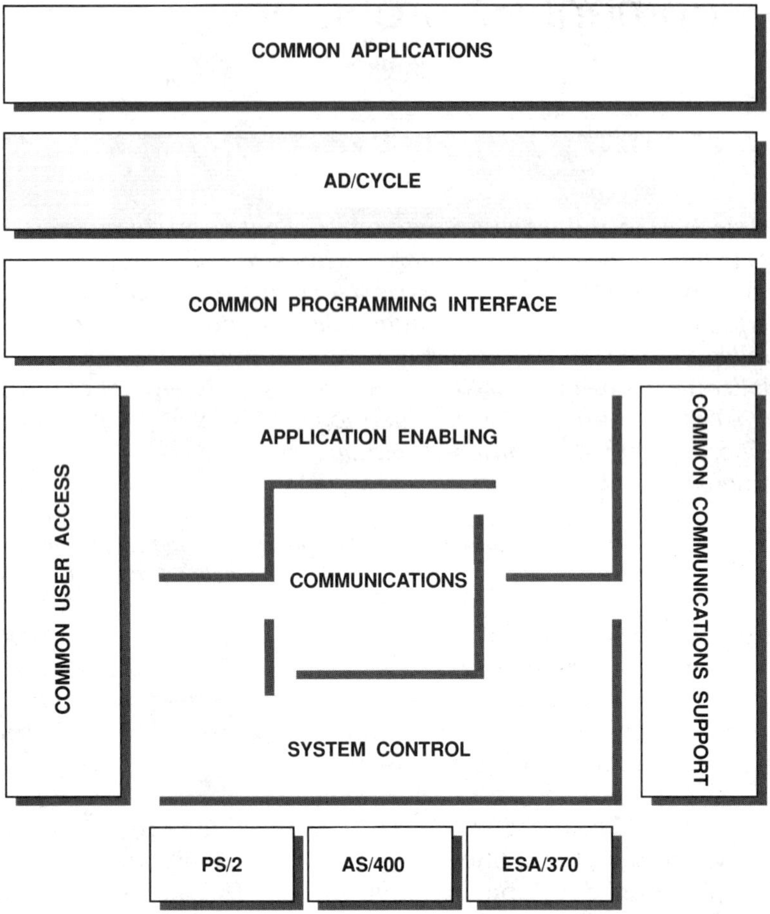

Figure I.45 AD/Cycle and SAA

The tools in AD/Cycle do not form an integrated whole, nor do they encompass all of the tools one might want for full life cycle coverage. IBM's strategy in this regard is threefold:

- to provide a central data repository through which true integration can be achieved;

- to encourage other vendors to provide tools that use the repository and thus integrate with others; and

- to provide additional tools itself.

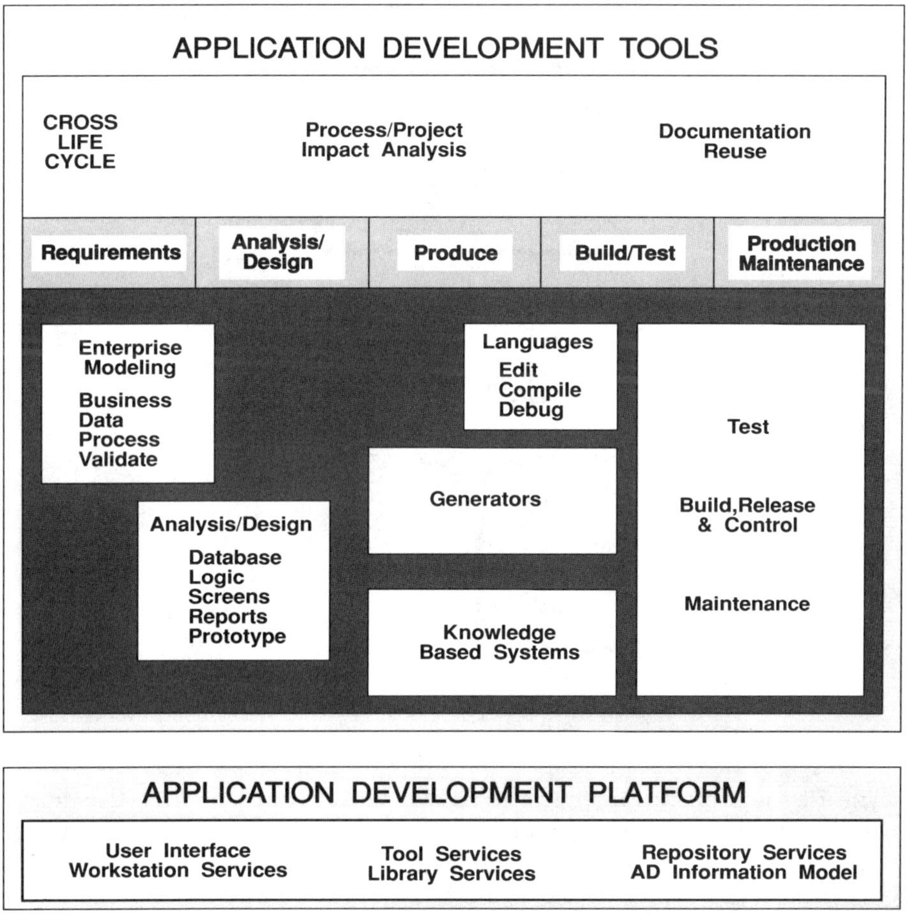

Reprinted courtesy of IBM Corporation

Figure I.46 The Tools of AD/Cycle

The central data repository is key to the concept of AD/Cycle. In the long run, all tools will put information into and take it out of this central repository. Tools will use the central repository for long term storage and control of the information that describes your business, your applications, and your technical environment. The repository will manage everything you produce throughout the systems life cycle: during strategic planning, design, development, and maintenance of systems; from business models to process and data designs to source code to test data.

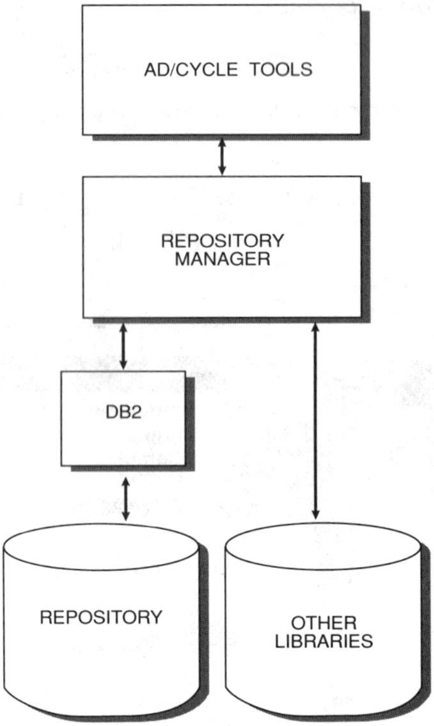

Figure I.47 The Repository in AD/Cycle

The Repository Manager is the IBM product that provides the central repository function. The associated AD/Cycle Information Model defines the types of data that will be shared by AD/Cycle tools, and stored in the repository. Some types of data, such as source code, will be stored in other libraries but will be managed via Repository Manager functions (and control entities contained in the repository database). Figure I.47 is a conceptual view of AD/Cycle tools using the Repository Manager to gain access to the repository.

At this time, the only version available is Repository Manager/MVS. IBM has indicated its intention to implement Repository Manager for VM and OS/400 systems and to provide access to Repository Manager services from OS/2 EE.

AD/Cycle is meant to be SAA compliant. The tools in AD/Cycle provide a common user interface conforming to CUA (or will in the near future). Some operate on the workstation, some on the host, and some in host-workstation distributed and cooperative processing modes (see Figure I.48). With the Repository Manager on the mainframe, all the tools of AD/Cycle will operate in a cooperative processing environment. [For the foreseeable future, the repository will be host-based (System 370 or AS/400) with cooperative processing interfaces to the workstation.] As in OfficeVision, the workstation will provide the primary window into the world of CASE.

[And a big window that will be. The announcement of AD/Cycle carried a recommendation for a workstation consisting of a PS/2 Model 70, with 12 Mb memory and a 115 Mb disk.]

AD/Cycle will help in developing SAA compliant applications. Some of the tools in AD/Cycle already are oriented to the SAA languages, environments, and databases. Others will be added to assist in creating CUA compliant screens and cooperative processing applications. It remains to be seen what form these will take.

In its current form, AD/Cycle is first of all a concept. IBM has told us how different tools (from potentially different providers) will work together in the future. In the meantime, system developers and maintainers will have to deal with products that are just being modified to work with a central repository and which currently provide little help in transferring work from one phase of the life cycle to the next. It is this sharing of data, implemented via the Repository Manager and the AD/Cycle Information Model, that will provide the greatest benefit to software developer productivity and system quality.

AD/Cycle will take several years to mature. Chapter 15 discusses some practical steps that you can take now to move in the direction of the integrated CASE environment that AD/Cycle promises.

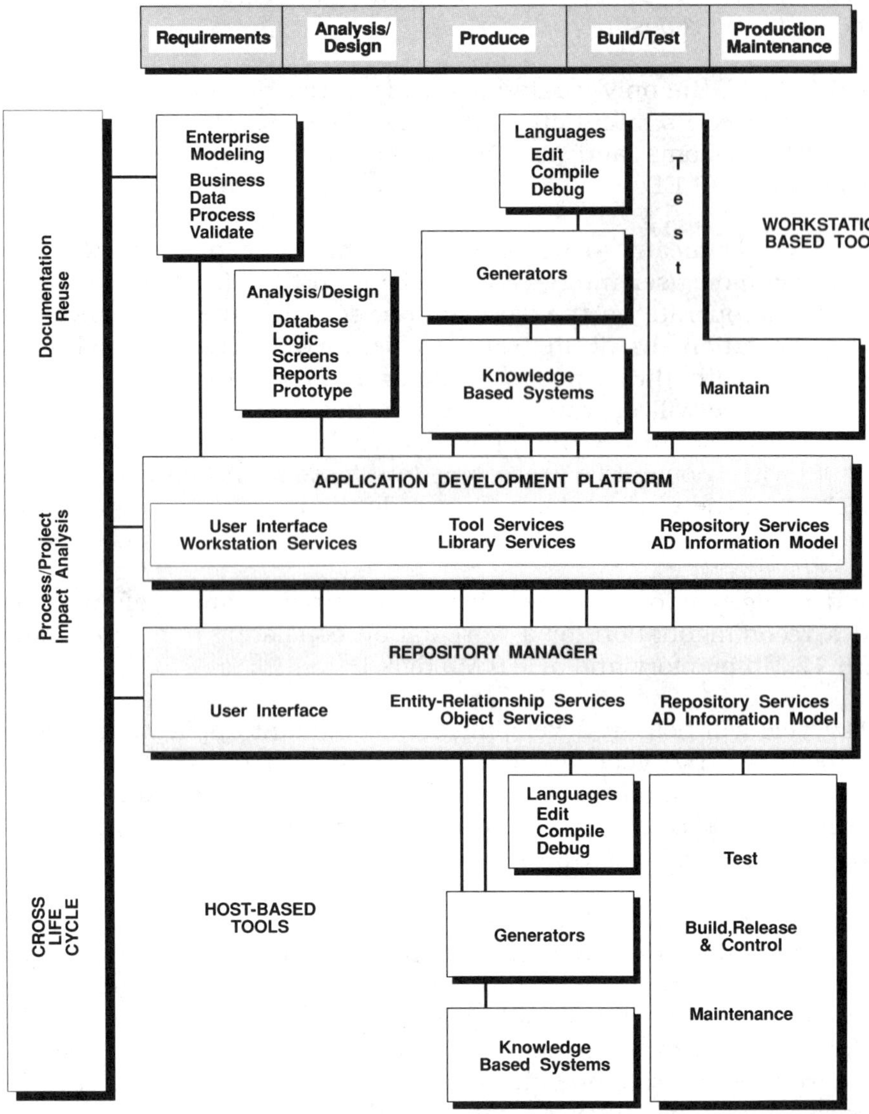

Figure I.48 Cooperative Processing in AD/Cycle

7.1 The Tools of AD/Cycle

IBM announced eight tools as part of the initial AD/Cycle introduction, but some 30 other vendors simultaneously announced that they would be integrating their offerings with AD/Cycle in the future. The tools included by IBM and their place in the life cycle are:

Cross Life Cycle Tools

- Application Development Productivity System (ADPS): a mainframe based process management system introduced by IBM Europe several years ago.

- Source Code Library Manager (component of ISPF/PDF): VM and MVS versions provide library management functions via an ISPF user interface, mainframe APIs, and workstation APIs. [This product was not referred to by name in the AD/Cycle announcement but the functions it performs were listed. A new release was announced simultaneously with AD/Cycle.]

Enterprise Modeling

- Application Development Workbench (ADW)/Planning Workstation: PC-based business modeling tool from KnowledgeWare, Inc. [KnowledgeWare's DOS-based tools go under the Information Engineering Workbench (IEW) label. The OS/2 tools in AD/Cycle use the ADW label.]

- PC Prism: PC-based modeling tool from Index Technology Corporation.

- DevelopMate: a cooperative processing application for creating entity-relationship models of the business and prototyping the rules that govern them. [The planned availability of this product is December 28, 1990.]

Analysis and Design

■ ADW/Analysis Workstation: another component of the ADW product which assists in creating software designs.

■ Excelerator: the flagship product of Index Technology provides a full range of graphics, dictionary, and analysis tools for creating software designs.

■ Re-Engineering Product Set: PC-based tools from Bachman Information Systems for creating data models and physical database designs for DB2, either from previously existing databases (IMS or IDMS) or from scratch.

Languages

■ Third generation language compilers implementing the SAA CPI occupy this box in AD/Cycle. [PL/I was announced as an addition to the SAA CPI as part of the AD/Cycle introduction in September 1989. This packaging was more a matter of convenience to IBM and its desire to announce something in every box on the AD/Cycle chart rather than a statement of PL/I occupying a special place in IBM's development strategy.]

Generators

■ Cross System Product is IBM's AD/Cycle application generator, although several application generator vendors (including Sage Software, Pansophic, and Netron, the three largest independents) have announced future compliance with AD/Cycle.

■ IBM Easel: originally developed by Interactive Images, IBM has been promoting this product as a way to develop workstation-based, CUA-compliant, stand-alone and cooperative processing applications. Its program and screen generator allow you to develop OS/2 applications without having to learn Presentation Manager.

■ Synon/2E: AS/400-based product for defining and generating applications in COBOL and RPG; also produces External Source Format for interfacing with CSP and transferring applications to or from the AS/400.

Knowledge-based Systems

- The Integrated Reasoning Shell: family of products for developing knowledge-based applications. The development environment is available for both OS/2 and AIX, and will produce applications which can additionally be run under MVS and VM.

Testing and Maintenance

- Workstation Interactive Test Tool: a PC-based tool for testing mainframe applications via captured scripts; demonstrated at CASE conferences over the past several years as an IBM internal tool.

- Software Analysis Test Tool: a mainframe test coverage and analysis system for PL/I and COBOL.

- COBOL Structuring Facility: a mainframe product for creating structured COBOL code from existing unstructured programs.

IBM's AD/Cycle business partners promised to have SAA compliant versions of their applications available during 1990. These products will subsequently interface with the Repository Manager and be able to use a host-based repository in conjunction with their own workstation repositories. IBM has also announced delivery dates for SAA compliant versions of some of its own tools. None of these as yet interface with the host-based repository.

7.1.1 Characteristics of AD/Cycle Tools

AD/Cycle is an open architecture. Participation in AD/Cycle is open to all tool vendors and to users who develop their own tools. For practical purposes, there are only four requirements for being considered "enabled" to AD/Cycle (official inclusion in AD/Cycle is obviously up to IBM):

■ the tool complies with SAA, particularly CUA and the cooperative processing approach;

■ the tool interfaces with the Repository via the Repository CPI;

■ the tool shares data in the repository using the AD/Cycle Information Model; and

■ the tool helps in producing systems that are SAA compliant.

With this definition, most major CASE vendors will want their tools to be part of AD/Cycle. Over 30 have already announced their intentions; we should see the results of those intentions beginning to hit the market in late 1990.

7.2 Application Development Platform

Application Development Platform, or AD Platform, is a concept that ties together the services and technologies needed to create an integrated tools environment. AD Platform is defined to include (see Figure I.49):

■ SAA Common User Access, guidlines for creating a user interface;

■ Workstation Services, routines for establishing a single-system image on the workstation for local and cooperative processing tools;

■ Tool Services, service routines addressing consistency and integration of tools, e.g. program invocation, window controls, and data transfer;

■ Repository Services, routines for accessing information in the central repository;

■ Library Services, routines for accessing information (such as source code) stored in an associated library system; and

■ The Information Model, the description of the data entities, relationships, and controls stored in the repository and shared across AD/Cycle tools.

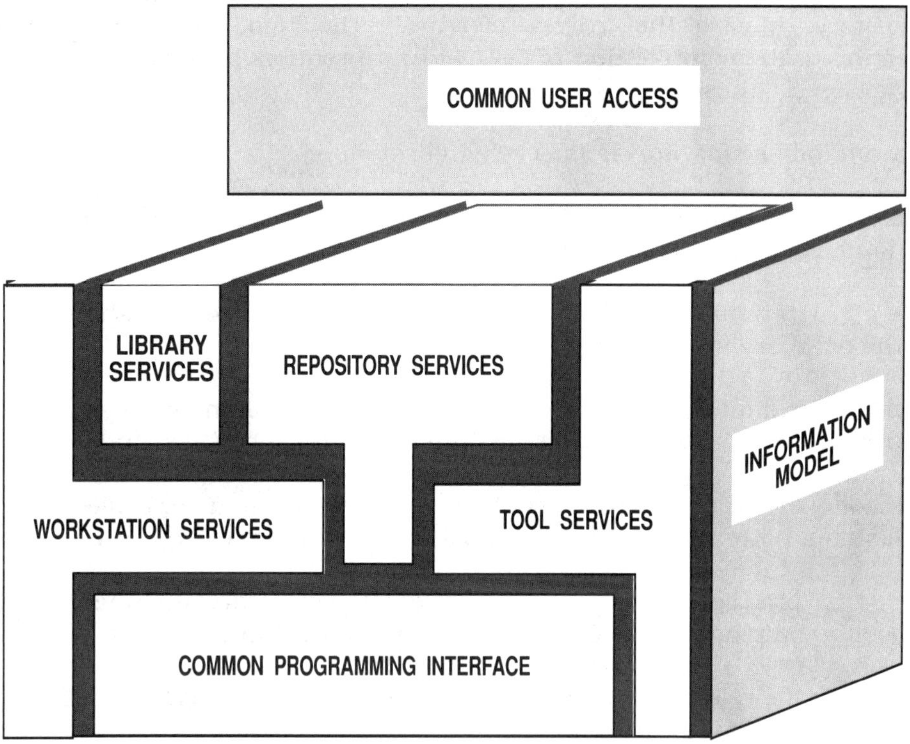

Figure I.49 The AD/Cycle Application Development Platform

The combination of services with CUA and the Information Model provide a foundation for CASE tool builders to use in incorporating their products into AD/Cycle.

7.3 The Repository

For at least two years, the industry has been anticipating "the" IBM repository. Most of the articles referring to the "Repository" are actually referring to the combination of several IBM products and concepts. At a "logical level," these are:

- a database for storing life cycle information;

- an "information model" which describes the entities stored in the database and their relationships to each other;

- a programming interface for defining entities and relationships to the database system;

- a programming interface for defining how and when entities can be updated and how these updates interact with each other; and

- software for accessing the data in the database in a controlled fashion, both at an entity-relationship level and at an object level.

At a "product level," several of these facilities are included in the Repository Manager, with other IBM products providing the rest:

- DB2, the relational database manager used by the MVS version of the Repository Manager;

- the IBM Repository Manager, comprising the software to define and access a relational database, including:

  - an Information Model which provides the entity-relationship model for the data to be stored in the repository database;

  - Entity-Relationship (E-R) Services, routines tool builders use to specify and access data in the repository database at the entity and relationship level;

  - Object Services, routines which access the repository at an "object" level, i.e., by applying specific "methods" in accessing entities and relationships;

- Tool Services, generic functions provided for the benefit of tool builders, e.g. routines that support workstation access to data in the repository or library, and that extend the service of the OS/2 operating system;

- an enhanced version of the Query Management Facility (Version 2 Release 4) which provides prompted query and report writing capability to the repository database; and

- Workstation Services, the basic facilities on the PWS used in building AD/Cycle tools (e.g. Presentation Manager, Database Manager, and Communications Manager).

Figure I.50 shows how these components fit together. The basic repository database is implemented in DB2 and will hold a general "information model" (supplied by IBM) of data to be shared in AD/Cycle. The information model specifies the types of information ("entities") that will be accommodated in the repository, the attributes of each, and the "relationships" among them. This "entity-relationship" model can be accessed via the E-R Services of the Repository Manager. Typical entities contained in the information model will embody design and development information, including system data models, process definitions, program module definitions, record contents, element definitions, screen layouts, and job control specifications. Typical relationships might be "elements contained in a record," "elements derived from other elements," "programs calling programs," and "process uses data entity." The information about a full system's life cycle will consist of several hundred entities (perhaps thousands of individual occurrences) related in hundreds of ways.

In addition to the E-R Services, the Repository Manager also includes Object Services. These access routines provide an "object-oriented" interface to repository data. Using Object Services, a CASE tool might automatically ensure that inconsistencies are not created when a data entity used in two different data models is changed.

[In other words, the Repository Manager comes very close to implementing a true "object-oriented database." I wonder what other products will begin to use it for managing their own "information models"?]

Tool Services will be provided by IBM CASE tools developers. Typically, tool developers will include the Tool Services routines with their products, or with a special "repository version" of their products. Tool Services are even higher level interfaces between a software development tool and the repository.

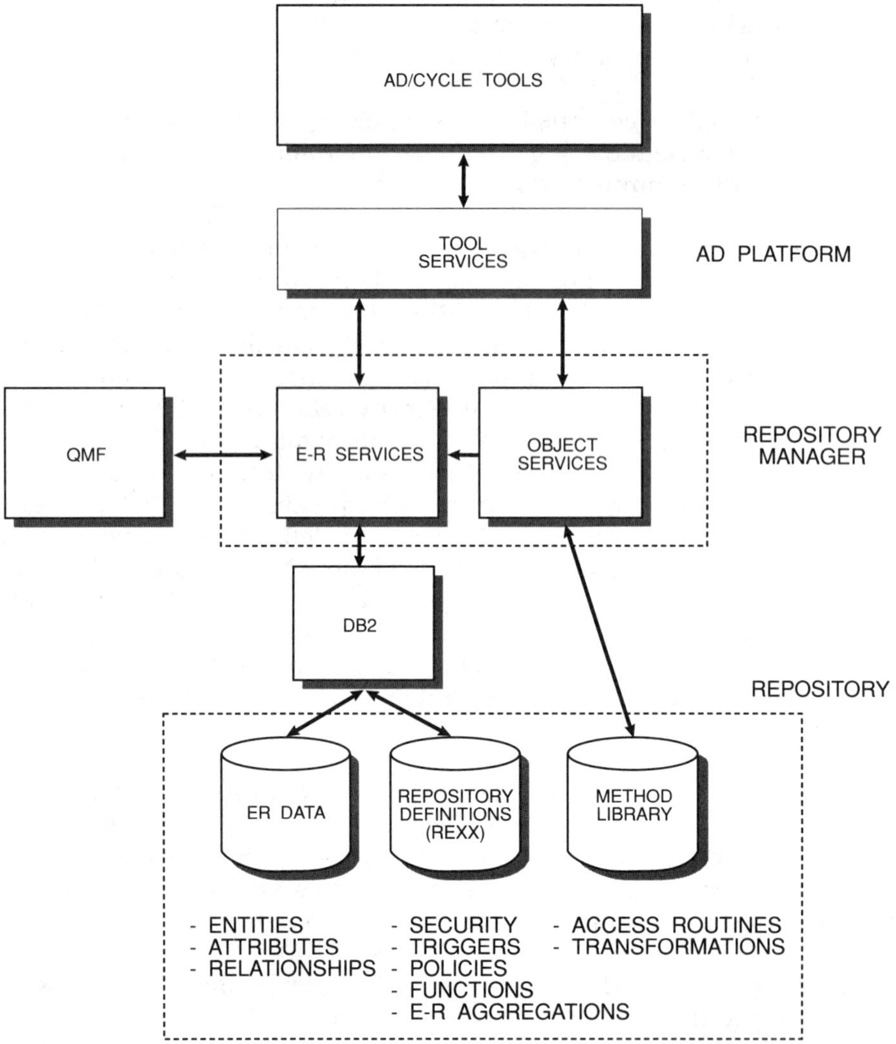

Figure I.50 The Components of the IBM Repository

The Workstation Services component of the Application Development Platform refers to the facilities provided primarily by OS/2 EE that enable the construction of CASE tools. Workstation Services is not a separate product, *per se*, although some functions are provided by the Workstation Platform for OS/2 feature of ISPF/PDF Version 3.2. In the future, Workstation Services will allow tool builders to provide tool users with facilities to access repository and library information without regard to where it resides on the network. The workstation will be the "window into the network" for applications developers, mimicking the concept of a "single system image" for application users. In the interim, tool builders will have to provide their own coordination between the workstation and the host-based Repository Manager.

7.3.1 The Repository Environment

Figure I.51 shows some of the IBM enabling products involved in implementing the repository concept. Many developers have already noted the number of products that are necessary. Some of these products are already in place in large information systems shops (MVS, ISPF, perhaps DB2). The others are available, for a price, from IBM.

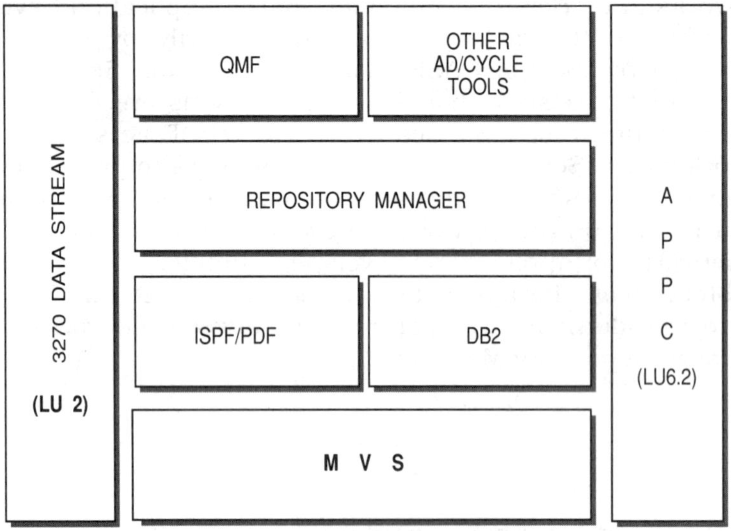

Figure I.51 IBM Repository and Related Products

7.3.2 Migration Products

IBM also announced several related products which will assist in migrating to a centralized repository controlled by Repository Manager.

The Dictionary Model Transformer is an interface between the IMS Data Dictionary (OS/VS DB/DC Data Dictionary) and Repository Manager. It allows the developer to specify selected information to be extracted from the IMS Data Dictionary, reformatted, and loaded in the DB2 repository via the Repository Manager. Most information in the IMS Dictionary can be moved to the Repository. There may be some cases when special programming is required (via defined user exits in the extraction process) to move data to the desired repository entities.

If you have existing design or development information stored in other repositories or databases, IBM's Data Extract products can be used to capture that information. The DXT family of products allows extraction from such databases as IMS, ORACLE, and INGRES in a form which can be loaded into DB2 tables. Via user exits, you can write routines to convert data into a form acceptable to the Repository. DXT/D1 is particularly interesting since it allows data to be moved from DEC VAX data files and databases onto IBM mainframes. If that data happens to be system design information or even source code, it can obviously be used to assist in converting VAX-based applications to IBM environments.

Part II: Implementing SAA

When spider webs unite, they can tie up a lion.
African Proverb

Systems Application Architecture provides a conceptual framework for an effective enterprise-wide computing environment. Implementing a strategy based on that framework will engage all parts of your organization in a coordinated effort over several years. Planning for that implementation will involve many of your key staff members for several months. Part II addresses the questions you will encounter as you begin this effort.

Chapter 8 deals with implementation planning issues from how to organize the planning process to measuring its success. Chapter 9 suggests a basic strategy, or "statement of direction," for SAA implementation. The following chapters deal with topics that will become agenda and decision items as you formulate your implementation plan. Each chapter begins with an "issue locator" which indicates the key issues discussed and their page references.

This part of *SAA: A Guide to Implementation* discusses topics that have themselves been dealt with in entire books. Without trying to condense a library into each chapter, I introduce the essential elements of each subject and how they relate to implementing SAA. Use Part II as a guidebook, a reference to topics that require further investigation, as you proceed through the maze of technical and managerial issues leading to successful implementation of the SAA approach.

8. The SAA Implementation Plan

The longest journey begins with a single step.
Chinese Proverb

8.1 Issue Locator

8.2 Major Steps in the Implementation of SAA

Implementing SAA means different things to different people. To the information systems manager, it means developing a strategy for distributed computing, creating a sophisticated application development environment, selecting new hardware and operating systems, re-training users and developers -- all while continuing current operations and planning the migration of existing systems. To the information systems staff, it means the beginning of an ongoing effort that will involve everyone in the department, most of the users of their systems, and many vendors and outside consultants. To computer users, it means easier to use and more sophisticated software, but also learning a new user interface. For some of these people, it also means some long hours as they try to grapple with the issues to be analyzed and the alternatives to be evaluated as they establish the organization's SAA plan.

This is obviously not "just another implementation project." The implementation of SAA will impact every project and task in your shop. You will need someone to be your "SAA implementation guru" (some organizations might want a czar) to guide the effort to success. You will have to back him or her with a team willing and able to understand both the technical and business sides of SAA. You will also need to instill an understanding of your approach and its importance to the organization in everyone, user and developer, who is involved with computer applications.

☛ *Issue: What are the major steps in implementing SAA?*

There are five major steps in implementing SAA in your organization (see Figure II.1):

1. Publish an "SAA Statement of Direction."

2. Develop an SAA Implementation Plan.

3. Identify and execute organization-wide projects.

4. Incorporate SAA concepts into new applications development projects.

5. Re-engineer existing application systems.

Making a comparison to a typical system life cycle, step 1 is the concept, step 2 is the design, and steps 3,4, and 5 are the implementation.

The Statement of Direction establishes the context for what is to follow. It lays out the broad strategies and policies, e.g. use of cooperative processing, graphical user interfaces, etc. It explains why SAA concepts will be implemented and how they will benefit the organization. Chapter 9 provides a sample SAA Statement of Direction.

The SAA Implementation Plan brings these concepts to the level of specific tasks. What does the organization actually have to do to bring these ideas to life? What organization-wide project must be accomplished to set the stage for implementation of application systems? In what time frame will this be accomplished? And what resources will be necessary? Organization-wide projects create the infrastructure for SAA implementation. Typical projects include those listed in Figure II.2. The key characteristic of these projects is that they cross the boundaries of individual applications and, for the most part, must precede the development of applications which implement the SAA strategy.

Application development projects will be planned as before, but their designers will be starting with a new paradigm. They will use a common architecture across all systems; they will assume that applications will operate on multiple hardware platforms; and they will learn how to comply with new and emerging standards for user, programming, and system interfaces. Developers will use new tools and follow the Common Programming Interface. The result will be applications which incorporate the organization's approach to SAA.

Existing systems must be included in the plan for SAA implementation. In some situations, a re-engineering approach will preserve your investment in useful systems. Architectural re-engineering will take many forms, e.g. introducing workstation cooperative processing with a graphical user interface, or re-implementing a database on a remote server. Other types of re-engineering may also be performed at the same time (code restructuring, reverse engineering of program code into a design repository).

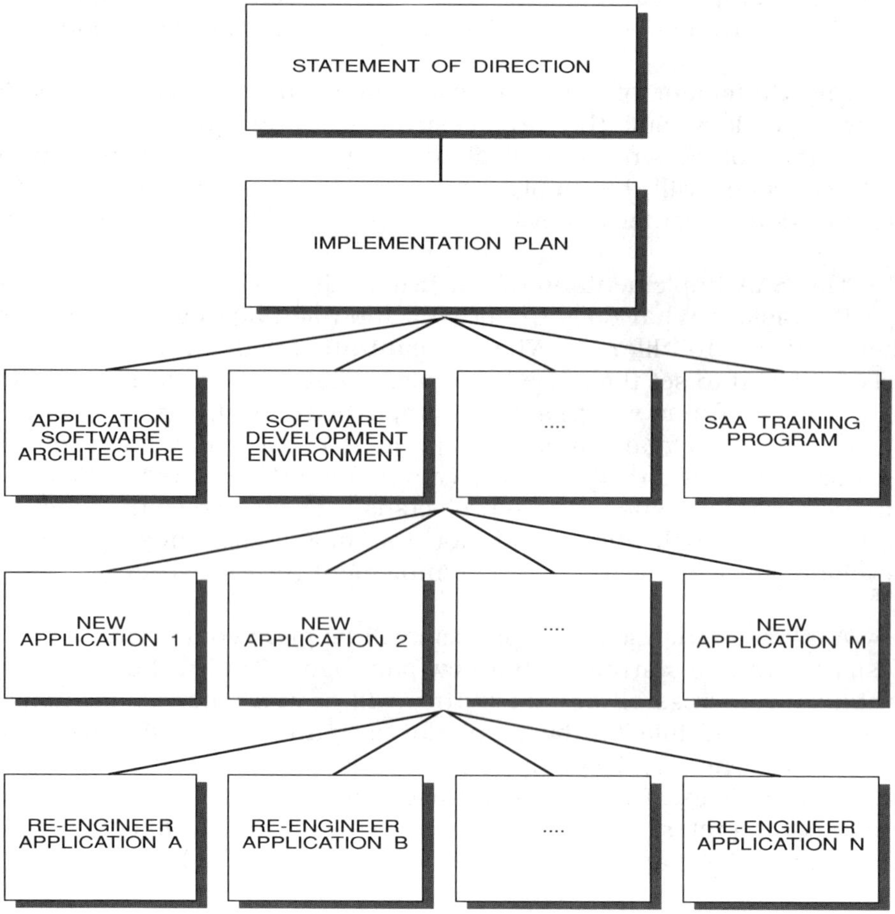

Figure II.1 Steps in SAA Implementation

Implementing SAA will take years. Some of the results will be immediately visible; others will take much longer to see. But the entire process starts with the formulation of an SAA Statement of Direction.

- Design an overall application architecture.
- Create an application development environment (workstations and CASE tools).
- Establish a training program.
- Select hardware and operating system software.
- Define a repository information model.
- Revise development methods.
- Set standards for and implement a wide-area network.
- Set standards for telecommunications protocols in distributed systems.
- Create a "style guide" for user interface design.
- Create an "SAA expert" group in your Development Center.

Figure II.2 Cross-system Projects for Implementing SAA

8.3 Implementing the Plan

Implementing SAA will require many changes in your organization: changes in the way you develop systems, changes in the way you use systems, changes in the way you maintain systems. Since changes of this magnitude do not occur very often, most organizations do not have the mechanisms in place to deal with them. A major factor, therefore, in SAA planning is managing the process of change, finding the balance between change and status quo, and creating the proper vehicles for introducing SAA concepts into the organization. Your SAA plan must fully address "change management" as well as specific implementation tasks.

The first step in change management is selecting the person in charge, the "change agent." The second step is selecting the project team and associated steering committee. Getting them started will itself be a key accomplishment, but it is like starting the Indianapolis 500: they will have to navigate around innumerable turns, deal with the caution flags, even avoid a crash or two, and still be in the running after 200 laps to say that they have finished.

8.3.1 Creating the SAA Planning Committee

☛ *Issue: Who should participate in the SAA planning process?*

The Information Systems Department has to take responsibility for creating the SAA implementation plan, but it needs review and counsel from a much broader group. The potential impact of SAA is so broad that there must be "buy in" from almost every area of the organization. The team for this planning project should have both a Working Group from the Information Systems Department and a broadly based Steering Committee.

The Working Group needs participation from the various groups within the IS Department:

- Strategic Planning
- System Development
- System Maintenance
- Software Engineering
- Software Architecture
- Quality Assurance

- Technical Support

- Hardware and Telecommunications

- Operations

The chairperson (project manager) should be someone with a broad understanding of systems and systems development, and who can deal both with long term issues and short term priorities. It should be a person with enough experience and seniority to be able to bring the concepts of SAA into the reality of the functioning organization. You should provide this person with expert assistance to ensure that the widest possible range of issues is raised and addressed.

The Steering Committee should include representatives from:

- major user organizations, such as Accounting and Finance, Production, Marketing, Engineering, and Distribution;

- field organizations; and

- the Chief Executive Officer.

This last person is someone, perhaps a key assistant, who can represent the views of the CEO, bringing back any cross-organizational issues that may need direct review. This is essential to showing a high level of ongoing management commitment to the process.

The Working Group will function best with a full time staff. While some members can participate on a part time basis, committed staff should number one to five persons (depending, of course, on the scope of their charter and somewhat on the size of your organization). These people will also perform staff work for the Steering Committee, whose members participate primarily at scheduled meetings.

Assuming no major impediments, the Working Group should produce a statement of direction and a preliminary implementation plan within a period of four to six months. This allows sufficient time for education, study, discussion, and issue resolution. Without full time assigned staff, this time frame will expand significantly and the delay may be unacceptable in meeting the needs of the organization.

8.3.2 Technology Transfer Issues

Introducing any new technology into an organization creates some degree of upheaval. For SAA, that upheaval will come about due to change in the use of:

- a standard architecture across many applications;
- a standard user interface design to conform to Common User Access;
- shared, re-usable code as a result of object orientation and other new development techniques;
- PCs both in development and as application workstations;
- distributed and cooperative processing architectures;
- relational database technology; and
- new tools and techniques to implement SAA conforming systems.

Preparing the organization for these changes and getting the organization and the people in it to embrace them as their own are hard work. The sociologists call this the process of "technology transfer." The key thing to remember is that the technology itself is useless unless it can be integrated into the organization. And that requires much more than good technology: it requires good people and good management.

8.3.2.1 Impact on the IS Department

The Information System Department will bear the brunt of the immediate changes coming from the implementation of SAA (user departments will see these changes some time later). By adopting the software development strategy inherent in the SAA approach, you are changing every aspect of the functioning of this department. Development methods, techniques, and tools will all change as you make the switch to common user interfaces, common programming interfaces, and common application architectures.

Every group in the IS Department will be affected, as will every level of person from programmer to analyst to manager. The "lone programmer" will all but disappear into the sunset (not totally disappear: there will always be a need for the "fastest code slinger in the East/West/North/South"). The roles of System Architect, Data Modeler, and Repository Manager will take on increased importance. The job of system maintainer will come much closer to that of developer, and developers will spend greater percentages of their time in design than ever before.

These changes will not come easily and will not necessarily leave everybody happy with their new roles. It is the function of management to make the transition as smooth as possible and to ensure, through various people acting as change agents, that there is a balance between positive change and negative disruption.

In short, implementing SAA is a way of turning the work of the IS Department into *software engineering* in the true sense of that phrase. What this also means is that the IS Department will be a focal point of productivity and quality improvements that will extend throughout the organization.

8.3.2.2 Who Is the Agent of Change?

[See Barbara Bouldin's book for a thorough discussion of this and related topics.]

When dealing with the impact of technological change on the structure of the work force and the nature of jobs, you will also have to deal with the possibility (certainty?) of resistance to some of those changes. This is where the "change agent" comes in, someone who views it as their responsibility to work with *all* the people involved in or impacted by the planned changes. Whether you are talking about changing the development methodology used in the IS department or the user interface given to the Purchasing Department, you will have to deal with those people who would rather leave it the way it was.

The person (or persons) performing the role of change agent have to be carefully selected. If they are to overcome resistance, or at least deflect it, they have to have particularly well-developed senses of dealing with people. They have to understand the details of the technology, why it is important, how it can help people, and how it can be used to greatest advantage. They have to be able to develop strategies for introducing new ideas and techniques in the least threatening way and for dealing with individual perceptions about that introduction. In short, they have to be both technologists and psychologists -- a rare breed, indeed.

But change agents already exist in your organization. They are the people that others look to for advice. They are the ones solving problems, rather than using them as excuses. They are the ones turned on by new ideas, rather than looking to perpetuate old ones. They are there, you simply have to identify them and bring them into the SAA planning process.

8.3.3 Assessing the Risks in the Plan

SAA was introduced over three years ago. Since that time, there have been numerous announcements of IBM products and several "statements of direction." Some of these have expanded the reach of SAA; a few have contracted it. At a strategic planning level, you can consider the definition of SAA fairly stable. At a tactical or detailed level, you can expect significant change as product announcements are made over the next several years. The question to deal with is how to minimize the impact of future announcements on your SAA plan.

At a strategic level, the SAA planning group must be able to draw the line on which technologies it will consider. Speculating on if or when DOS/VSE will be officially brought into the SAA fold is of little use. Deciding on whether to stick with PL/I as a key implementation language, even though it is not yet implemented in all environments, is another matter. One is strategic, the other is tactical. IBM may change its mind regarding DOS/VSE (it is currently *not* an SAA environment), but you are taking a big chance if you bet your organization's strategic direction on that happening. PL/I will be available, and that fact can be relied upon. The tactical question is *when* to migrate from VSE and *when* PL/I will be available on the OS/400 and OS/2. Uncertainty at this tactical level is a fact of life in our business.

There is a significant difference in the two examples in the previous paragraph. The planning group cannot let any individual member go off into outer space on whether or not his or her favorite operating system or database will eventually be part of SAA. Nor can it limit discussion only to those environments and software products already delivered (as the federal government does in its procurements). Speculating on IBM's strategic direction is inherently more risky than speculating on its tactics.

The planning committee should rely on IBM's published statements (not on rumors of those yet forthcoming) and assume that anything announced, whether or not a delivery date is specified, will be available in the time frame of the plan. IBM has indicated that all SAA-compliant products will be available within two years of their announcement. While this may be optimistic, the fact that IBM has made such a statement is a good indication of their commitment. Allow some slack (perhaps as much as a year) and you are not likely to go wrong.

Similarly, if a specific statement of direction has been issued by IBM, it is reasonable to assume that that direction can be relied upon for the duration of your SAA implementation plan. That statement of direction may be enhanced, as in the addition of another networking protocol to CCS or another language to the CPI, but the general direction will remain intact.

Following these straightforward rules will eliminate most of the strategic risk and a good deal of the tactical risk associated with changes in the SAA definition.

8.4 The Cost of SAA Implementation

A billion here, a billion there, pretty soon we'll be talking about real money.

Senator Everett Dirksen, referring to the defense budget

Implementing a program to introduce SAA will cost (although not "real money" according to one of our late Congressmen). Management will properly ask what those costs will be and how the resultant benefits can be measured. Not only will benefits be difficult to estimate (many are "intangible," like increased user efficiency due to easier information access), but even the direct costs will be hard to ferret out.

The basic approach to solving this problem is to look at costs and benefits as two sides of the same coin: rather than trying to determine costs and benefits separately, look at the impact of SAA implementation in terms of either an increase or decrease in already planned for costs. In this way, you can determine the net tangible effect (costs and benefits) of the SAA implementation program before having to deal with any intangibles.

☛ *Issue: What will it cost to implement SAA?*

Figure II.3 lists the major categories of implementation costs and the reasons for expected increases or decreases. Some of these categories may show up as specific line items in your information systems budget (e.g. operating systems software). Others represent functional areas that would be further broken down into line item components (e.g. application development activities are composed of labor, computer, and other costs).

Baseline Cost Effect	Incr	Decr	Comments
Hardware			
Host computers		✓	Offload some work to PWSs
Workstations	✓		Significant
Network	✓		More people connected to the network
OS & Enabling Software			
Operating systems	✓		Small difference (OS/2 costs more than DOS)
Database management		✓	Included in OS/2 EE
Communications		✓	Included in OS/2 EE
Office automation	✓		More will be used
Applications			
Analysis			No difference
Design		✓	CUA, CPI, CCS will reduce
Development		✓	CPI and architecture will reduce
Implementation		✓	Standards will help
Maintenance		✓	CPI, OOP will simplify
Training			
Manuals and books	[I]	✓	Long-run reduction
Technical courses	[I]	✓	Long-run reduction
User courses	[I]	✓	Long-run reduction
[I] = Initial outlay will be required.			

Figure II.3 SAA Cost Factors Summary

High-power programmable workstations will be one source of higher costs. The assumption is that you are not currently providing developers or users with workstations powerful enough to run OS/2 EE and compatible applications. Office automation costs will also be higher because people will want and use more software in doing their jobs. Costs will also be higher for initial purchases of books, manuals, and training.

User training for each new system should be reduced significantly after users become familiar with the CUA environment. Preparing a "CUA user" manual will be an incremental cost, but it will serve every system from then on by reducing the size of their user manuals. These SAA "costs" will actually show up as *decrements* rather than increments to your baseline.

Cost Factor	Direction	Reason
Workstation hardware	UP	Need more sophisticated PC
Workstation software	UP	Need more sophisticated software
Network	UP	Higher speed is probably needed to handle increased traffic
System development	UP	Staff must be trained in new techniques; currently available enabling products are more complex than those for traditional centralized environment
User training	DOWN	Initially, users will have to be trained in the new standardized interface, but this training will be useful across all applications
System maintenance	DOWN	Application is more effectively modularized; use of standardized programming interfaces will make applications easier to understand and enhance
User costs	DOWN	Higher productivity expected due to standardized user interface; higher quality in performance of duties expected due to more sophisticated user interface

Figure II.4 Cost Factors for CUA and Distributed User Interface

One way to analyze the total cost picture is to specify several "implementation scenarios" and look at all the costs associated with each approach. For example, what are the cost factors associated with:

> *using programmable workstations with a graphical user interface as front ends to distributed processing applications.*

Since this scenario does not deal with host processing or distributed database (other scenarios can be constructed to deal with those or other implementation approaches), only some of the cost factors will be affected, as shown in Figure II.4.

8.5 Measuring Success

If you can't measure it, you can't manage it.

Unknown

Unfortunately, only a small percentage of today's IS organizations will be able to measure the success (or failure) of implementing SAA -- assuming that the current lack of interest in measurement continues. Over the past three years, I have asked approximately 2000 managers from over 300 major organizations how they measure productivity (and quality) in their IS department. Only 1% to 2% had any idea what their productivity was. Fewer still had ongoing programs in place to take productivity and quality measurements. Until this situation changes, it will be impossible to *measure* the validity of statements like the one at the beginning of this section.

"The main advantage of following SAA is that productivity of developers, maintainers, and users will improve." This statement is made in various ways throughout the literature on SAA (including this book). Unfortunately, nobody can prove its truth since SAA is only now becoming a reality. It is important to you and to your organization, however, that you prove its truth *at some point in the future*. Only then will the critics be satisfied that your investment in training, hardware, and software was justified.

It is not the purpose of this book to show you how to set up a productivity measurement program (for that, I recommend Grady and Caswell's text). However, deciding on productivity measures and setting up a productivity measurement program, assuming one does not already exist, is an appropriate task on your SAA implementation plan.

8.5.1 Quality and Productivity in the Organization

The impact of computer technology is evident in almost every function of the modern enterprise. Whether you produce a product, supply a service, or manage what others do, computers affect the productivity of your staff and the quality of their work. Computer technology is so pervasive that it is almost impossible to judge the totality of its impact.

Implementing SAA will clearly impact productivity in the IS Department. It may be more difficult to sort out the impact of the several changes all taking place concurrently, but SAA will be the catalyst. All of these impact productivity, usually by different amounts in different time frames. Initially, you may see productivity decline as your staff first learns about the SAA Common Programming Interfaces and the rules of CUA. As they become familiar with the style of programming called for by object-oriented user interfaces and cooperative processing, they will also become familiar with tools and techniques that will help them. Defining common object libraries and using higher level development tools will all contribute to a higher level of designer, implementer, and maintainer productivity.

In the long run, improvements in productivity will go hand in hand with even greater improvements in quality. In the data processing department, the use of standard designs and software will improve the quality of systems as measured by a higher level of user satisfaction and fewer reported problems. In the user departments, easy to use systems providing expanded capabilities will help improve the quality of work.

This can be at least partly measured by increased demand for computer power throughout the organization.

If you measure the quality of systems by the satisfaction of their users, then SAA will improve quality in three ways:

- easier to use, consistent user interface;
- cooperative processing applications which merge the facilities of personal workstations with mainframe computers; and
- shorter development and maintenance cycles via the use of common programming tools and interfaces.

The issue at this stage is how to measure these improvements so that they can be managed and encouraged.

8.5.2 Establishing Productivity and Quality Measures

☛ *Issue: How can the success of the SAA implementation be measured?*

Figure II.5 shows productivity and quality measures that can be used in gauging the effect of your SAA implementation program. These are measures to be taken at the project and departmental level to see the impact of major changes on the functioning of the IS Department. Whether you use these measures or others, it is important to define the measures up front and to measure and report on them on a regular basis.

What you are looking for in the measurement program is the trend line. Establish where you are now and then measure periodically in the future. This will allow you to see whether the various productivity and quality measures are improving and at what rate. You can use this information in judging success and in justifying changes in your implementation program.

Measure	Comments [See text]
Productivity	
Lines of code per person month	Outdated, may yield misleading results.
Function points per person month	Requires consistent measurement to be effective.
Function points per dollar	Includes dollar value of labor and capital.
Quality	
User satisfaction	Subjective user surveys need interpretation.
Number of problem reports per month	Easy to collect and very visible.
Number of enhancement requests per month	Measures quality of system design.

Figure II.5 Typical Productivity and Quality Measures

8.5.2.1 Productivity Measurement

Productivity measures are calculated as:

$$\text{Productivity} = \frac{\text{Output}}{\text{Input}}$$

In the case of data processing productivity, the "output" can be measured in "DP terms," e.g. lines of code, or in "user terms," e.g. the number of systems delivered. While there is no generally accepted "standard," the best compromise to date is a measure called "function points." The function point measure was first studied by Allan Albrecht of IBM in 1979 and has since achieved a good measure of acceptance, even spawning the International Function Point Users Group.

Function points measure the output of the IS Department by counting the "functions" delivered to users. To establish a degree of uniformity, proxy measures of functionality are used. Number of input transactions, reports, queries, and files are summed to arrive at a "function count" which is then adjusted by various complexity factors. [For more information on function points, see the IFPUG publication listed in the References.]

The primary "input" in developing information systems is labor. While not ignoring the cost of computer hardware and tools used by system developers, management is often trying to measure the "labor productivity rate" as it changes various factors in the environment.

In existing measurement studies, labor input is most often measured in "months of effort" (person months). Unfortunately, this equalizes the contribution of all personnel (one month is as good as another), often skewing the results. A more useful measure is "total labor cost." This measure distinguishes people by skill and experience as evidenced by their salaries. (If we introduce a new tool or technique which allows us to implement the same system with less experienced people, haven't we improved productivity?) This allows us to express productivity in terms of "labor dollar input."

You can expand the measure of inputs to include non-labor items if you measure everything in dollars. Treating the cost of hardware and software as a monthly amortization or usage figure, and adding in telephone, xerox, and supply charges, you arrive at the total dollar input to the development process.

Putting everything together, you have what I consider the best measure of IS productivity available today:

$$\text{Productivity} = \frac{\text{Functions points}}{\text{Dollar value of all "inputs"}}$$

or "function points per dollar." While better measures will undoubtedly be developed in the future, tracking function points per dollar over many projects and for the organization as a whole (adding in general and administrative costs) will provide a consistent base for analyzing the trends in productivity and impact of changes in your environment.

8.5.2.2 Quality Measurement

No one has yet defined a formula for measuring quality; in fact, there are bookshelves in the library devoted to this topic. In the IS world, we have only to define the quality of systems, rather than dealing with the whole "quality thing."

> *Definition: High quality systems operate reliably, support people in fulfilling their responsibilities efficiently and effectively, and, in general, contribute to the functioning of the organization. Low quality systems do not (in varying degrees).*

This definition leads immediately to several possible measures of quality. The first and most obvious is derived from surveys of users: just ask people whether they think the systems they use are of high quality. User satisfaction surveys are remarkably useful instruments in assessing the general state of health of systems. An annual questionnaire will give you at least a subjective view of system quality and whether it is improving.

There are other, somewhat more objective measures that can be made. Analysis of problem reports and change requests will yield some overall statistics (a trendline of change requests per month, for example) as well as answers to questions, such as:

- Are systems installed today experiencing fewer start-up problems than systems installed a year ago?

- Do change requests indicate user dissatisfaction with current system features (low quality systems) or expanded ideas about how successful system features can be improved (high quality systems)?

Each answer contributes to your understanding of system quality and how it is changing over time.

None of these measures is foolproof. They can, however, provide a view of quality in the IS Department that will help in measuring the impact of SAA.

8.5.2.3 SAA Impact Measurement

The measures discussed above are general measures of productivity and quality in a data processing organization. It is possible to establish other direct measures of the impact of SAA. These measures are directly related to the effects of SAA on the data processing environment.

As more and more systems are implemented under your SAA implementation plan, you should see the impact of the move to cooperative processing, the introduction of Common User Access, and the use of the Common Programming Interface. Figure II.6 lists some indicators of the expected results of SAA implementation.

Measure	Comments [See text]
Mainframe MIPS vs. distributed MIP	Should see shift toward distributed MIPS with overall decrease in cost/MIP.
Percentage of new vs. reused routines	Software reuse (in whole or in part) should expand.
Amount of cross-application documentation	Common interface and functions should allow documentation reuse.
User training time per application	Should decrease due to CUA.

Figure II.6 Additional Measures of SAA Implementation

If cooperative processing applications are being developed, more of the MIPS needed to perform an application should be coming from workstations and distributed servers. By tracking the shift in MIPS from mainframe to other processors, you will measure the introduction of cooperative processing.

As more and more of your applications take on similar display and user functions, some of the routines developed by your staff for one application will find a home in others. One measure of SAA's impact, therefore, would be a count of routines in a new system that are developed from scratch versus those based on previously developed routines.

Similarly, some of the user documentation normally associated with each individual application should now be useful across applications, i.e. there should be "common documentation." This documentation will be a direct outgrowth of the use of CUA in establishing a common user interface across multiple applications. If you are not producing some common documentation, perhaps some part of your SAA implementation plan is running into difficulty. This may also apply to application and system level documentation, although to a lesser extent.

One of the goals of Common User Access is to make it easier for users to learn new applications. If user training time for new applications is decreasing, it may be an indication that CUA is taking hold.

These measures will show the introduction of SAA into your systems environment. All other things being equal, they should correlate with improvements in the productivity and quality measurements you are also collecting.

9. A Basic SAA Implementation Strategy

"Would you tell me, please, which way I ought to go from here?"
"That depends a good deal on where you want to get to."
Conversation between Alice and the Cheshire Cat

9.1 Issue Locator

9.2 Outline for an "SAA Statement of Direction"

By the very nature of SAA, your organization's SAA Statement of Direction should be one of the most encompassing documents of computing strategy and tactics you write. Of course, you could do less, but then you would be missing some of the potential impact of Systems Application Architecture.

☛ *Issue: What is the scope of the SAA Statement of Direction?*

Figure II.7 and the remainder of this section is an outline that can be used as a starting point for your SAA Statement of Direction. Section 9.3 presents a basic strategy in this form. The specific situation in your organization will, of course, require you to add, delete, or change some of the items.

I. Management Summary
II. Commitment to Systems Application Architecture
III. Overall Implementation Strategy
IV. Common User Access
V. Distributed and Cooperative Processing
VI. Common Programming Interface
VII. Operating Systems and Applications Enabling Software
VIII. Hardware and Communications
IX. Software Development Environment
X. Training and Education
XI. Remaining Issues

Figure II.7 Statement of Direction Table of Contents

SAA Statement of Direction

I. Management Summary

Discusses the role of SAA in implementing an "enterprise computing strategy." Provides motivation by discussing the impact SAA will have on both the suppliers and consumers of computing resources.

Provides a brief statement of the key strategic decisions that have been made and of the ones remaining to be resolved.

II. Commitment to Systems Application Architecture

Indicates the organization's commitment to follow the concepts of IBM's Systems Application Architecture. Specifies any general departures from that commitment or any specific cases when departures will be allowed, e.g. to use a fourth generation language already known by the organization.

Specifies that a common "application architecture" will be developed to make compliance with SAA easier.

III. Overall Implementation Strategy

A. Strategy for New Systems

Indicates in general terms what aspects of SAA are to be followed in new system development projects.

B. Strategy for Existing Systems

Indicates when and how (or if) existing systems will be brought into conformance with SAA. There may be several different strategies, each applicable to several existing systems.

IV. Common User Access

A. Strategy for New Applications

Establishes the appropriate CUA models to be followed in developing new applications. Also indicates organization-specific standards.

B. Strategy for Existing Applications

States whether existing applications will be modified to conform to CUA, and, if so, on what timetable. May also indicate what approach will be taken to this migration, e.g. use of front end software products.

V. Distributed and Cooperative Processing

Discusses the various types of applications and the different types of cooperative processing that should be considered for each.

A. Strategy for New Applications

Specifies the general architecture of new applications; e.g. display processing on PWSs with most processing functions and database access performed on a mainframe.

B. Strategy for Existing Applications

Lays out a strategy for migrating existing applications into the types of cooperative processing most appropriate to each. May indicate specific systems to be changed.

VI. Common Programming Interface

Specifies the languages and operating system interfaces that will be used in developing systems, i.e., the SAA CPI elements.

Indicates where non-SAA language or interfaces may be used, e.g. Natural 4GL to create user inquiries to DB2 databases.

VII. Operating Systems and Applications Enabling Software

A. Operating Systems

Identifies when each applicable operating system should be used. Specifies when non-SAA operating systems (DOS, UNIX, VSE) are allowed.

B. Language Compilers

Specifies which language versions will be used, e.g. VS COBOL II, Microfocus COBOL Workbench.

C. Database Systems

Specifies which database systems will be used in each operating environment. Specifies whether migration from any other existing databases will be made and under what conditions.

VIII. Hardware and Communications

A. Hardware Strategy

Indicates preferred or standard hardware configurations for mainframes, mid-range, and personal computers.

B. Telecommunication and Networking

Specifies the overall networking strategy and the classes of telecommunication hardware and networks that will be used in different situations.

IX. Software Development Environment

Lays out strategy for use of computer-aided software engineering (CASE), including analysis and design tools, application generators, etc. Indicates the role to be played by a centralized development repository and where it will be located.

May also specify any expected changes in system development methods which will accompany the adoption of SAA and the use of CASE.

X. Training

Emphasizes the organization's commitment to provide training in all areas. Specifies some of the types of training (e.g. classroom instruction, computer-based training) which will be provided. Lays out a basic curriculum of courses and seminars.

XI. Remaining Issues

Lists any known issues that will be dealt with in future additions to the Statement of Direction.

9.3 A Basic Strategy

This section presents a basic strategy for a phased implementation of SAA concepts in a medium to large organization. You can follow this approach or use it as a "strawman" against which to judge your own plan.

The basic strategy was formulated for a hypothetical, but typical, organization. This organization has an Information Systems Department of 100 or more people and is supporting 20 to 50 major and many minor application systems. Its other characteristics include:

- an application portfolio that addresses most core operating functions;
- most (if not all) of its current applications operating in a host-only environment;
- some of its users equipped with personal computers running in terminal emulation mode;
- some specialized applications operating in environments which are not SAA operating environments (either on IBM or other computer manufacturer's equipment);

- the majority of its Information Systems Department staff engaged in maintenance and enhancement of existing applications;

- system development done primarily on the host, but with some use of personal computers;

- structured methodologies employed, but not consistently or completely;

- some automated tools available, both on personal computers and the host computer, but not widely used.

This scenario is typical of many corporate and governmental organizations using IBM mid-range and mainframe computers today.

9.3.1 Commitment to the Systems Application Architecture Approach

The organization commits itself to implementing systems that follow the approach described by IBM's Systems Applications Architecture. This commitment does not imply a blind adherence to SAA standards and IBM implementations of software products. Rather, it indicates the organization's understanding and appreciation of the benefits that can be achieved by efforts in the directions specified in the SAA approach.

This approach encompasses several key concepts:

- implementing systems that use all types of computer resources effectively in a "cooperative processing" environment;

- creating a common application structure or "architecture" to encourage a consistent approach to creating systems;

- providing a common user interface for all systems; and

- the use of standard languages and software interfaces (supplied by IBM and others) across different computer environments.

The benefits of implementing systems that conform to a common architectural approach and that present a common interface to the user can be substantial. They will be seen in improved productivity and quality of work, both in the Information Systems Department and in the departments which use computer applications. But it will be several years before that payback on the organization's investment in training, equipment, and systems will be realized.

The commitment to SAA will take different forms in the short, medium, and long terms.

In the short term (one to six months), the Information Systems Department will:

- train its staff in the concepts and facilities of SAA;

- analyze the organization's current applications portfolio to assess the degree of conformance with the common approaches of SAA;

- determine which components of SAA will become immediate and future standards for the organization;

- begin work on an overall "application architecture," a framework for application structure which utilizes the common approaches of SAA;

- include vendor plans for conformance with SAA as a selection criteria for purchased software; and

- begin to create an application development and maintenance environment that is conducive to producing and enhancing systems that follow the SAA standards.

The organization's application architecture will become a blueprint for developing applications that have common components and structure. SAA will define the interfaces to the operating system that will help developers in creating systems that follow the architecture.

In the medium term (six months to one year), the staff will become familiar with the concepts of SAA. They will define an overall application structure, or "architecture." They will begin to learn about application development and maintenance tools that will help implement conforming systems. The workstations they use will be upgraded to accommodate these tools.

When these tasks have been accomplished, the organization's application architecture and Systems Application Architecture will become the basis for new system development. User staff will be trained in the use of interfaces which follow Common User Access. The IS Department will also develop user manuals and training which explain the common user interface.

In attempting to reap the maximum benefit from its portfolio of existing applications, the organization will investigate the use of re-engineering techniques to modernize its systems. Systems that do not require complete redevelopment in the short to medium term will be candidates for re-engineering. The re-engineering tools and techniques used will also bring these systems into some degree of conformance with the concepts of SAA.

In the long term, all systems will become candidates for redevelopment. When systems are redeveloped, the new systems will conform to SAA. Not all systems will conform to SAA, at least not for many years. Recently completed systems will not be due for major enhancement for some time and may exist in their current state for ten years or more.

Implementing the SAA approach is not an all or nothing proposition. Some aspects of SAA's common approaches are already being followed in the organization. Others will take many years to find their way into the majority of systems. The direction is clear; the commitment is there. But it will take time, money, and hard work.

9.3.1.1 Viewing Computing as an "Enterprise" Resource

A strong computing capability is crucial to the continued success of the organization. The growth of strategic computer applications and their use across the enterprise will depend on effective sharing of resources at all levels.

Computers of all types must be used together for the benefit of the organization. Mainframe computers managed by the Information Systems Department have always been a corporate resource. Now, they must be used in close cooperation with computers managed by individual departments. To accomplish this, mainframe, mid-range, and personal computers will be connected via an enterprise-wide communications network. Applications will be developed which use the capabilities of the network to share hardware, software, and data resources.

Data is a corporate asset. Existing central databases represent only one part of that asset. Other databases, created by analyzing data both internal and external to the organization, are being created every day. New efforts to catalog and share such data will result in better information to manage and guide the enterprise. One of the key goals of the enterprise network will be to establish a data repository to serve as a basis for expanded application systems.

In the enterprise-wide computing strategy, the largest possible number of staff members should have access to the widest possible array of computer applications. To further this end, all applications should use standard methods of presenting data and providing services. Users should be able to learn "how to use the computer" once, and apply what they have learned to many applications. In this way, computer applications will truly become an enterprise-wide resource.

9.3.1.2 Creating an Application Architecture

IBM's SAA provides only some of the software required to create applications which truly exploit common approaches and structure. What is needed is a tier of software or application components *above* that provided by IBM to deal with commonalities in the applications themselves. The implementation of this "application architecture" will be a key factor in improving the maintainability of the organization's portfolio of application software.

The application architecture will provide a framework for the internal structure of application software systems. The overall structure will include many common programs interacting with programs specific to the application function. The common programs will isolate the application function from the specifics of the hardware and operating system environment and will provide capabilities generally needed by most application systems (data entry, reporting, security, error processing, etc.). These programs will also isolate the application functions from the specific data needed to perform common functions so that the common programs can be improved without affecting existing applications. This architectural approach will result in the creation of programming "objects" which can be reused across a wide variety of applications.

Creating an object-oriented application architecture will yield long term benefits in terms of decreased application development and maintenance complexity and costs. This approach is consistent with the concepts of many components of IBM's Systems Application Architecture.

9.3.2 Overall Implementation Strategy

Where possible, new applications will be developed to conform to SAA standards. This means using enabling software (languages and services) which conform to the SAA Common Programming Interface. Where such software is not yet available, software with comparable or similar functions may be used. Regardless of operating system or hardware platform, precedence will be given to the use of languages and services which follow the CPI or can operate in conjunction with other software which does. In this way, new applications will form the nucleus of the enterprise computer network.

☛ *Issue: Will existing applications be enhanced to conform to SAA? If so, will there be multiple levels of compliance?*

Existing applications will not be scrapped, but will be brought into conformance with SAA as they are upgraded over time. Depending on the magnitude of the upgrade or enhancement, SAA compatible languages and services will be worked into the application structure. Since many applications will not be significantly reworked for several years, organization-wide conformance with SAA will be an evolutionary process.

9.3.3 Common User Access

Common User Access is the "visible" part of SAA. Where the type of user interface defined by CUA will be of immediate benefit to users, those systems will become candidates for immediate re-development.

CUA compliant user interfaces can be implemented on programmable workstations (the CUA Graphical and Workplace Models) and on non-programmable terminals (the CUA Text and Entry Models). The direction is toward the use of the more sophisticated graphical interfaces available with PWSs. However, the organization will follow a strategy of phasing in programmable workstations and will have applications which use non-programmable terminals for many years. New applications may implement a "dual interface" strategy, providing both NPT and PWS interfaces, if this is deemed appropriate for the intended user community.

Existing applications will be brought into compliance with CUA via a "front end" cooperative processing strategy. Development tools are available for creating workstation-based user interface modules which work in conjunction with existing host applications. This approach will bring CUA Graphical Model interfaces to a wide variety of applications and users in a relatively short period of time.

The NPT screens of existing applications will continue to be used "as is." As tools become available for re-engineering these screens to conform to CUA (using the Entry Model), such approaches will be investigated.

In the long term, the organization's application architecture will provide a framework for generic workstation-host cooperative processing with CUA conforming interfaces on the workstation.

9.3.4 Common Programming Interface

Many existing systems will be found not to follow the SAA CPI. New systems will be developed in one of the languages specified in the CPI. Language compilers will be used that validate compliance with the CPI elements for the particular languages used.

All new procedural programming (batch files, command files, etc.) will be done in the CPI Procedures Language (REXX).

Application generators currently in use will continue to be used. These application generators need not follow the SAA CPI element for application generators as long as they produce code in one of the CPI languages.

CPI service elements (Presentation Interface, Dialog Interface, Database, Query, Communications, Repository) will be followed by using enabling software which implements those services.

New CPI services will be used as soon as practical after implementing software is made available by IBM.

9.3.5 Distributed and Cooperative Processing

There are many approaches to distributed and cooperative processing. In each approach, parts of the application or database are distributed among multiple hardware platforms. The general modes of cooperation which will be implemented are as follows:

- Workstation-host cooperative processing, where user interface processing executes on the workstation while applications processing and the database reside on a host;

- Distributed processing, where parts of applications working in conjunction with each other may reside on different machines on the network; and

- Distributed database access (sometimes called client-server processing), where the applications (including user interface processing) reside on a workstation and parts of the database and data access routines reside on other machines on the network.

The organization will assess the benefits of these different modes of processing and their variations, and will incorporate them into its overall application architecture.

In the short term, workstation-host cooperative processing will be implemented for existing applications that will benefit from an improved user interface. Distributed processing and distributed data access will be implemented where the distribution of computing power can be justified for improved reliability, security, or flexibility.

9.3.6 Operating Systems and Applications Enabling Software

Certain operating systems have been designated by IBM as "SAA operating environments." This ensures IBM's commitment to continue to improve these systems and to implement on them new components of the SAA common architecture. Wherever possible, the organization will develop applications which use these operating systems, i.e., OS/2 Extended Edition, OS/400, MVS/ESA (TSO, CICS, IMS/TM), VM/SP, and VM/XA.

The UNIX operating system provides many of the capabilities called for in the SAA CPI, CUA, and CCS specifications. While not a part of SAA, UNIX systems will be able to interoperate with SAA systems. Any version of UNIX which provides appropriate functions, e.g. conforming languages, OSF/Motif (for presentation services), relational database, and LU6.2 communications, will be an acceptable operating environment for the organization. IBM's AIX provides all of these services.

Some applications will be implemented on IBM-compatible personal computers using the OS/2 operating system. Some inquiry and data entry applications will additionally provide DOS user interfaces. These applications will use development tools which provide CUA-like capabilities to provide as much consistency as possible with OS/2 versions.

The OS/400 operating system allows the operation of System/36 and System/38 applications. It is thus appropriate to migrate to this operating system (which runs on AS/400 hardware) for mid-range systems.

Mainframe systems using MVS and VM will continue on their current evolutionary paths. VSE-based systems will be evaluated for possible conversion to the MVS environment. Sufficient SAA-conforming enabling software exists on VSE to allow its participation in the enterprise network at the current time.

9.3.7 Hardware and Communications

☛ *Issue: How will hardware decisions be affected?*

SAA compliant software is not currently available for some of the computer hardware used in the organization. Every attempt will be made to continue to use this hardware for its maximum useful life. New hardware purchases will be examined in the light of their ability to use operating systems which participate in SAA, or to interoperate with SAA environments.

Over time, IBM mid-range and mainframe systems will be upgraded so that they can use one of the SAA operating environments. Mainframe systems from other manufacturers may be used when specific processing needs dictate. However, a strong emphasis will be placed on their ability to participate in a cooperative processing network using protocols prescribed in SAA Common Communications Support.

New personal computers will be purchased which have the ability to be upgraded to operate OS/2 Extended Edition, although they need not have that ability in their initial purchased condition. Non-IBM compatible personal computers will continue to be purchased where specific processing needs dictate. Workstations using the UNIX operating system will be upgraded so that they are capable of participating in cooperative processing applications. As in the case of mid-range and mainframe computers, a strong emphasis will be placed on the ability of all hardware to participate in an SAA cooperative processing network.

No new non-programmable terminals will be purchased. Application users who do not require programmable workstations will be supplied from existing inventory as other users upgrade to PWSs.

The existing local area network will continue to expand over time. Existing Ethernet, TCP/IP, and token-ring networks will be connected with bridges and gateways to form an interconnected "wide-area" network. This network will be capable of operating cooperative processing applications using protocols prescribed in SAA Common Communications Support. There is no need to rework existing networks to support a single network type, although standards for new networks will be established.

9.3.8 Application Development Environment

The organization will continue in its efforts to implement a sophisticated application development environment using advanced computer-aided software engineering (CASE) tools. This strategy will be expanded to include the creation of enterprise and project data repositories as central collection points for all information relating to the design and implementation of systems.

IBM's AD/Cycle specifies two key standards for CASE tools: conformance with SAA and implementation of a central repository interface. These standards are consistent with the direction of the organization's approach to CASE. Any tools which are included in AD/Cycle, or which follow its standards, will be considered for inclusion in the application development environment. Additionally, the specific use of IBM's Repository Manager will be considered as the mechanism for implementing the development data repository.

Development methods will be reviewed and upgraded in light of the intended implementation of cooperative processing applications. New techniques, such as object-oriented design, will be included in these methods where they add significant value to the design and development process.

9.3.9 Training

Training is key to the implementation of SAA. Computer users and developers alike will need education and hands-on experience in the SAA components of Common User Access, Common Programming Interface, and Common Communications Support.

Training in development methods and tools will be expanded significantly to ensure that the information systems staff is adequately prepared to implement SAA. Training for this group is most critical due to the lead time in creating new applications.

User training will include introduction to SAA concepts, such as Common User Access and cooperative processing, and to systems which implement these concepts. Ensuring that users understand the implications and benefits of SAA will advance the successful implementation of SAA in the organization.

10. Creating a Strategic Software Architecture

10.1 Issue Locator

☛ Issue: What does "Registered in IBM's SAA Catalog" mean? Page 224

10.2 Developing An Application Architecture

☛ *Issue: How do I develop an "application architecture" for my organization?*

SAA attempts to establish a framework for interfacing to the user, to the operating system, and across hardware platforms. How do the various elements of SAA relate to what might be called a "common application architecture," a framework for interfacing among different software components within the application itself?

The answer is that SAA deals with applications as if they consisted of only two types of software: components that "do the work" from a user point of view (e.g. provide the function or purpose), and those that deal with the hardware and provide various services independent of the specific purpose. In this view of an application's internal architecture, SAA today deals primarily with the "systems architecture," an integral component of the overall "applications architecture."

10.2.1 Defining Application Architecture

An application's architecture is the overall framework that describes its structure, how its different pieces fit together. A general "application architecture" is an overall framework that describes the structure of a large number of systems, such as business systems or manufacturing systems. One way of expressing that architecture is as a series of "tiers" and levels, each identifying a class of system functioning. Figure II.8 shows an architecture with four tiers, some horizontal, indicating a tier which isolates two others, and some vertical, indicating parallel tiers. The application function tier is what might be thought of as the substance of the application system. Each tier consists of programs that provide certain services to those at the next higher level and to parallel tiers, and that call upon services from the next lower level tiers via defined interfaces.

Following such a layered architectural concept allows you to create application systems that reuse common parts. Viewing each program in a system as a constituent part of a particular architectural tier serves to isolate programs in one tier from changes in the others. A significant result of this view is to simplify design and maintenance of applications by encouraging the reuse of entire tiers of software. With two or three architectural tiers, the amount of reuse can approach 50% of a new application system.

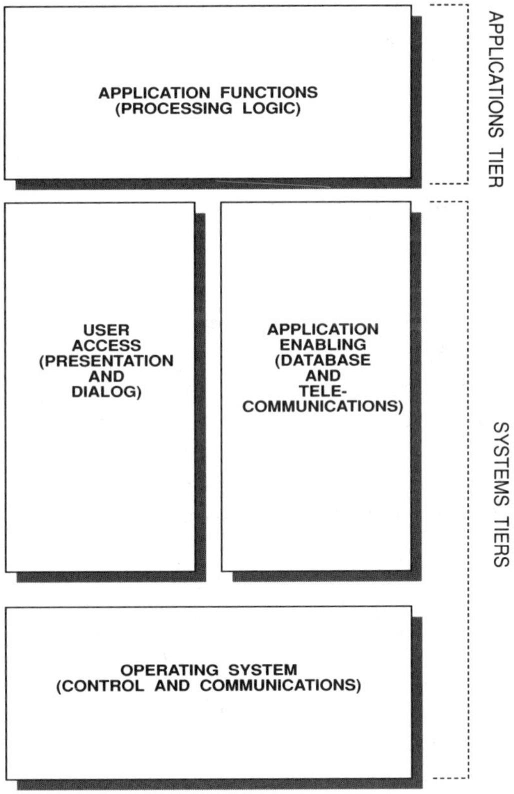

Figure II.8 Application Architecture Tiers

For example, the application enabling tier provides database access services to the application function tier while calling upon the operating system tier to perform its functions. Programs in the application function tier should not have to call upon services in the operating system tier directly to perform data access -- that should all be provided through the application enabling tier. If the application enabling tier is general enough, it can be used across a wide range of application systems.

The existence of many generalized database management systems is one proof that this concept is followed by many software developers. The tiered application architecture has also proven useful in hundreds of applications across all functional areas of hundreds of organizations. Experience shows that strict isolation of each level is a somewhat idealized concept, but this is a normal translation of a theoretical construct into actual practice.

10.2.1 Tiered Application Functions

More detailed study indicates that application function tier of a system can itself be divided into levels. For example, in Figure II.9, the application function tier has been divided into four, with "application specific programming" now representing the substance of the particular application. The lower tiers represent services of increasing generality used by the application specific programs. The stair-stepped shape of the boxes indicates that the application specific programs may need access to each of the lower levels. Analysis of IBM's OfficeVision products (Chapter 6) shows that they have architected the OS/2 version of this product according to this exact model.

Functional area services are those facilities commonly needed in many applications in a particular functional area. The contents of this tier will be industry-specific.

In the financial services industry, many different systems need to associate a customer number with the different account numbers assigned to that customer for different loans and deposit accounts. A program to perform the required database accesses and validations might become part of a functional area services architectural tier for financial industry systems. In the oil industry, a similar requirement might be to find the wells and properties owned by a particular individual. In the telecommunications industry, it might be to find a person's multiple telephone numbers. Each function is common to the systems in its functional area, but not to the others.

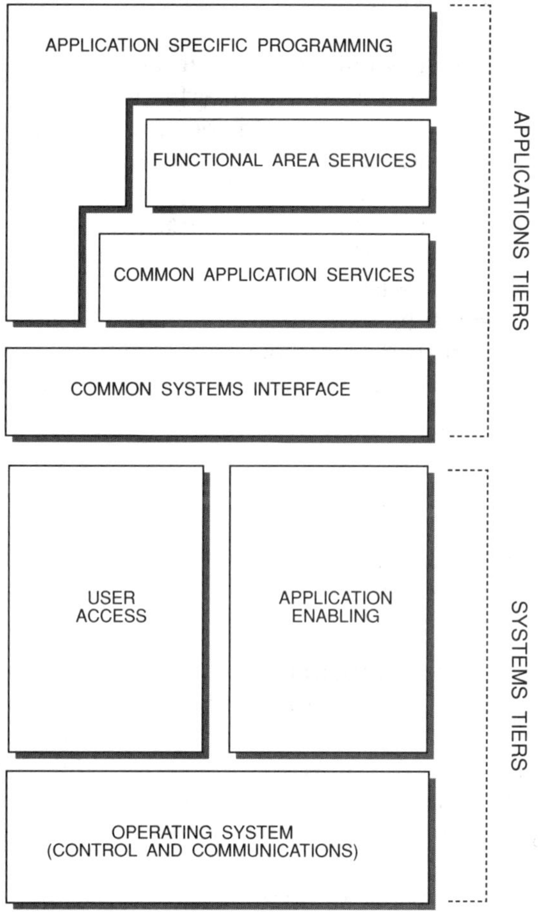

Figure II.9 Further Breakdown of Application Tier

Cross-functional area services such as security control, transaction error processing, report production, and many others can be contrasted with the previously described functional area services. These services would be provided by programs in a "common application services" tier of the architecture. This tier could be used in a wider variety of application systems, without regard to the functional area. There might still be different common application services for applications which were totally different in nature, such as transaction processing applications versus decision support applications.

The next tier shown is called the "common systems interface." This tier provides high level language interfaces to the systems layers. Examples of such interfaces would be presentation subroutines to display application windows at a particular location on the screen, communication subroutines to send a user's transaction input to another computer, or a generic data request interrogating part of a relational database. All of these functions require multiple calls to the systems tiers and serve to isolate the application programmer from many of their details. User interface functions would typically be part of this tier. Subroutines in the common programming interface would be applicable in *all* applications, regardless of type or functional area.

10.2.3 SAA and Application Architecture

SAA defines key components of a comprehensive application architecture, i.e., the interfaces to enabling and system control software. Referring to Figure II.10, the SAA components provide an architecture for the systems tiers and the lowest application tier. The structure of OfficeVision for OS/2 hints at the introduction of higher level interfaces. Perhaps these will become extensions to SAA in the future.

Common User Access defines a strategy for that part of the programming interface dealing with user access. The Common Programming Interface defines the interfaces between the application tiers and the systems tiers. Common Communications Support and various parts of the CPI also deliver the functions of the systems layers of the architecture to the application layers. Other than general guidance in the direction of object orientation, however, nothing in the current SAA definition prescribes the structure or function of the application function tiers. In terms of Figure II.10, SAA deals with the systems layers and programming interfaces, but not with the application architectural tiers.

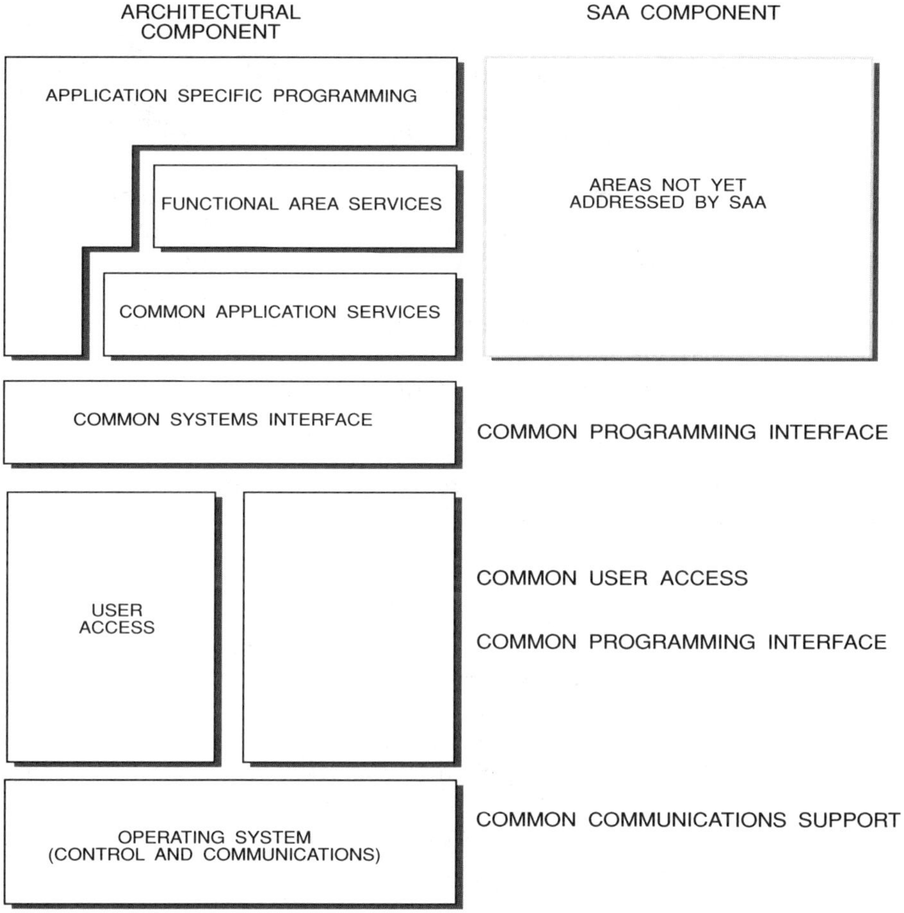

Figure II.10 SAA Components Compared to Application Architecture Tiers

10.3 What Does "Object-oriented" Really Mean?

Which statement is true?

[A] The object-oriented revolution has begun.

[B] Object-oriented evolution has begun.

Regardless of whether you subscribe to the revolutionary or evolutionary view, you would probably agree that the term "object-oriented" has irrevocably entered the vocabulary of computing. Usually appearing as an adjective (as in, object-oriented design, object-oriented programming, object-oriented system, etc.), we see the term applied to everything from a technique to a tool to an application. Unfortunately, as seems to have happened to the "structured approach," one industry pundit observed that:

Everyone will soon subscribe to an object-oriented approach. And no one will know just what it is.

☛ *Issue: Does adopting SAA also mean adopting "object-oriented" stuff?*

SAA does not explicitly require object orientation in applications. Some of the SAA interfaces allow an object-oriented style of development (for example, using the Presentation Interface). Furthermore, OfficeVision, IBM's first SAA application, presents an object-oriented user interface. There is little doubt that understanding object-oriented "stuff" is important, but adopting SAA does not mean that you are (or must be) object-oriented.

The Summer 1989 issue of *American Programmer (Ed Yourdon's Software Journal)* contains eleven articles by the gurus of system development methodologies, names associated with all of the methods in common use and with most of the new books on object-oriented approaches. Their observations are enlightening, both for their differences and similarities. Some are of the revolution school, going so far as to say that current development techniques and languages must be thrown out. Others believe that object-orientation is an evolutionary step which builds on established methods and which will result in evolutionary development in today's computer languages and tools. I am of the evolutionary school, in as much as most so-called "revolutionary" ideas in our field can be shown to have evolved from a number of other sources. Given the people nature of our business, and the way in which people generally respond to any change let alone revolutionary ones, I hope that we "evolutionists" are correct.

American Programmer is an excellent source for those wanting a broad view of object-oriented issues. The references in the Summer 1989 issue include a wide variety of articles and books. For those interested in a more condensed introduction to object orientation, and to its implications for software strategy, read on.

10.3.1 A Brief Tutorial on Object Orientation

☛ *Issue: What is an "object" anyway?*

"Objects" are abstractions of real world things. In user terms, typical objects might be pictures on a screen representing documents, files, accounting transactions, purchase orders, mail boxes, or telephones. In programming terms, objects are combinations of data structures and procedures which perform certain functions on that data.

Object-oriented analysis, design, and programming deal with the development of systems based on "objects" as the basic building blocks, rather than on the data structures or procedures individually. Object-oriented systems contain data structures and procedures, as do all systems, but it is the objects that are the fundamental focus.

You can think of an object-oriented system as containing a large number of these procedure-linked-to-data objects floating around in "object space" with their receptors humming as they wait for messages from other objects telling them to do some work (Figure II.11). Contrast this with the traditional view of a system as a hierarchically structured set of programs, each performing its work in turn as the system proceeds from start to finish. Revolutionary or evolutionary? Perhaps some of both.

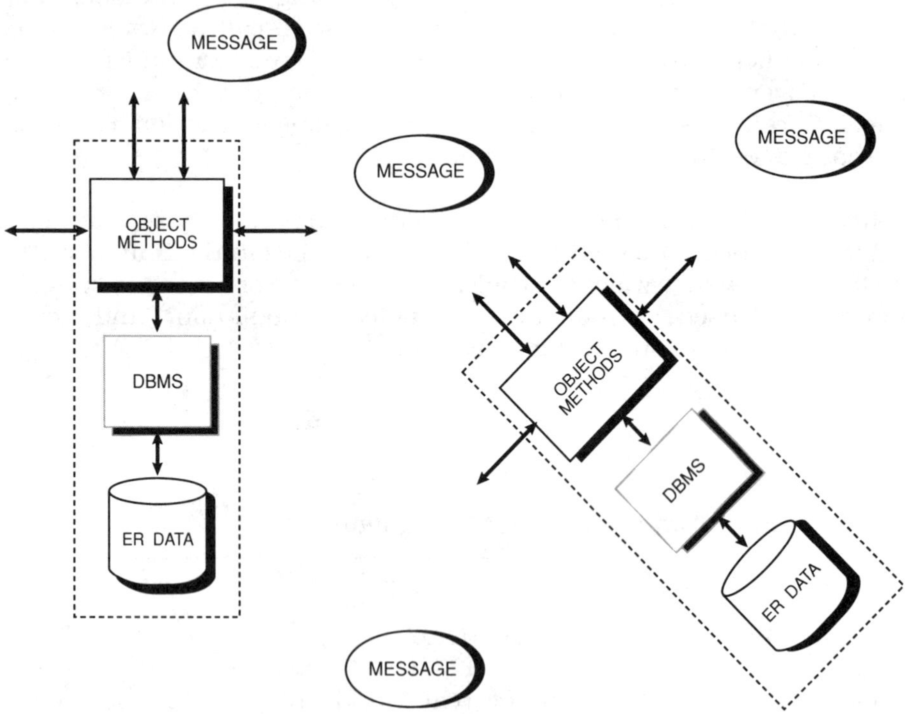

Figure II.11 Object Space

10.3.1.1 Formal Definition

An "object" is the combination of a set of procedures and the data on which they operate and which behaves in certain defined ways based on its inputs ("messages") and its heritage ("object class").

An "instance" of an object is one which has specific values for the data attributes.

The functions an object's procedures perform are called "methods."

An "object class" (also called "object type") contains objects having some similar methods and attributes.

Object orientation is further defined by the properties that objects have. These properties are:

- abstraction
- encapsulation
- modularity (information hiding)
- hierarchical inheritance

The data in an object represent "abstract data types." An abstract data type is a data structure defined for the commonality of the operations performed on it. An "accounts payable voucher" is an abstract data type; a "four character string" is not. An instance of an abstract data type can only be looked at and manipulated by the common operations that are defined on it.

Thus, the data in an object are "encapsulated" by the procedures of the object, i.e., the procedures provide the only way in which the data can be accessed and manipulated. Procedures that are outside of a particular object can only access its data via the methods contained in that object.

Object methods have the property of "information hiding." Their defined interfaces reveal as little as possible about how they are implemented.

Objects have the property of "inheritance." They inherit data attributes and methods from other objects in the object class to which they are hierarchically related. "Accounts payable vouchers" inherit many attributes and methods from the "accounts payable transactions" class, which in turn inherits from the "accounting transaction" class.

Other properties which have been included in some definitions of object orientation include:

Objects communicate with each other via "messages." Objects may, therefore, operate asynchronously or synchronously.

Object classes should have the property of "multiple inheritance" through multiple levels and paths in a class hierarchy.

> *Many object classes should be able to use the same messaging protocol, although the underlying method implementation will vary from class to class. This property is called "polymorphism." It allows the design of general purpose algorithms that can be applied to many different types of data (object instances).*
>
> *Object-oriented systems are constructed from objects contained in object libraries. Many of the objects in an object library should be re-usable across multiple systems.*

Applying these definitions, an object-oriented system appears in many ways similar to any structured, modular system. After all, a well-designed modular system can be expected to employ techniques such as encapsulation and information hiding, two key properties attributed to object-oriented systems.

The single most significant distinguishing factor between a traditional modular system and an object-oriented one is the property of hierarchical inheritance. This property can be illustrated in a simple order entry system. If the designer defines an "order" object, then "mail order," "telephone order," and "walk-up order" would all be members of the object class "order." Procedures to add orders, change orders, and modify orders could be implemented as part of the order object and yet be available to all types of orders. The data structure associated with a generic order would form the core of the data structure of specific types of orders. Only the additional attributes of a telephone order (e.g. the telephone number of the caller and the time of the call) need be added to the generic attributes of an order (e.g. the name and address of the person placing the order). This additional property extends the concept of modularity to include reuse of data and procedures to a very broad extent.

Without inheritance, object-oriented systems are not much more than could be accomplished using more traditional tools and techniques. For this reason, object-oriented systems can be viewed as evolutionary to structured, modular systems. To the extent that the designer's basic thought processes and mind set are different in working with an object orientation, object orientation can also be viewed as revolutionary.

10.3.1.2 Design and Analysis

Development of object-oriented systems requires an object-oriented development methodology, i.e., one in which the definition of objects and their interactions is the key design step. This does not mean that all of the techniques used in structured analysis and design need to be thrown out (although some writers do advocate this). Entity-relationship models are useful for defining objects and for specifying the relationships among objects in the system. They can further be used to specify the attributes in objects that are hierarchically related. On the other hand, they would have to be extended to indicate the methods that are associated with the data in the object. Structure charts may be acceptable for developing a detailed design of these methods, but they do not get across the higher level interaction among objects. Data flow diagrams could be used either at the method detail design level, or to show the passing of messages (data flows in the DFD) among objects (processes in the DFD). State transition diagrams can show the state of objects as well as they can show the state of data entities, so they appear to be useful as well.

None of these diagrams is perfect for designing object-oriented systems (many people would say that they were not perfect even for designing structured systems either). As a result, there have been a number of suggested diagramming techniques to aid in the analysis and design of object-oriented systems. (The references in the cited issue of *American Programmer* contain most of them.)

The biggest problem in creating object-oriented systems is the definition of objects. In some ways, this is akin to defining entities in a data model. There are as yet no established methods for determining what constitutes an object, rather than just part of an object or an object class. But rest assured, the methodology gurus are hard at work.

10.3.1.3 Development

You can use any language for object-oriented development as long as it supports the properties of object-oriented systems. Since traditional languages do not support the properties of object-oriented systems, you can only use one of the "object-oriented languages" for implementing object-oriented systems. Unless, of course, you (or someone else) develop the infrastructure to permit traditional computer languages to handle object-oriented constructs.

That about sums up the situation in object-oriented development. The proponents of Smalltalk and similar languages argue that they were designed from the ground up to handle objects. They allow you to define objects as being members of objects classes with inheritance of function and data; they handle message processing among objects; and they enforce encapsulation of data. The Smalltalk developers and their followers claim that it is only by true object-oriented languages that you can implement true object-oriented systems. The proponents of C++, an "objectified" version of C, have added constructs to a traditional procedural language to deal with object management, inheritance, and message passing. They claim that this will result in perfectly good object-oriented development.

And then there are those who note that most people who program do so in COBOL or FORTRAN and that sooner or later, someone will figure out how to produce object-oriented systems using these languages as well. [There is already a proposal before the appropriate ANSI committee to add object extensions to COBOL.]

In my opinion, what is most likely to bring object-oriented systems to everyone's attention is the development of "object environments" which will accept procedures written in any language, but will control their invocation and operation in an appropriate object-oriented manner. After all, does it really matter that a procedure to update an accounting balance is written in COBOL if it appropriately hides the structure of the balance database, responds to applicable requests to update it, and automatically invokes other procedures which are hierarchically related to it? The development environment provided by Smalltalk/V PM (Smalltalk in the OS/2 Presentation Manager environment) provides a superb set of tools for object-oriented development -- if you know Smalltalk. What about using those tools to invoke other language procedures to perform certain business functions?

In other words, what we need is an object-oriented "run time" environment to control our procedures and data, regardless of the specific implementation language used. Interestingly enough, the IBM Repository Manager product applies this strategy in controlling the repository database and its associated methods.

10.3.2 What About Object-oriented Databases?

Just as data processing departments are becoming comfortable with relational databases, someone goes off and develops "object-oriented databases." Does this mean that all those systems being written with relational databases are already obsolete? Should systems written in hierarchical databases such as IMS be re-written using object orientation? The answer to all such questions is "it depends."

In general, it is neither necessary nor appropriate to reprogram existing applications just to use the latest technology. In the case of object-oriented databases, this is even more true. Object-oriented databases (OODB) provide facilities for implementing object-oriented systems, i.e. they are database management systems which allow access to complex data structures only through the filter of a program. The database encapsulates the data and the program by forming an "object" which is then referenced by sending a message to it. In addition, they deal with the object property of "inheritance" by re-introducing the concept of hierarchy in the database (see, there really isn't anything new in the world). The world of OODB is still immature, however, and the capabilities provided by different vendors vary widely.

There is a growing belief in the data processing community that object-oriented techniques will provide major improvements in development and maintenance productivity. Industry experience in this is limited, and does not begin to address systems performance in high volume production environments. Like all technology decisions, therefore, the issue is whether the tool fits the problem, not whether the tool is the latest to hit the street.

10.3.3 Why Are Object-Oriented Systems So Important?

If object orientation is "just another" development paradigm, why all the fuss? Theorists will ramble on about totally new ideas which will revolutionize the design and construction of systems; pragmatists will talk about the use of new programming languages and finally getting out from under the weight of COBOL. There are probably as many answers to why people are making a fuss as there are people answering the question.

The real answer (of course this is the *real* answer) has to do with a basic truth about systems: the more code you write, the more it costs. If you could find a way to write a lot less code (not just for one application, but forever), you would have something worth making a fuss about. Object-oriented methods are the first paradigm which seems to address this fundamental point in a concrete way.

Whether during initial development or the much longer maintenance period, cost is directly related to the number of lines of code written for a system. There are several ways to write less code for a system. One of the most promising is to reuse code written for a previous system. Unfortunately, until the development of the object-oriented paradigm, there has been a lot more hot air than hot ideas about how to do this. Creating a library of objects which can be readily referenced and whose contents can be drawn upon to create new applications is one of the more promising concepts for improving reusability. Not only does it promise to provide reusable code, but reusable data models and designs as well.

Cost is what all our methods are really about. Modularity, structured design and programming, information models, and all the other techniques for reducing system complexity, simplifying development, or reducing maintenance are all ultimately directed at reducing the cost of doing whatever it is you are trying to do with systems. Until we start to see some really large systems (in today's terms typified by one million lines of code or more) implemented using object-oriented techniques and incorporating libraries of reusable objects, it will be difficult to tell if the cost savings are really there. But there are a very large number of very practical people betting a lot of money on the fact that they are.

10.4 Selecting a Programming Language

In 1969, Jean Sammet's definitive history of the topic listed over 120 different programming languages in public use. FORTRAN, COBOL, PL/1, and LISP were among them. Ada, C, Pascal, REXX, RPG, and Smalltalk were not. More recent estimates are that the number of languages enjoying some degree of use is double or triple the number of 20 years ago. Yet, for the most part, the choice of programming languages for "industrial strength" applications boils down to a handful. Since most of the common procedural languages are included in the SAA CPI (Ada being an exception), the issues arise in selecting which one to use. [The absence of languages for creating artificial intelligence applications from SAA has been noted by more than a few observers. IBM has indicated that this is an area that will be covered in the future.]

☛ *Issue: How do you decide which computer language to use in which environment?*

Criteria that can be used in selecting an appropriate programming language include:

- features of the language
- availability of experienced programmers and designers
- ease of training programmers and designers
- availability of development tools like optimizing compilers, debuggers, editors, etc.
- efficiency of programming and debugging
- efficiency of program operation
- understandability and ease of maintenance of programs written in the language
- consistency of the language with current and emerging software architecture and design concepts

■ number of languages in use in your shop (and the ability to assimilate more)

At a more detailed level, each of these expands into many individual questions. At a strategic level, comparing the strengths and weaknesses of the various languages for just these questions will allow you to focus in on an answer.

10.4.1 C vs. COBOL

For business applications, mainframe programmers use COBOL and microcomputer programmers use C.

While this statement has been generally true, it was often a matter of programmers using the languages that were available to them. And that is changing. C is available on all the SAA platforms and so is COBOL. The choice of language now rests on other factors.

There are more experienced COBOL programmers in the world than C programmers by a very large multiple. If you limit your looking to commercial shops using IBM hardware, that multiple may be 100 or greater. One criterion that must be considered in choosing a development language is the number and level of programmers experienced with that language and COBOL wins hands down.

[This situation may be changing. More and more university graduates are entering the work force with C in their repertoire. Simple demographics show, however, that C-experienced programmers will not overtake COBOL-experienced programmers until the COBOL programmers retire. By that time, we may all be programming in Smalltalk -- or in English.]

Luckily for progress, there are other considerations in picking a programming language, features for instance. The facilities in COBOL for defining complex data structures are limited compared to C. COBOL is similarly limited in its string handling abilities. While C was designed as a block structured language, these features were relatively recently added to COBOL and are not in use in all shops (you have to use VS

COBOL II to get them on an IBM mainframe and there are many shops that have not yet migrated from prior versions). In addition, COBOL is extremely verbose compared to C (even its name is five times as long).

C's compactness, however, sometimes works to its disadvantage. While there is little hard evidence, it appears to be more difficult to train a journeyman C programmer than it is a COBOL programmer. Furthermore, C code is inherently less easy to read than COBOL code, a factor in program maintenance and enhancement.

The approach to writing systems in C is much more dependent on libraries of common routines than is COBOL. This is viewed as an advantage when overall productivity is considered. The ability to reuse C routines is indicated by the number of C routine libraries that are available for purchase. In its much shorter life span than COBOL, C shops have spawned thousands of routines that are really reused, and not just in the shops that created them. How many commonly available libraries of COBOL routines have you seen recently?

Perhaps because of the features in C, several of the recent object-oriented languages are based on it. C++ is enjoying a degree of popularity, as is Objective C. C programmers thus have a migration path to full object-oriented systems without complete retraining.

One of the chief reasons C has achieved popularity in the microcomputer world is the availability of relatively compatible versions on a large number of hardware and software environments. Almost all of the major microcomputer application products were originally written in C or have been re-written in C to achieve portability. More recently, good COBOL compilers and debugging tools have become available on the PC (MicroFocus COBOL Workbench being a key example) and COBOL programmers have started to port existing applications and do new work in COBOL on the PC. SAA will further equalize the availability of C and COBOL in the IBM world, but not necessarily in the broader world of multi-vendor systems.

So which should you use? One approach to answering this question relates to the creation of a reusable "application architecture." Those "layers" of the application system that represent system control and application enabling system interfaces can be written in C. They are written once (and used by many applications), by a group of specialists, to get maximum advantage out of the platform software and to separate some of the most complex program logic from the application "substance." The remaining application functions can then be written in COBOL. This approach plays to the strengths of both languages, and deals with knowledge and complexity issues by limiting the amount of work to be done in C. The desirable mix may change over time, but for now this is a reasonable way to deal with the trade-offs.

10.4.1.1 What Happened to Pascal?

Pascal was developed primarily as a teaching language to illustrate a number of modern concepts of good language design. As the students who learned Pascal in school spread into the community, and as teaching versions of Pascal began to be supplied with early microcomputers, its use spread throughout a segment of the software development community. As C implementations became available, professional programmers generally switched to avoid some of the constraints of the Pascal language.

While Pascal continues to enjoy popularity among a large number of PC programmers, C is the choice of professionals. No doubt Apple will continue to keep some version of Pascal alive (their Macintosh system software is written in a variant), but even they are coming out with a C++ (which will include a preprocessor to integrate with their Pascal operating system routines). It is unlikely that Pascal will ever surpass C in the IBM world, and certainly not in the UNIX world where C is the standard.

10.4.2 Scientific and Engineering Languages

FORTRAN is part of the SAA CPI. It is probably the most widely used programming language and is the first language to have an ANSI Standard definition. It was designed for solving numerical problems and is mostly used in scientific and engineering applications. There are alternatives to FORTRAN for dealing with certain application areas, so-called "domain specific languages," but none approach it in generality.

[It is interesting to note that FORTRAN has been used (although not necessarily by desire) over the years for almost every type of programming imaginable, from business systems to compilers to decision rule processors (i.e., "knowledge-based systems"). The very popular fourth generation language FOCUS was itself originally (and until recently) written in FORTRAN. This is a tribute both to the flexibility of the language and to the ingenuity of programmers using the only tool they had available in ways that its designers never dreamed of.]

The inclusion of FORTRAN in SAA and, therefore, the planned availability of consistent versions across the SAA environments, assures its continued use for years to come.

10.4.3 A Role for Ada

Ada was designed under contract for the Advanced Research Projects Agency of the Department of Defense to provide a common language for DOD systems. Over a decade later, it is still in the growth stage within DOD and with DOD's contractors, and has not achieved significant visibility outside of that community.

Ada contains many constructs which make it desirable for programming systems of all types. Its ability to create structured programs, using some of the same principles applied in object-oriented programming, is well understood. Data abstraction, encapsulation, and information hiding are all concepts known to the Ada programmer. Since inheritance is not built into Ada, it is not an object-oriented language in the strict sense. Extensions will undoubtedly move it in this direction.

The continued support of the Department of Defense and the many aerospace and weapons contractors will ensure a place for Ada. Whether IBM supports Ada in all its environments or not, third party developers will. There is even an Ada for OS/2 which implements an interface to the Presentation Manager (see *IBM Personal System Developer* magazine for information on third party development tools for OS/2).

10.4.4 Artificial Intelligence Languages

The two main languages used in artificial intelligence programming today are LISP (List Processor) and PROLOG (Programming in Logic). Neither is widely used on IBM mainframes (there are implementations, at least under VM) although they are widely available for use on PCs. Initial AI work seems almost universally to have been done on Digital Equipment Corporation hardware (the first computer in the AI Lab at MIT was a PDP-1, followed by a PDP-6, and then a PDP-10) and many variants, particularly of LISP, were created for those machines.

Perhaps because of IBM's reputation for providing the workhorse machines for business processing, rather than machines whose strength lay in their interaction with on-line users, AI has only recently become an issue for the IBM mainframe. Mainstream AI today (as opposed to experimental work) involves the link-up of complex decision tree processors with large databases of information ("knowledge-based systems"). There are a number of vendors providing programming engines for this type of work, including IBM itself. IBM's The Integrated Reasoning Shell (TIRS) is available in several SAA environments and AIX and is a component of AD/Cycle. Whether this leads to an SAA CPI or not, AI work will increasingly insert itself in the enterprise-wide computing strategy. In the near term, the language issue is more likely to boil down to one of finding the desired application solution and using whatever language or AI engine it is implemented on.

10.5 Other Architectures

☛ *Issue: What about "industry standard" architectures?*

SAA is IBM's definition of a standard software architecture. Not everyone, especially other hardware manufacturers, will want to view SAA as a standard. Many of them, individually and as members of industry consortia, are hard at work developing their own application architectures. There are so many industry groups (sixteen by one count) that it is almost impossible to sort them out. IBM is a member of some of these, and others have certainly influenced the SAA designers. Even so, it is unlikely that the SAA standard will be exactly the same as any other. Our interest is in how these other efforts will impact on and co-exist with SAA. The brief synopses below show some of the parallels with the SAA architecture.

10.5.1 The UNIX Strategy

There are as many UNIX implementations as there are hardware and software vendors selling them.

The UNIX world may not have as bad a problem as IBM with its multiple operating systems, but it does not have a single standard either. In fact, there are two key groups, the Open Software Foundation and UNIX International, trying to develop that standard. Other groups, such as the X/Open consortium and the Institute of Electrical and Electronics Engineers (IEEE), are working on pieces of the standard that both other groups will adhere to.

The AT&T-led UNIX International is proposing that the AT&T version of UNIX become the standard. The Open Systems Foundation was formed to counteract this move, attempting to create an alternative to what its members felt was the growing proprietary nature of AT&T's UNIX. While AT&T has made overtures, the battle of the UNIX standards continues to rage.

OSF is a non-profit consortium with over 100 member organizations, representing hardware and software manufacturers, large computer users, universities, and other research organizations. IBM is a member. So is Digital Equipment Corporation, Hewlett-Packard, Data General, Apollo, Hitachi, and Groupe Bull. Its stated purpose is to develop and provide to its members software that implements a common environment that can be ported to a wide variety of computers. This environment is to be based on the IEEE POSIX standard, the MIT X Window System, and ANSI Standard C.

The base operating system technology for "OSF/1" was originally going to be IBM's AIX. That was subsequently rejected due to inadequate multi-processing features, although many commands and libraries will still come from AIX. OSF then announced that OSF/1 would be implemented using Carnegie Mellon University's Mach operating system. The concept for OSF/2, based on a totally different architecture, was also announced (just to keep things interesting).

With IBM a key player in OSF, the industry is very interested in what it will do to keep AIX consistent with the OSF standard. The announcement of AIX Version 3 specifically states that software's conformance to the IEEE POSIX standard, upward compatibility from UNIX System V, and IBM's intent to conform to the X/Open Portability Guide for its Common Applications Environment (CAE). OSF is not mentioned.

10.5.2 Digital's Application Integration Architecture and Network Application Support

Digital Equipment Corporation has been a leader in creating a consistent hardware and software architecture over a wide range of computing platforms. Its VAX series of computers ranges from a desktop model to one which challenges some of IBM's largest mainframes. Most importantly, applications using the VMS operating system will operate on all machines in the VAX line -- they are compatible and portable at the binary level. In addition, DECnet provided a broad spectrum network architecture that allows these (and other) computers to be tied together.

But Digital began to face a wider challenge in the late 1980s. Its solutions did not go far enough. The standard on the desktop was not a VAX, but rather an IBM compatible PC or an Apple Macintosh. It still had not been able to unseat IBM in the "workhorse mainframe" category. And more and more users were hearing the UNIX call by shifting to Digital's ULTRIX as an alternative to VMS. Its architecture for the 1990s would have to encompass more than a VAX running VMS.

Application Integration Architecture (AIA) is Digital's attempt to define standard operating system interfaces that will allow the creation of applications operating in a heterogeneous distributed computing environment. In that sense, it is much like SAA. Unlike SAA, however, the architecture encompasses Digital's standard operating system (VMS) and their UNIX (ULTRIX), and provides interoperability with MS-DOS, OS/2, and the Macintosh Operating System.

The implementation of the AIA strategy is in Network Application Support (NAS). NAS is the marketing name for Digital's enabling software (operating system interfaces, toolkits, subroutine libraries) to implement AIA. NAS is being rolled out over a period of several years for both VMS and ULTRIX, with appropriate subsets for PCs and Macintoshes.

AIA deals with the interfaces among users, systems, and applications (as does SAA). It defines overall architectures and application programming interfaces. The implementation of AIA in NAS is divided into three areas:

- application access
- communications
- information/resource sharing

Figure II.12 lists the services defined in each area. The specific vehicles for delivering these services are Digital products which, in general, follow or provide a superset of industry standards. For example, DECwindows is the product which provides windowing services. It is a superset of the OSF/Motif graphical user interface on top of the MIT X Window System. Similarly, compound document services are provided by Digital's CDA (Compound Document Architecture) products which expand upon the ISO Office Document Architecture (ODA) and SGML. In general, Digital is implementing its own standards on top of other standards.

Service	Purpose
Application Access	
Windowing Services	Graphical user interface
Forms Services	Data entry and inquiry
Terminal Services	Character-mode terminal emulation
Graphics Services graphics	Two- and three-dimensional
Application Control Services	Cooperative processing
Communications	
Messaging Services	Electronic mail
EDI Services	Business document interchange
Information/Resource Sharing	
Compound Document Services	Office document interchange
Data Access Services	SQL access to relational data
Repository/Dictionary Services information	Design and development
File Sharing Services	Distributed file management
Print Services	Device independent printing

Figure II.12 Digital's Network Application Support Services

AIA is clearly not SAA. It is not as broad in terms of interfaces or enabling products (at least not yet), nor is it as likely to have anywhere near the impact of SAA. It also has a different purpose. AIA is Digital's attempt to bring VMS and UNIX together, at least from a user and application perspective, and to allow users a wide variety of workstation choices in communicating with Digital's mid-range and mainframe computers. The real question is whether there will be "interoperability" between AIA and SAA (probably) and when (probably not for a long time).

10.5.3 UNISYS's Solution Generation Environment

UNISYS has a problem: 16-bit and 48-bit Burroughs machines, 36-bit Univac machines, and 32-bit RCA machines, all with operating systems to fit. Over the years, all of these have come under the UNISYS umbrella. The announced Solution Generation Environment is a common development environment (based on UNISYS's very successful MAPPER product) that will be able to generate code for all of these operational environments. Add a common communications interface (based on OSI of course), and voila...U-SAA.

Not really an "architecture," Solution Generation Environment does deal with some of the same issues as SAA. Based on announced capabilities (nothing is delivered yet), the UNISYS strategy is more akin to providing the features of IBM's Cross System Product than to full SAA.

10.6 The Importance of SAA Compliance

☛ *Issue: What does it mean for software to comply with SAA and why is that important?*

Complying with SAA means:

- using the languages and interfaces defined in the SAA CPI;
- developing user interfaces that follow the CUA definition;
- architecting your application for cooperative processing;
- using one or more of the included operating environments; and
- using communications mechanisms specified in CCS.

SAA compliance, however, is not an all or nothing proposition. Some or all of an application can comply in whole or in part with some or all of SAA. The answer to the question "how much compliance is enough?" depends on who is asking the question and who is listening to the answer. The answer will be different if you are a commercial software developer trying to interest a customer in your products, or if you are a systems designer in a large organization trying to justify the redevelopment of a major system. In fact, the entire issue of compliance may need to be treated on several different levels, from concepts down to specific rules and standards.

What SAA is really about is productivity and quality. It is not so much an issue of strict compliance with rules and standards for their own sake, as it is what we can expect as a result of complying with them. Underlying the whole SAA approach is a fundamental belief that productivity of developers and users alike will improve when we use standard approaches to implementing systems and delivering their functions. And that the quality of our work, measured in every way from number of errors to customer satisfaction, will also improve from the use of these same standards.

In some sense, you "comply with SAA" when you achieve the benefits of improved productivity and quality that will come from cooperative processing, common user access, and common programming interfaces. We are all in this together (IBM, other hardware manufacturers, independent software vendors, and computer user organizations) so the more we can agree on a set of standards that all can use, the more we will all come out winners.

10.6.1 Viewpoint of a Software Vendor

Software vendors have a very important role in implementing IBM's SAA strategy. Without the support of a large percentage of the software industry, SAA could easily fade into obscurity. IBM being IBM, this is extremely unlikely to happen, and independent software vendors (ISVs) are lining up to embrace SAA. Of course, embracing SAA conceptually and for marketing purposes is different than restructuring and re-implementing software, although this is also taking place.

It is much more important for software vendors to be able to say that their products strictly follow SAA than it is for a systems group in a user organization. It is equally as important for software vendor's products *actually* to follow SAA as it is for a user organization. *Saying* that you follow SAA will help sell products for a while; *following* SAA will help improve profitability forever.

[One of the largest independent software vendors decided to switch, not fight. It made a public showing of scrapping a $25 million investment in its own software architecture and implementing an SAA-based strategy. That organization clearly thought the long term payoff was better with SAA.]

One of IBM's goals in formulating SAA was to improve its *own* productivity. IBM was (and still is) wasting countless hours and dollars in re-inventing variations of languages and operating system interfaces for four (or more) different operating systems. Having a Common Programming Interface which it can implement on all platforms will result in major savings in design, training, testing, documentation, and maintenance. Creating a common multi-layered software architecture will go even further in reducing the redundant programming effort across different applications. The same is true for software vendors, at both the system and application levels.

Forward thinking software vendors are already moving in the direction of common user interfaces across multiple applications, and common software across multiple platforms. Peruse almost any of the trade publications and you will see these capabilities touted in the advertisements of the major application vendors. With the advent of SAA, they have the added legitimacy of IBM's strategic direction to pursuing goals of improved productivity and quality via better software architecture.

10.6.1.1 What Will They Really Do?

Aside from the marketing hyperbole, what will the vendors really do? The first group to sign on to SAA compliance demonstrated their prototypes at IBM's May 1989, press conference. At that point, SAA compliance meant following the graphical model of Common User Access implemented via OS/2 EE Presentation Manager. Some vendors also showed compliance with the CUA Workplace Model as it ties in with OfficeVision. Some showed cooperative processing among workstation and host. Some used non-standard languages in their implementations but no one made any noise about it. No one used the CPI for Communications because the system software to implement it was not yet available.

It takes most application vendors two or more years to implement major changes in their products. This is a normal cycle of concept, design, development, implementation, and marketing. The first IBM applications to embody a full set of SAA interfaces became available in 1989, so it will be late 1990 and 1991 before application software which is fully SAA compliant becomes generally available.

Based on 15 years of following the application software market, my prediction is that:

- Vendors will all claim SAA compliance, some long before they actually have it.

- CUA will be the first SAA component to be followed; it is the most visible part of SAA and the implementing software is available. However, there will be fairly wide variations in what different vendors interpret as "complying with CUA" (see below).

- Cooperative processing will begin with workstation front ends to previously existing mainframe applications; distributed databases will be in second or third releases.

- Non-SAA language use will be phased out over a number of product releases since few, if any, vendors, will re-write older software until they really have to.

- Every software vendor serving the IBM market will move further in the direction of SAA compliance with each new release of their software.

Application Structure

- ❑ **Standalone**
  - ❑ Host With Non-Programmable Workstations (NWS)
  - ❑ Programmable Workstation (PWS)
- ❑ **Cooperative**
  - ❑ Host With Programmable Workstation

Common User Access (CUA)

- ❑ **CUA 1987**
- ❑ **CUA 1989**
  - ❑ Basic Interface Design Guide
    - ❑ *Entry for NWS*
    - ❑ *Text for NWS*
    - ❑ *Entry for PWS*
  - ❑ Advanced Interface Design Guide
    - ❑ *Graphical*
    - ❑ *Workplace*

Environment

- ❑ **OS/2 EE**
- ❑ **OS/400**
- ❑ **VM/CMS**
- ❑ **MVS**
  - ❑ TSO
  - ❑ CICS
  - ❑ IMS-TM

Common Programming Interface (CPI)

Languages	**Services**
❑ **Application Generator**	❑ **Communications**
❑ **C**	❑ **Database**
❑ **COBOL**	❑ **Dialog**
❑ **FORTRAN**	❑ **Presentation**
❑ **PL/1**	❑ **Query**
❑ **Procedures**	❑ **Repository**
❑ **RPG**	

Figure II.13 SAA Compliance Checklist - Structure, Environment, CUA, and CPI

Common Communications Support (CCS)

Data Streams	Application Services	Session Services
❑ RFT:DCA	❑ DIA	❑ LU 6.2
❑ 3270 DS	❑ DDM	
❑ IPDS	❑ SNA/DS	
❑ CDRA	❑ SNA Network Management	
	❑ DRDA	

Network	Data Link Controls	Open System Interconnect Protocols
❑ LEN	❑ SDLC	❑ OSI
	❑ Token Ring	
	❑ X.25	

Figure II.14 SAA Compliance Checklist - CCS

10.6.2 How Can You Tell If Software Is SAA Compliant?

☛ *Issue: How can I tell if purchased software complies with SAA?*

IBM provides *A Guide for Evaluating Applications* to help you in verifying SAA compliance. This manual supplies a convenient checklist listing the major components of SAA (reproduced in Figures II.13 and II.14 with permission of IBM). Anyone developing software can check off those features of the SAA definition that are used in their applications. This, like most checklists, provides only a superficial view of how the application is implemented. It does not show what non-SAA software or standards are also used, nor does it indicate how much of an application uses the standard. If one set of queries uses SQL, but the rest of the application is written in assembler, does that make it SAA compliant (i.e., allow the vendor to check the box)?

IBM is leaving the answers to this type of question up to us, but my answer is NO. We need to perform a finer grain analysis to determine what *parts* of an application conform to what *parts* of SAA. Only in this way will developers and users establish a common understanding of what they are providing and getting.

10.6.2.1 SAA Compliance As a Software Selection Criterion

Software vendors have been feeling the heat about SAA compliance from their customers and prospects. It seems that almost everyone has added

> *"Does your software comply with IBM's Systems Application Architecture? If not, what are your plans?"*

to their software selection checklists. But if IBM is not independently verifying vendor claims, how good are the answers going to be?

At this point in SAA's history, major applications vendors should have fairly well-developed plans for bringing their software into line with SAA. At the very least, you should be able to see a prototype or get a presentation on their plans. If the vendor is unwilling to provide a written plan or cannot make a creditable presentation, you should take a dim view of its commitment to SAA compliance. At this date, over three years after SAA was announced, that would make me very leery of committing my organization to that vendor's products.

Once a vendor has presented its SAA plan to you, you should be able to compare it with your own organization's plans. You should be careful to distinguish between short-term and long-term differences. In the long term, it should not matter whether your preference is for PC-based LAN servers or mainframes acting as database servers. Vendors complying with SAA will be able to provide both. In the short term, this could be a big issue. For example, if your organization is making a move in the direction of token-ring LANs with heavy emphasis on LAN-server cooperative processing architectures, it would not make sense to buy application software whose vendor puts that type of processing at the bottom of its implementation priority list.

Select vendors with an eye to long term relationships. In the long run, compliance with SAA will reduce the importance of the types of issues cited above (after all, isn't that what SAA is all about?). In the short term, it could make all the difference in the world. Using a form like that in Figure II.15 may help in organizing your review. Factors can range from "use of CUA text model" to "some use of non-SAA language." You can array the vendor's strategy for software migration in current and future releases and in long term plans.

Time Frame	One Year	Two Years	Future
Overall Application Factor 1 . Factor n			
Application Area 1 Factor 1 . Factor n			
. .			
Application Area n Factor 1 . Factor n			
Fill in the columns with vendor plans regarding each SAA compliance factor			

Figure II.15 SAA Factor Analysis

10.6.2.2 IBM's Role

IBM is leaving it up to software vendors and purchasers to determine if and how specific software conforms to SAA. They will not audit or even certify compliance, except for their own offerings (some of which will not be fully SAA compliant for some time). This puts a significant burden on you as a software developer or user to understand the issues underlying compliance and to insist on it where it is important.

If IBM is taking a generally passive role in enforcing SAA compliance, even among those vendors publicly proclaiming it, does this mean that SAA will devolve into chaos as everyone puts their own interpretations on what the standards mean? To a certain extent, yes, particularly in the area of the user interface.

Apple doesn't certify compliance with the Macintosh interface, but users agree that almost all applications look and function in basically similar ways. There are minor annoying differences which presumably would have been eliminated if there were an audit program, but it is questionable if the benefit would have been worth the cost. In general, the marketplace served to police the consistency of the interface with most vendors falling into line or out of business. [Even now, there is a group of vendors attempting to establish standards for the Mac interface to eliminate, or at least limit, some of those differences.]

IBM is not totally passive, however, on these matters. For example, it does have, in effect, "CUA police." Members of the CUA design team helped ensure that the first vendor SAA applications had consistent user interfaces. They reviewed designs, studied screen prints (even videotaping the user interactions), and highlighted non-conforming features. While IBM could afford to do this with a dozen ISVs (who were willing to allow it, given the benefits associated with being first), there is no reasonable way to carry this kind of audit or certification to the thousands of potential vendors who might want IBM's *imprimatur*. But it does make sense for IBM to provide assistance and consulting (although not necessarily for free) to those vendors and users who want it and need it. Maybe the CUA police will be reconstituted as the CUA consulting force.

IBM has also had a few words to say to ISVs about their advertising. Almost everybody and his brother was claiming "SAA compliance" from the day SAA was announced, even though very few knew what that meant. There are far fewer general pronouncements now that SAA compliance can be measured, and now that at least some software is available to set the standard. Although IBM won't admit it, it is clear that "suggestions" have been made to vendors to be more specific in their advertising, for example stating that software "follows SAA/CUA" rather than the blanket "complies with SAA."

☛ *Issue: What does "Registered in IBM's SAA Catalog" mean?*

IBM is publishing a catalog of current and announced products that comply with SAA. The first edition of this catalog includes applications that support SAA as to:

- application structure
- environment
- common user access

as shown in Figures II.13 and II.14. Listing in future versions of the catalog will require adherence to CPI and CCS components of SAA as well.

Listing in the SAA Catalog permits the vendor to specify "Registered in IBM's SAA Catalog" in advertising and on the products themselves. However, only the vendor makes the judgment as to whether a product follows SAA guidelines in a particular area. IBM reviews requests for catalog listing but not the actual software, and presumably will catch only blatant misrepresentations.

11. Designing for Common User Access

11.1 Issue Locator

11.2 What CUA Means

Providing a consistent user interface is a key component of architectural strategy. By following the SAA Common User Access specifications, you are accepting IBM's definition of this interface and saving yourself the effort of creating your own standard. The CUA standard, however, does not answer every possible question about application "look and feel." It allows significant variation in the application area of a window to accommodate the widest possible number of application types.

The key to successful application of this standard is understanding the principles underlying CUA and how to apply them in designing systems. From that base, you can create additional standards to ensure that your applications provide the level of consistent user access that you need.

11.2.1 Providing Consistency

When a user wants to perform some function, for example, printing a document or searching a database, that function should be accomplished in the same way regardless of the application the user is working with or the hardware he or she is working on. "Providing a consistent user interface" means that common functions are always there, are always presented in the same way, and can always be used in the same way. Software today more frequently shows examples of *inconsistent* user interfaces rather than consistent ones.

A common example of inconsistency is in application menu design. There are certain commands that show up in a wide variety of applications, almost always with minor (and sometimes major) differences in implementation. One of these is the "print" command. If I want to print something (a document, a form, the screen I am looking at), the command to do that:

- should always be called "print" (not "display," "show," "output," or anything else);

- should always be on the same command menu (not hidden in different menu levels in different applications) and be selectable with the same letter or key;

- should always require me to enter the same information (e.g. what pages I want printed, how many copies I want); and

- should actually do what I expect (i.e., print the document on a previously selected printer in the previously selected fonts and style).

Keyboard usage and reference are other areas where consistency can be improved. It goes without saying that having the same keys mean the same thing in all applications would greatly reduce user frustration at all levels. DEC once tried to implement this concept in hardware by having a separate key labeled "HELP" on their personal computer keyboards. They also had a "GO" and a "PAUSE." Unfortunately, their machines never caught on and this concept seemed to have been lost. I guess we just have to content ourselves with "F1" (which at least 50% of all PC applications use as the "help" key), "enter" (newer keyboards actually use this word, rather than just having a symbol that is supposed to indicate a carriage return), and "Ctrl-Break" (isn't it strange that just pressing the "Break" key doesn't do *anything* in most applications?). Even if their meaning is not intuitively obvious, if developers use keys consistently, most users will catch on.

Direct reference to keyboard labels is another way to establish consistency. Every key has a label, although admittedly some are quite cryptic (at least to the uninitiated), e.g. "Ctrl" or "Esc." The user dialog appearing on the screen and in the user manual should use the label appearing on the appropriate key whenever it references that key (although, in the manual it is possible to have much more supporting text to explain deviations). If you want the user to hold down the key marked "Ctrl" and then press the key marked "F1," why not say exactly that? Sure, you as designer will have to know what the label is on any keyboard the user might have, but that information can be determined once, as part of the application installation or setup process, so that the user doesn't have to do a mental translation every time he or she wants to do something.

Another aspect of consistency concerns the basic ways in which actions are performed. In the CUA graphical model, the "object-action" sequence is specified for most user interfaces. An "object-action" sequence is one in which the user first selects some data item, group, etc. and then indicates the action to be performed. While an action-object selection method might work as well (and in some cases better), CUA has selected object-action for its standard and the user will come to rely on applications acting in that way. [There are certain cases where CUA explicitly allows a deviation from standard, e.g. in creating a "tool box" for a drawing application. This and other special cases are discussed below.]

There are certain cases where consistency can be carried too far, particularly in trying to implement the same user interface across all manner of workstations. Beginning with the description of CUA in 1987, 3270 (non-programmable terminal) users wondered how they were going to implement the fancy pull-downs and pop-ups that were supposed to be commonly used. By 1989 they realized that this wasn't really practical:

> *To balance the value of consistency between NPT and PWS with the advanced capabilities of the PWS, CUA defines two user interface models, Entry and Graphical. Where practical, similar base components are used across the models to enhance user transfer of learning.*
>
> *IBM Programming Announcement 289-219*

The differences and similarities that can be achieved in these two situations are discussed further below.

11.2.2 Allowing User Control

Allowing an application to be "user-driven" rather than "system-driven" is another aspect of the CUA standard. Many computer applications lead the user through allowable sequences of functions via a series of hierarchical menus (see Figure II.16). While this gives users some flexibility of action, it also inhibits other sequences that an individual might find more appropriate to his or her personal style. Even the best designers will not be able to anticipate every useful sequence of function for every potential user of the system.

When people first learn an application which automates previously manual tasks, they should be able to interact with the computer using sequences of steps that closely follow what they are used to doing. As they become more familiar with the computer's capabilities, they can begin to vary these steps and perform their tasks more efficiently. In fact, they will be adapting the tasks they perform to the new medium they have for performing them. This kind of progression demands a high degree of flexibility in the design of the system so that users can perform whatever functions they want in whatever order they want.

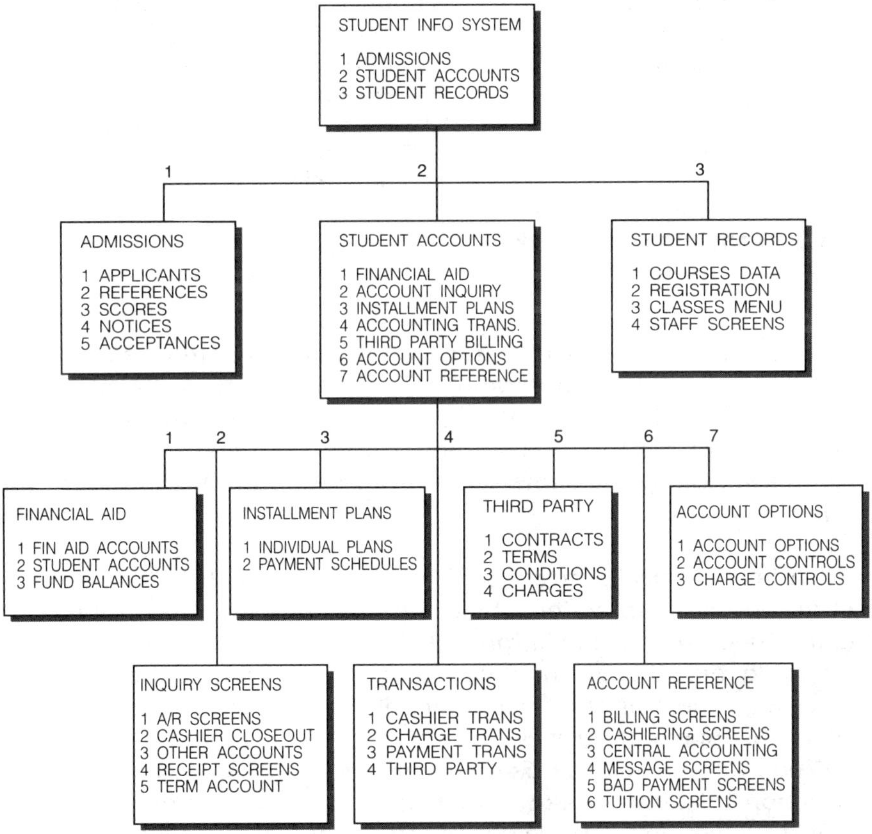

BASED ON INFORMATION PROVIDED BY AMERICAN MANAGEMENT SYSTEMS, INC.

Figure II.16 Hierarchical Menus

Another aspect of user control is the ability to "undo" something:

As you press the "delete" key, you realize that you are about to lose two hours' work and there is nothing you can do about it.

CUA deals with this kind of problem by specifying that actions that are logically reversible should be able to be "undone." In general, the user interface should be forgiving of user missteps. This will not only make users feel more comfortable in the environment, but will encourage their exploration of its features.

When computer users *know* that they are in control and that moving the mouse or pressing a key has a predictable result, then they will quickly learn common actions and be able to transfer their knowledge within and across applications. By allowing the user to control the flow of interaction, rather than having the computer control the flow, developers introduce a new level of usability to their products.

11.2.3 Providing Feedback

Dialog sequences, whether initiated by moving a mouse or pressing a key, will be easier to understand if the user is given visual clues and immediate feedback as to what is going on. To a veteran computer user, it is very frustrating to select an action and then see a blank screen, or worse, to see exactly the same screen that was there before you made the selection.

CUA is very specific in prescribing what users should see when they select an object or an action. Selected objects should be emphasized by changing their color or background (CUA specifies when to do each). The user should also be given a visual indication whenever an action is selected, e.g. selecting the "delete" action for an object should cause that object to disappear from view. If the action is "hidden," a "dialog box" should pop up and tell the user that it has been completed successfully. If the action is likely to take a long time, a progress indicator should be displayed. Ergonomic studies have repeatedly shown that users perform much better and have a higher tolerance for system delay when they are given immediate feedback. The message is obvious: treat your users as you would be treated -- tell them what is going on at every step of the way.

Even Apple found ways to improve on the visual feedback in the Macintosh interface. When a user selected an action, the cursor representing the mouse position on the screen changed from an arrow to an hour glass. Although this was helpful in knowing that the action had indeed been initiated, it gave no indication of continued progress.

Later versions of the Macintosh operating system could display a watch with a moving hand. This showed continuing progress but still didn't give an indication of how much work remained to be done. Still later versions display dialog boxes (pop up windows) with messages such as "x files copied out of y total" where x is updated each time a file is copied.

The best visual feedback of progress on long running applications, in my view, is that provided by Lotus in many of their products, and also specified in CUA 1989 (CUA 2). Figure II.17 shows a horizontal bar graph with percentage completion indicated by the amount filled in. This is updated every few seconds until the task is complete. Very few people ever complain about not knowing what is going on with this type of display. (By the way, a CUA dialog box with this type of display should also have a CANCEL button.)

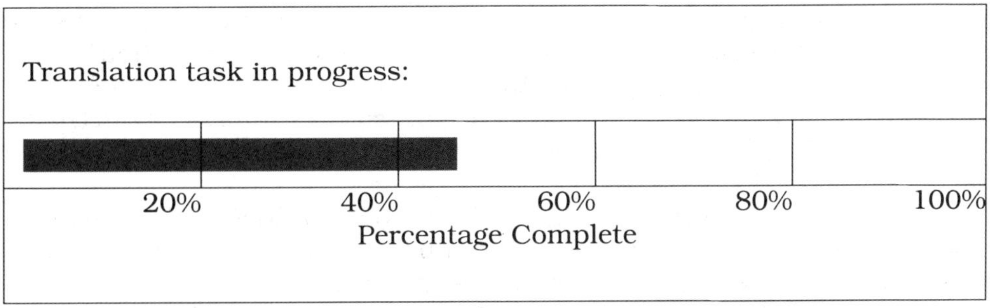

Figure II.17 Visual Progress Display

11.2.4 Hiding Complexity

Providing an "undo" capability makes the user interface more forgiving. It also significantly complicates application programming. One of the reasons that so few applications have a good "undo" is because it is so difficult to program. From a user's point of view, it is an obviously useful function. The complexity of the program is, in most senses, irrelevant to the user and should be entirely hidden from view.

Rather than giving users a complex interface which may be easy to develop, give them a simple interface although it may be harder to develop. Users will be more likely to use all the features of your application if its complexity is hidden behind a simple interface. Manufacturers of television sets have figured this out; manufacturers of VCRs haven't.

11.2.5 Object-Action Orientation

The CUA Advanced Interface Design Guide specifies an "object-action" dialog sequence for most applications. At one level, this is obvious: the user selects an "object" and then selects some "action" to be performed on it. The CUA Basic Interface Design Guide indicates that this may not be appropriate in many NPT-based user interfaces. Perhaps this issue of object-action needs some further exploration.

[This use of the term "object" is related, but not identical, to the use of the term in the phrase "object-oriented programming." In that context, a programming object is a program that provides access to and certain operations on a defined set of data. We will use the term "programming object" to avoid confusion where necessary. This section is discussing "user objects," objects that are selected by a user via the user interface. User objects are the visual presentation of certain programming objects.]

To create an object-action interface, you first have to define an appropriate set of objects and actions. Figure II.18 shows typical user objects for three different types of applications.

Airline Reservation System	**Word Processing Application**	**Accounting Application**
Seat	Character	Data field
Flight	Word	All index fields
Airplane	Sentence	Group of data fields
Passenger	Paragraph	Entire transaction
Checked luggage item	Column	All transactions in an "accounting event"
Reservation	Document	
Ticket	User selectable area	Selected group of transactions

Figure II.18 Typical User Objects

In an airline reservation system, the real world objects immediately stand out: seats, airplanes, passengers, luggage, etc. Different users select different objects and then perform actions on them. A reservation agent selects a flight and checks space availability, or selects a person and verifies his or her itinerary. A check-in agent selects a seat (on a particular flight) and reserves it.

In a word processing application, user objects include individual characters, words, sentences, paragraphs, documents, or even groups of related documents. User objects could also be defined dynamically, by the user selecting a group of words, characters, or columns. Users should be able to select any type of object and expect to have actions on them operate in a consistent manner.

In an accounting application, the definition of the user objects might not be so obvious. One definition would treat each field on an accounting transaction as an object. However, there might be groups of fields that must always be acted upon together, and these could also be defined as an object. For example, the accounting "key," the set of fields that uniquely specifies an accounting event, could be defined as an object. The entire transaction could also be defined as an object for some types of actions.

Once an object is selected, the user would then indicate what action he or she wants performed. Actions might include moving, re-sizing, or deleting the object, or using the contents of the object to look something up in a table. In the word processing application, the selected object might be used to create an index key. In the accounting application, the selected accounting object might be used as a key to look up a table of current account balances.

The table in Figure II.19 shows a possible list of objects and actions for a word processing application. Only some actions will be permissible for each type of object. It would not make sense to use an entire sentence as an object to access a word thesaurus, although using a word or perhaps part of a word would. [Using a portion of a word might bring up a list of words beginning with those letters so that a further selection could be made.] Similarly, selecting part of the accounting key as the object might be acceptable to look up account balances (you would be presented with a list of multiple entries), but might not be allowed for an action which OK'd an expenditure (which would require a fully specified account code).

Actions **Objects**	**Allowed**	**Not Allowed**
Character	D,M	P,S,T
Character group	D,M,S,T	P
Word	D,M,S,T	P
Word group	D,M	P,S,T
Sentence or group	D,M,P,S	T
Paragraph or group	D,M,P,S	T
Column	D,M,S	P,T
Document	D,M,P,S	T

D = Delete; M = Move; P = Print; S = Spell check
T = Thesaurus lookup

Figure II.19 Word Processing Objects and Actions

Looking at the list in Figure II.19, you can also see that actions do not have to have exactly the same meaning when applied to different objects. When applied to a group of characters, the "move" action would take that object and relocate it within a document. However, when applied to a group of documents, "move" would take the documents and move them elsewhere in the file system directory hierarchy. The concept is still one of "moving," but it has been applied in a different context.

The general concept of user interface design is that users are less likely to lose track of where they are and what they are doing if they first select an object and *then* an action. There are exceptions to this rule, of course, some of which are discussed in the next section.

11.2.6 Avoiding Modes

We don't need no stinkin' [mode switches].
"Blazing Saddles," the movie [with apologies]

Many application programs in use today provide so many functions that they require the user to select a "mode" of operation. For example, in many data entry applications (even some older word processing applications), you are either in "entry" mode or "edit" mode (in the former you enter new text, in the latter you modify something that is already there). Once in that mode, you can perform allowable functions and must then cancel the mode or select another to perform other functions. Some people find this approach helpful in simplifying complex applications. Others find it confusing, usually because it is difficult to remember what mode you are in.

CUA's general advice is to avoid creating modes in the user interface. "Modes force users to focus on the way an application works, instead of on the task they want to complete" (*CUA Advanced Interface Design Guide*). There are certain situations where modes simplify the interface, however, and these are specifically prescribed.

An obvious situation where modes are useful is when a user wants to perform the same action repeatedly. For example, in creating a program structure chart in a computer-aided software engineering (CASE) application, you may want to define the control data elements for each of several program modules. You should be able to select the "define control data" function and then apply it to each module on the diagram by moving the cursor and pushing the mouse button. When you are finished defining control data, you can cancel this mode or select another one. There are many other applications where this kind of functional, or "tool driven," mode is applicable.

[One system designer I know distinguished between a single-object selection mode and a group selection mode by displaying the cursor as chopsticks for one and as a butterfly net for the other. He got an "A" for creativity and may even have established a new standard for intuitive user interface design.]

Another kind of mode is the "spring-loaded" mode. This is easy to identify because the user is directly causing the mode change. Pressing and holding a mouse button to drag an object on the screen puts you in the spring-loaded "drag" mode. Releasing the button releases the mode. Holding down the shift key while moving the mouse is another example of a spring loaded mode which is frequently used in workstation applications (usually to allow you to select multiple objects on the screen).

Simplicity is the key issue in deciding to use modes in the user interface. If modes simplify the interface for the user, use them. In any case, providing visual feedback, such as changing the shape of the cursor, is a must so that users always know what mode they are in.

11.3 Picking the Right CUA Model

☛ *Issue: How do we decide among the various CUA models?*

CUA 1989, with its four user interface models, makes a clear distinction between applications using PWSs (advanced personal computers as workstations) and NPTs (3270s). The CUA documentation makes this split obvious. The *CUA Advanced Interface Design Guide* is targeted to applications using workstations capable of running OS/2 Extended Edition. The *CUA Basic Interface Design Guide* is targeted to 3270 applications developers. The CUA Graphical and Workplace Models are for PWSs. The CUA Text and Entry Models are for 3270s. Although clearly a secondary approach, CUA Text Model implementations are also allowed on PWSs.

In the world of programmable workstations, there really is no choice about which CUA model to use: the Workplace and Graphical Models complement each other. The Workplace Model is an extension of the Graphical Model which allows applications running in different windows to interact with each other using "direct manipulation." The Workplace Model defines the total user environment; the Graphical Model is the basis used in each application.

Dealing with 3270 applications is more difficult. The issue usually is how to move in the *direction* of common user access without wholesale rewriting of all existing applications. This is where understanding the concepts behind CUA is important. The CUA Text Model provides some of the advanced user interface of the Graphics Model, as much as can be accommodated on a character-oriented workstation (although this model can also be used on a graphical workstation). The Entry Model is designed to accommodate the typical data entry application -- no action bars and pull-downs, just enter the data. In the NPT world, user and computer performance issues will dictate which model to use.

The Text Model is a subset of the Graphical Model. This implies that Text Model applications should be upgradable to use the Graphical Model (only on PWSs, of course). This may sound easy in theory, but it is quite difficult in practice (as will become evident as you read the discussion on Implementation Alternatives).

Multiple user interface models, such as exist in CUA 1989, dilute the concept of "common" user access. IBM is trying to regain the concept of a single user interface by strongly encouraging the use of PS/2s as user workstations, regardless of where the main part of the application is running. In this way, all users can have a common user interface or "single system view" into their applications.

Until the widespread acceptance of advanced function PCs as replacements for 3270s or other non-programmable terminals, there will continue to be a role for multiple user interface models. CUA 1989 describes the SAA approach to this situation.

11.3.1 Performance Implications of the Text Model on NPTs

The CUA Text Model requires you to emulate many of the components of the Graphical Model on a character mode terminal. Since most IBM mainframe shops are using 3270 terminals or equivalents, it is important to understand the performance implications of this approach.

All data entry, correction, and cursor movement is handled solely between the 3270 and its controller until the Enter key or a function key is pressed. Pressing enter indicates that some or all of the contents of the screen should be sent to the mainframe for further processing. Pressing a function key indicates that the mainframe should perform some action (such as sending the next or previous screen). [Communications can be limited to only the unprotected fields or even to only those fields that have changed.] A mainframe program is invoked to determine what to do next. This mainframe interrupt is very costly (in relative terms) and is the source of a perceptible delay in response.

Using the Text Model in a host/3270 environment, mainframe intervention will be required for many actions that would be processed locally by a PWS. Actions such as:

- changing the highlighting of an action bar;
- scrolling a scrollable window area;
- "popping up" a pop-up window;
- "pulling down" a pull-down menu; and
- getting help

will all require execution of mainframe programs. The basic object-action selection sequence will take three mainframe interactions, one to select the object, and at least two to select the action (one to pull-down the menu, one to select). Each one of these interactions is a source of processing costs and delay. While this delay may not always be apparent (especially in carefully constructed vendor demonstrations), users will often be treated to wildly varying response times from the workstations on their desks.

The Text Model provides many of the common features of the full Graphical Model. These features are designed to improve ease of use and training and are desirable to have. However, providing these features must be weighed against the cost, particularly in terms of response time, in providing the best interface for your 3270 users. For many applications, the Entry Model, which does not include action bars and the requirement for an object-action orientation, will be more appropriate.

11.3.2 Designing Applications to Use Multiple Windows

Designing applications for use with CUA, particularly on a PWS, is not just a matter of rethinking what goes where on a screen. The ability to display multiple windows, to have a virtual screen area many times larger than the physical screen, to copy and move information easily among windows, and to do multi-processing means that the application functions and how they are organized has to be rethought as well.

Many of today's applications are constrained by the fixed and limited size of an NPT screen. Application designers have taken many approaches to dealing with this problem, from splitting single "transactions" over multiple screens, to jamming twice as much information on a screen as is easily readable. On the input or data entry side, it is not unusual to have to page through three or more screens, sometimes with no way of backing up to handle what is perceived by the user to be a single transaction. On the output side, inquiry results are often shown in abbreviated form, on multiple screens, or in summary and detail screens. This lack of presentation space has also led to the use of a variety of inventive abbreviations on field and column labels. Not only does this contribute to the generally "unfriendly" nature of many of today's NPT applications, but also to general user confusion.

Scrollable windows used in the CUA Graphical Model provide an essentially unlimited "logical" area for displaying user information, although not necessarily all related information will be on the screen at once (there is still a physical size limitation). This type of user interface presents opportunities to the designer and, of course, another set of constraints. What used to take three or four 3270 screens, each requiring mainframe interaction, can now be put in a single scrollable window. Users can easily navigate up and down using the scroll bars. On the other hand, the visual overhead of the windowed approach (space for scroll bars, action bars, etc.) may force undesirable changes in user interaction or in the application itself. What could have been done on a single 3270 screen 24 rows by 72 columns wide may not be viewable in a single window on a similarly sized PWS screen.

Users of windowed systems still see the limitation of physical screen size. Even with overlapping windows, there is only so much information that you can display on a 12-inch or 13-inch screen (pity the poor Macintosh user, most of whom have barely more than 9 inches, and in black and white at that). The designer of a windowed application has to be cognizant of the context in which the application will be used. The designer needs to know how many windows the user will typically be viewing at once -- both from this application and from other applications used with it. It does not do any good to add integration with spreadsheets, electronic mail, and word processing if the user has difficulty seeing related data from multiple windows simultaneously.

[UNIX systems, many of which have had windowed interfaces for several years, often come with 16-inch or 19-inch high resolution displays (often costing as much as a good size PC). As your users experience the windowed application approach, they will begin to demand larger, higher resolution displays on their PS/2s.]

11.4 Implementation Alternatives

11.4.1 Presentation Manager, Dialog Manager, and Easel

An issue that will be raised immediately among your programming staff is whether to use the Presentation Manager, Dialog Manager, or Easel for creating PWS CUA applications. The issue is whether to use "native" PM, or to use one of these higher level tools to mask PM's complexities (both DM and Easel use PM calls internally for performing their work). Each provides a way of implementing CUA; each has its pluses and minuses.

☛ *Issue: When do I need to use Presentation Manager, Dialog Manager, Easel?*

Presentation Manager provides a full set of application program interfaces (APIs) for creating windowed user interfaces under OS/2. It supports (but does not enforce) use of the CUA Graphical Model. Programmers will have to learn the PM routines and create programs using an "event-driven" paradigm. [Many programmers use object-oriented techniques in creating PM applications, but this is not a requirement.] While the PM APIs are available for COBOL and FORTRAN, the language of choice for PM applications is C. Based on industry experience with the Macintosh and with Windows, even journeymen programmers will require a training period measured in months (prior experience with the Mac or with Windows would shorten this significantly). Using PM allows the most flexibility in creating applications, but also requires the greatest understanding of OS/2, CUA, and the event-driven programming style.

Dialog Manager supports the creation of CUA Text Model (subset of the Graphical Model) applications. It provides APIs for controlling window usage and a language (Dialog Tag Language) for defining window contents. Through its limited number of APIs, DM enforces a specific set of CUA standards. DM only provides for primary windows and dialog or message pop-ups. Only textual data and literals can be placed in a window. [PM can be invoked directly from within a DM application to add some graphics.] DM application programs have a more familiar structure than will PM application programs since the event-driven nature of the user interaction is handled in the run-time DM core itself. Based on the popular ISPF system on the System/370, DM application programming will be familiar to many mainframe programmers and far easier to learn than PM to others.

Easel is a combination of a screen painter, application generator, run-time system, and language. It was originally developed (by Interactive Images Corporation) to provide better user interfaces for 3270 applications. It is now a full-fledged application development tool for creating CUA Graphical Model applications. Programmers lay out a screen using the screen drawing tool which makes most of the PM "controls" available (pushbuttons, list boxes, radio buttons, etc.). Easel then generates a program (in the Easel language) to handle the user dialog (window placement, mouse movement, button presses, control selection, etc.). This program is then modified (either directly or by calling external routines) to handle other application functions. Programmers using Easel can create CUA Graphical Model applications with far less training and with far greater ease than by using PM directly.

[Easel also provides complete facilities for creating cooperative processing applications. Neither DM nor PM provide communication APIs directly, although you can use APPC or other communications routines from the same programs. You should consider these issues as well as the ones discussed above in deciding on a programming environment. Chapter 12 discusses the implementation issues for distributed programming in more detail.]

For most applications, Easel will provide the best trade-off of features, performance, and cost for application development. If you are already using ISPF, then using DM will be an appropriate evolutionary step. For some highly interactive applications, limitations of either DM or Easel may force your programmers to go directly to PM. Before actually writing any PM (or DM) code, however, you should investigate Easel and other available implementation tools (see Chapter 15).

11.4.1.1 SAA Compliance with PM, DM, and Easel

In creating applications using these facilities, two aspects of SAA compliance need to be looked at: CUA and CPI. The discussion is of both theoretical and practical importance.

PM is the implementation of the Presentation Interface element of the CPI (it is not implemented in any other SAA environment). It also includes some capabilities not in the CPI definition. It allows, but does not enforce, creation of CUA-compliant applications. Knowledge of CUA rules, therefore, is a pre-requisite for PM programmers.

DM is the implementation of the Dialog Interface element of the CPI (portions of DI are implemented by ISPF on the System/370). For the most part, applications implemented under DM will conform to the CUA Text Model (it is possible, but difficult, to create applications which violate its rules).

The Easel screen painter enforces compliance with the CUA Graphical Model. IBM has included Easel as part of AD/Cycle. Easel programs, however, are in a proprietary language which is not defined in the SAA CPI. In spite of this, IBM has been very aggressive in pushing Easel as the "development environment of choice" for the PWS. Obviously, it is easier to program in Easel's language than in C and Presentation Manager.

The bottom line: PM and DM are OK for hard-core programmers who understand the ins and outs of CUA. While the Easel language is not part of the CPI, it is the only tool (from IBM) that enforces CUA. If IBM clarifies the position of the language, then it will become "the programming tool for the rest of us."

11.4.2 Is Windows a Viable Choice?

[Company] Exec Tells of Ordeal: "Aliens Forced Me to Use MS Windows"

Column Headline, "InfoWorld," October 16, 1989

We have been hearing about Microsoft Windows as an add-in to MS-DOS (and PC-DOS) since 1983. It finally became viable with Release 2 in 1987. Starting in 1989, sales began to take off. Software developers had ported enough of the popular applications so that users could do all of their work in a Windows environment. [Two exceptions were Microsoft's own Word, finally released as Word for Windows in 1990, and Lotus's 1-2-3, still not available in a Windows environment.] The introduction of Windows Release 3 in mid-1990, while meaning more conversion work for software developers, added features that makes it a major competitor to OS/2 and its Presentation Manager. Microsoft has even announced that they intend for Windows Release 3 applications to run unmodified under OS/2. The choice for application developers now has another dimension.

[Windows' popularity is an interesting statement on the marketing power of Microsoft. Two other graphical user interfaces (GUIs) introduced at about the same time have more or less faded into oblivion. The GEM Desktop from Digital Research, the implementer of an early microcomputer operating system, was initially a contender, but never received the support it needed from vendors of application packages. IBM's entry, Topview, saw a similar fate.]

Windows provides application developers with a set of subroutine calls for implementing CUA-like user interfaces. The developer will find a rich set of subroutines with which to implement multiple windows, pull-down menus, pop-ups, mouse movement, and the direct manipulation of screen information across applications. While absolute compliance with the CUA Graphical Model is not guaranteed, applications come close enough for users to see Windows-based applications as providing the look and feel of those implemented under OS/2's Presentation Manager. The Microsoft Application Style Guide, similar in some respects to the CUA design guides, also provides standards for implementing Windows applications.

☛ *Issue: Is DOS with Windows a viable alternative to OS/2 and Presentation Manager?*

Given the range of capabilities of Windows Release 3 and the obvious support it is garnering in the marketplace and from Microsoft itself, the answer has to be yes, but with some qualifications.

Windows can be a starting point for implementing CUA-like user interfaces in many organizations. It becomes even more viable in organizations with large numbers of PCs equipped to operate Windows and using commercial Windows applications. For all its capabilities, Windows Release 3 is still missing some of the most important features of OS/2 Extended Edition:

- a simple memory management scheme (virtual memory is available in Windows Release 3 only if you have an 80386 processor);

- full multi-tasking, the ability to have two or more processes in progress at once (Windows Release 3 allows partial multi-tasking of non-Windows applications, only if you have an 80386 processor);

- the rich communications of the OS/2 Communications Manager (needed for cooperative processing applications); and

- the relational database of OS/2 Database Manager.

Almost all of these deficiencies can be overcome to some degree. Microsoft and third-party developers are supplying add-ins and add-ons that deal with these issues. However, it will never be as easy to develop very large programs in DOS as it is in OS/2 and many of today's applications are very large (1/2 Mb and up for the programs themselves, let alone any data).

IBM and Microsoft announced their joint position on DOS/Windows versus OS/2 in November 1989 (*Programming Announcement 289-625*). That announcement established Windows as an accepted environment if the software was targeted to operate on 286-based PCs with less than 2 Mb of internal memory. For larger machines (more memory or later version microprocessor or both), both companies agreed that OS/2 is their preferred environment. [It is too early for direct experience, but it appears that a dividing line of 4 Mb may be more appropriate. You will need almost that much for a high performance Windows Release 3 environment, and quite a bit more for OS/2 EE.] As part of the same announcement, Microsoft agreed to release new versions of its application software under OS/2 before it releases Windows versions. This announcement, of course, was before the introduction of Windows Release 3.

In other words, the jury is still out. If you are planning a full scale assault on enterprise computing and SAA, OS/2 is the right place to be. Windows will only buy you part of what you are looking for. If you are simply looking for commercial application packages which have a better user interface than the typical DOS-based package, Windows will be sufficient. In many ways, Windows Release 3 provides a look into the future, and an increasingly large one. OS/2 and Presentation Manager *are* that future.

11.4.3 Implementing the CUA Workplace Model

☛ *Issue: How do I implement the CUA Workplace Model?*

The only way to implement a CUA Workplace Model application at the current time is by using OfficeVision -- no other software product provides the necessary APIs (although you could write them yourself).

OfficeVision/2 provides the additional calls that allow straightforward implementation of workplace interactions. The OfficeVision Application Programmers Interface (API) uses the Presentation Manager CPI to create a higher level programming interface.

[Details of which APIs will be available in OfficeVision were not available at the time of publication. The OfficeVision/2 APIs are to be delivered with Release 2 of this product. IBM delayed general availability of this release until the fourth quarter of 1990.]

11.4.4 Implementing CUA on the NPT

As opposed to the SAA PWS environment's single operating system (OS/2 EE), NPTs can be found in five SAA environments: CICS, IMS/TM, MVS/TSO, VM/CMS, and OS/400. The tools for creating CUA-conforming applications in any of these environments are limited.

At the current time, there are no tools specifically designed for implementing CUA applications under CICS on the System/370. [Easel can be used with CICS OS/2 but this does not help the 3270 user.] This means that the interpretation and implementation of CUA rules is up to you. Basically, you continue to use whatever techniques and tools you used before CUA, but with the added knowledge of the CUA standards and guidelines for the Text and Entry Model user interfaces.

ISPF, available both under MVS/TSO and VM/CMS, provides many of the tools you need to implement CUA applications in these environments. The Dialog Tag Language in recent releases of ISPF duplicates that available in the OS/2 Dialog Manager. IBM redefined its approach to the Dialog Interface of the CPI in a June 1990 announcement, so that ISPF will not necessarily correspond to Dialog Manager in the future. This has little, if any, short term implication and ISPF will continue to be a viable tool for some time to come.

Standard development tools delivered with the AS/400 allow the creation of CUA-conforming applications. IBM's arrangement with the most popular third-party supplier of CASE tools for the AS/400 (Synon) also signals further assistance in this environment.

Compared to the PS/2, the CUA tools environment for the other SAA environments is weak. With the increased emphasis on the PS/2 as the single user interface for all applications on the enterprise network, this situation can only be expected to continue.

11.5 Implementations in Other Environments

☛ *Issue: Are there alternatives to CUA?*

Complicating the life of the information systems manager (as if you haven't seen enough complications already), a number of other vendors and industry consortia are developing competitors to CUA and its implementing software. As competitive pressures take hold, the capabilities and even the APIs they provide will become almost indistinguishable (or perhaps we will all be designing to a higher "GUI standard independent" interface). Since each started from a different place, they reflect their origins in different strengths and weaknesses.

11.5.1 The X Window System

The X Window System is a windowing standard developed at the Massachusetts Institute of Technology. It has been adopted by a broad range of software and hardware vendors as an underlying mechanism for implementing graphical user interfaces (GUIs) across multiple hardware platforms running variations of the UNIX operating system (although it is designed to be operating system independent). It is not in itself a GUI, but rather a foundation for building GUIs. The system's strength lies in its protocols for network-independent communication for implementation of cooperative processing in a client-server architecture. Some vendors have introduced X Window terminals with this protocol implemented in hardware and ROM to provide a low-cost graphical workstation for applications running on other machines. Other vendors have introduced X Window implementations that co-exist with PC-DOS.

The X Window System, unlike CUA and Presentation Manager, provides low level routines that require system developers to define their own "style guide" for the user interface. This means that applications written to the X Window "standard" can still look and feel quite different. UNIX International's Open Look and OSF's Motif are two X Window System-based GUIs.

11.5.2 OSF/Motif

The Open Software Foundation has developed a GUI standard that is very similar to the Graphical and Workplace Models of CUA. Since OSF is developing a standard UNIX, the only vendors interested in Motif view it as a GUI for UNIX-based operating systems.

The Motif design incorporates elements of Digital Equipment Corporation's graphical API, Hewlett Packards's NewWave, and Microsoft's Presentation Manager (used in OS/2). It is implemented using the MIT-developed X Window System and its behavior is "designed to conform to Microsoft's Presentation Manager." IBM's AIXwindows GUI for AIX conforms to the OSF/Motif standard.

11.5.3 NewWave

NewWave is an object-oriented user interface developed by Hewlett-Packard to sit on top of more primitive GUIs. The first implementation ran on DOS machines using Windows Release 2. OS/2 and UNIX versions have been announced, although NewWave will not add as much to an already sophisticated GUI like OS/2 with PM.

In many ways, NewWave provides the same functionality that the OfficeVision API does and that future versions of PM are expected to. It allows the user to perform a variety of functions by manipulating icons on the screen rather than typing commands. It implements cooperative processing capabilities (similar in concept to X Window) to give the user a single system image of cooperative and remote processing applications.

There has been a lot of industry excitement about NewWave, perhaps because it was the first iconic user interface to be delivered for use on IBM personal computers. The number of software vendors delivering applications which take full advantage of its capabilities (by using the NewWave APIs) is still very limited.

12. Designing for Distributed and Cooperative Processing

12.1 Issue Locator

☛ Issue: Should we wait for the CPIC or use APPC now? Page 284

12.2 Distributed Processing

A great myth seems to have grown up about distributed processing (and in a very short time): that distributed processing refers to a single mode of computer processing, that all modern systems should use it, and that implementing it is easy. None of these statements is always true (distributed processing refers to *many* types of processing), and the last one is never true (at least not yet). It is most certainly true, however, that distributed processing (and one of its many forms, cooperative processing) is a key concept underlying SAA and is essential to establishing an effective enterprise-wide computing resource.

Distributed processing occurs when an application system (programs and database) uses multiple computers connected over a network to complete its tasks. Sometimes the programs are distributed, sometimes the data, and sometimes both. The wide variation in distributed processing applications raises numerous questions about why, what, and how to distribute. And that is what this chapter is about.

12.2.1 Drawing the Line

Before discussing the "how" of distributed processing, you must understand the "what." Several classifications of distributed systems have been proposed, most of which follow a basic form. In the *IBM Systems Journal* issue on SAA, Allan Scherr defines four "modes" of distributed processing. An expanded version of his definition is presented here.

Scherr's concept of distributed processing begins with a simplified diagram of the components of an application (Figure II.20):

- user dialog and presentation component, used in the generic sense of management of display and user interface functions;

- application function, referring to the programs doing the "work" of the application; and

- data access functions, programs that control access to the databases (the database management system and any interface routines).

To round out the application environment, the diagram also shows:

- the workstation, and

- the database.

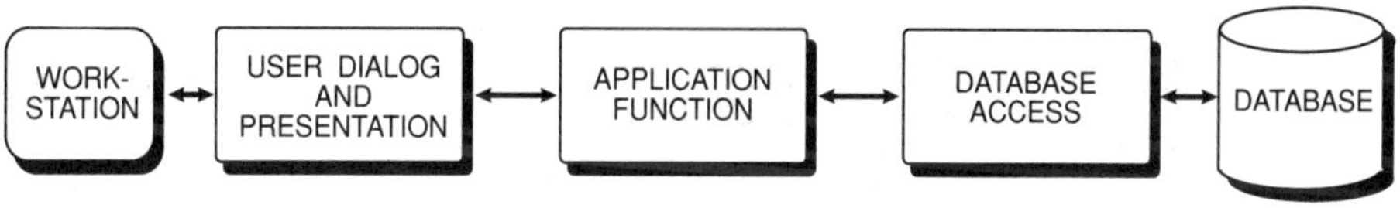

Figure II.20 Application Components

☛ *Issue: What are the different forms of distributed processing?*

Creating a distributed processing application can now be viewed as drawing a line to show which parts of the application will operate on which processors. The types or modes of distributed processing depend on where you draw the line (or lines). Since this line can be drawn anywhere, the distributed processing classification is really a continuum.

- If you don't draw any line, i.e., everything operates on a single machine, you have "local processing" (Scherr's terminology).

- If the dialog and presentation portion of the application (i.e., the user interface) is on a workstation and everything else is on other processors, you have "distributed user interface." [This and any other type of workstation-host distribution is called "cooperative processing" in the SAA literature.]

- If significant parts of the application are split between two or more computers, you are in the "distributed function" mode.

- If most of the database is separate from the application function, you have "distributed data access." Client-server architectures are distributed data access systems.

- If significant portions of the database are split between two or more computers, you have a "distributed database."

Figure II.21 shows this classification of distributed processing. Classifications can be combined so that, for example, you can have an application with both distributed function and distributed database.

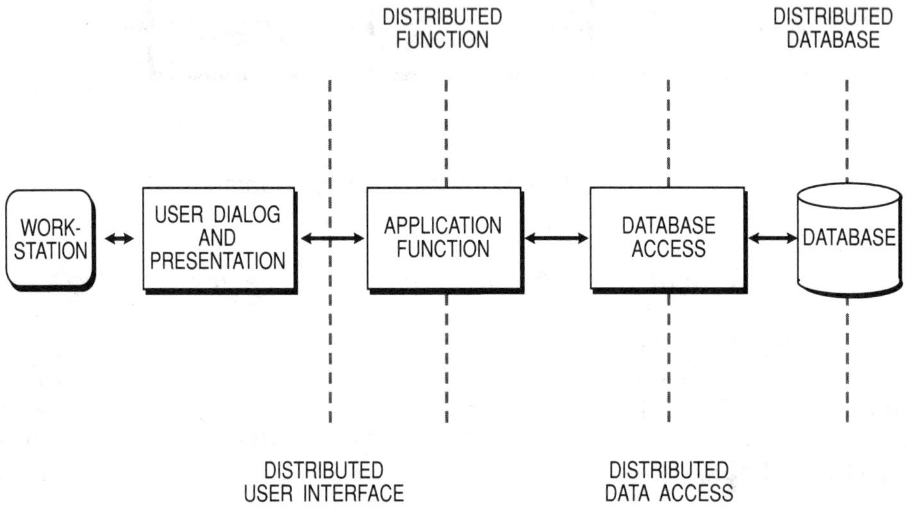

Figure II.21 Distributed Processing Modes

12.2.2 Developing a Distribution Strategy

The criteria for determining where to "draw the line" are many. Not all will apply in every situation, but you should at least review them all to make sure. Different distribution modes will result in differences in:

- processing costs
- communications costs
- system performance (response time and throughput)
- security and access control
- reliability
- flexibility
- system management

Each of these criteria may have different importance in different applications. Different types of distributed processing will impact each of these criteria differently.

A *distributed data access* system, for example, may allow you to have much better control over data security than a *distributed database system*, especially if some of the data is distributed to individual workstations. Flexibility may also be enhanced via distributed data access since the data access server is the only machine that needs to be changed if volume increases. There may also be better tools available for managing a distributed data access network than there are for managing distributed data. However, system performance may be lower and communications costs may be higher using distributed data access, because each request will require a response from the data base server machine. In a distributed data approach, many data requests may be able to be handled locally (i.e., on the same machine initiating the processing). Given the unlimited number of ways in which the distribution decision can be made, this type of analysis has to be carried out for each system you develop.

Distributed processing designs have to balance the effective use of multiple processors with the cost of communications flowing among them and the system performance (response time and throughput) that results. The greater the communications necessary among the different parts of a distributed processing application, the slower that application is going to appear to the user. It is always faster for programs to access data or other programs locally (on the same machine) than to access them on a remote processor via a communication line. If the applications are CPU-intensive, the total time to move data around the network and perform the processing remotely will only be faster if the remote processor is significantly faster than the local one. Speed and cost of processing and communications must be evaluated together in making distributed processing decisions.

Another point needs to be made about flexibility. Not enough is known about the performance characteristics of distributed processing to ensure that a design will work exactly as planned. Actual use of the system may also deviate from the assumptions made by the designers. For these reasons, flexibility is an extremely important criterion in distributed systems. Ideally, you would like to be able to determine the mode of distributed processing dynamically, or at least without having to make any programming changes. Some of the approaches to distributed processing system design allow this type of flexibility; others do not. If you take a more limited path, be sure you have thought through the consequences.

12.2.2.1 An Example

Using the classifications presented above, one could distribute the system functions across multiple modules in a variety of ways. Distributed processing strategies might include the following:

- User interface modules could reside on the workstation.

- Some on-line processing functions could be placed on the workstation, some on departmental machines, and some on a central host.

- Off-line processing functions (those not requiring user intervention) could be similarly divided.

- Regular reports could come from the host while special analyses could be run on the workstation.

These are just some of many possible ways of dividing an application. While it might be less efficient, you could, for another example, further distribute the user interface by putting data entry on the workstation while moving help and tutorial processing to a downstream processor. This might make sense if help and tutorial information were used infrequently but required a large database.

Examples can be created in a variety of other ways, all valid under some set of assumptions about the use of the data and the application.

12.2.3 Rules of Thumb for Cooperative Processing

In his article in the *IBM Systems Journal* special issue on SAA, Scherr notes:

> *In a well-designed distributed system, the local data processing mode is usually prevalent, because it offers the best performance and lowest cost.*

Scherr is saying that even in a distributed application, most of the processing and data should be on a single machine! In other words, in distributed processing, "less is more," i.e., less distribution often gives greater performance. This guidance is sometimes forgotten amid all the hoopla of cooperative and distributed processing possibilities.

☛ *Issue: What are the criteria for deciding among the types of distributed processing?*

In the absence of a generally accepted formula for deciding when the trade-off is in favor of local processing and when it is in favor of distributed processing, designers have to make these decisions based on analysis and experience. Although there are some rules of thumb that can be applied to this analysis, they are at best a general guide:

- If a small amount of data can be extracted and downloaded to another processor where it will then be accessed "locally" (i.e., on the same machine that is performing the processing function), do this rather than distributing the data access.

- If most of the data used is private, don't distribute it.

- When a high rate of user interaction is called for, try to put all of the underlying programs on the same processor, usually a programmable workstation.

- When a specialized processor is available, use it only for the specialized parts of the application. Vector processors, database machines, and graphics processors are examples.

These rules can be combined in a variety of ways, for example:

- If a small amount of data is needed in a CPU-intensive application (some scientific and engineering and a few business applications fit this scenario), download the data to a specialized processor.

- If a large amount of data is necessary for a CPU-intensive task (e.g. airline crew scheduling), keep the database on the same machine as the fastest CPU and distribute other parts of the application, for example the user interface.

Almost any possible combination of these rules will be useful in some situation.

12.2.4 Two-Tier vs. Three-Tier Architecture

Not only can you create distributed processing applications that have more than one distribution mode (distributed user interface and distributed database, for example), but you can also create multi-layered distributions. Why restrict yourself to having only two processors cooperating to process an application or limit yourself to only two places in which to store data, locally on whatever machine you are using, and on the host? Applications that have some of their data on a workstation, some on an intermediate level database server, and some on the host are practically implementable as well as theoretically possible. [Two meanings for "practically" may be applicable in this statement.] The software to implement multi-tier distributed processing or multi-tier distributed databases is available, but there are a variety of factors that may lead you to a more limited distributed architecture. At some point, the ability of the designer, developer, or maintainer to keep control of both application and data is impeded by the complexity of a distributed application.

Even with system software "assists," multi-tier distributed systems add a level of complexity to distributed processing that has to be carefully analyzed and justified.

12.2.5 Performance of Distributed Applications

The introduction of the network into the performance equation for an application complicates the already difficult process of predicting performance (response time as seen by the user or throughput of an off-line transaction). There are so many variables in determining the performance characteristics of distributed applications that even simulation results must be questioned. Benchmarks are even more troubling, unless they are based on applications very similar to the ones you are implementing. They purport to tell the truth (after all, they are based on actual operation of distributed systems), but often end up obscuring it. Several vendors have recently engaged in a "benchmark war" for their distributed database systems that is sure to leave potential users even more confused than before -- they even came up with different results for the so-called baseline.

The absence of analytical solutions to this problem may be discouraging, but it is not crippling. Common sense approaches often yield very reasonable results. It is only at the stress points that performance considerations will be important, and that is where any simulations, benchmarks, or other techniques should be concentrated.

In a typical inquiry system, it is almost always possible to predict that time of day when the load will peak and to estimate the number of database requests that will mean. Aided by vendor and independent benchmark data (carefully sifted for biases, of course), you can usually determine the *feasibility* of a particular distribution approach. In making a gross selection between a beginning-of-day download to each user's workstation and a request to the server for every inquiry, you can probably rely on vendor benchmarks -- particularly if your request rate is expected to be hundreds per second and the benchmark shows a maximum of 10.

For many types of information systems, rough estimates of system performance are sufficient. The basic strategy is to see if you are well within the ballpark or are beginning to push the limits of the system. Using estimates of volume and expected growth, you can prepare a chart showing upper and lower bounds and most likely transaction loads. Adding some actual performance data and some extrapolations from non-distributed systems (typical database access and processing times), you will be able to explore several solutions to your distributed system approach. In more time-critical applications (such as airline reservation systems where slower response results in lost business, or military systems where slower response may be deadly), these techniques will barely scratch the surface of the work you have to do. Even then, having a rough idea of how different approaches stack up can be a "reality check" on the results of more detailed analysis.

12.2.6 Distributed Processing and Network Traffic Patterns

Two aspects of distributed processing applications will have different effects on the network. The first is program-to-program communication and the second is remote data access (which may also be accomplished via program-to-program communication, but that is not the important point here).

Distributed processing applications come in many forms, but in general, direct program-to-program communication will increase. This traffic may not require lengthy transmissions (maybe only a few thousand bytes), but it will have to be accomplished quickly in order to maintain good response time to the application user. The need for high-speed, short transmission network capability will become more obvious as cooperative processing, in almost any of its forms, enters the picture.

The impact of distributed processing on database access is not as clear. When multiple users share a single database, there are several possible methods of moving data around the network. In the simplest case, a user may copy a file from a network file server to a local disk. This puts a high load on the network. Much of the data transfer is probably wasted since it is often the case that only a few records in the file need to be interrogated or updated. In a more sophisticated situation, the program may only read or write the needed records, thus putting a much smaller total load on the network as well as spreading it out over a longer period of time. Sophisticated cooperative processing is becoming easier to implement so more programs will implement record-at-a-time access instead of whole-file access. However, more and more files will be shared so that overall traffic may still increase. Furthermore, file transfers have typically been performed when an application started up in the morning and/or when it was shut down at night. Individual record accesses during the day were then accomplished totally locally, and thus at very high-speed as seen by the user. The network will now have to provide a similar level of responsiveness throughout the day, something that may require a revised view of network capacity.

The general expectation is that network traffic will increase as SAA applications come on-line (independent of and in addition to the increase due to an increase in the number of users and applications). Requirements will expand to higher speeds to handle short bursts of traffic.

12.3 Transparency and Single-system Image

One of the more interesting puzzles of distributed computing is that we spend a tremendous amount of energy figuring out how to design and implement distributed processing, and then we have to figure out how to make the user [and the programmer] believe the processing isn't distributed at all.

Anonymous MIS Director at a conference on distributed processing

☛ *Issue: Can distributed processing be hidden from the user and the programmer?*

A key concept in common user access and cooperative processing under SAA is that of "transparency." The fact that part of an application or its data may not be located on the same machine that the user is looking at, or that they may be on different machines at different times, should be transparent to the user. In addition, the programmer should be able to write programs without regard to the eventual distribution of function or data. SAA deals with both *user* and *programmer* transparency.

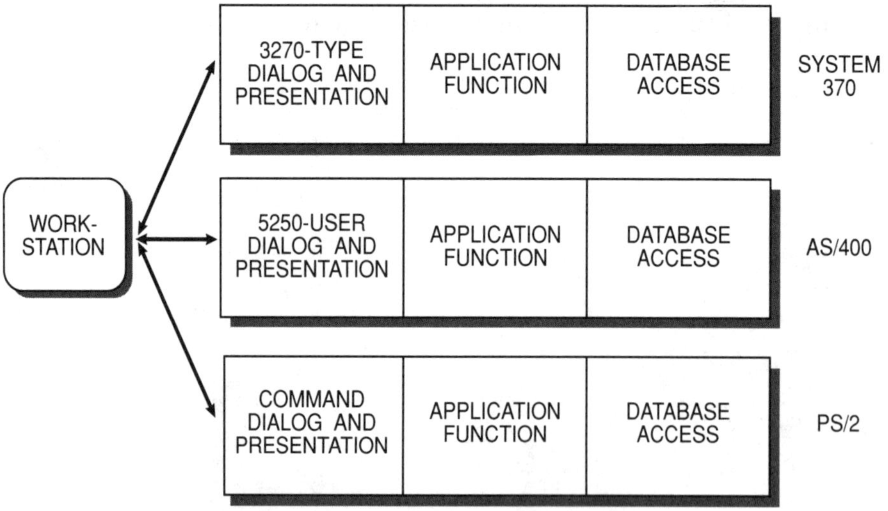

Figure II.22 Multiple System Image

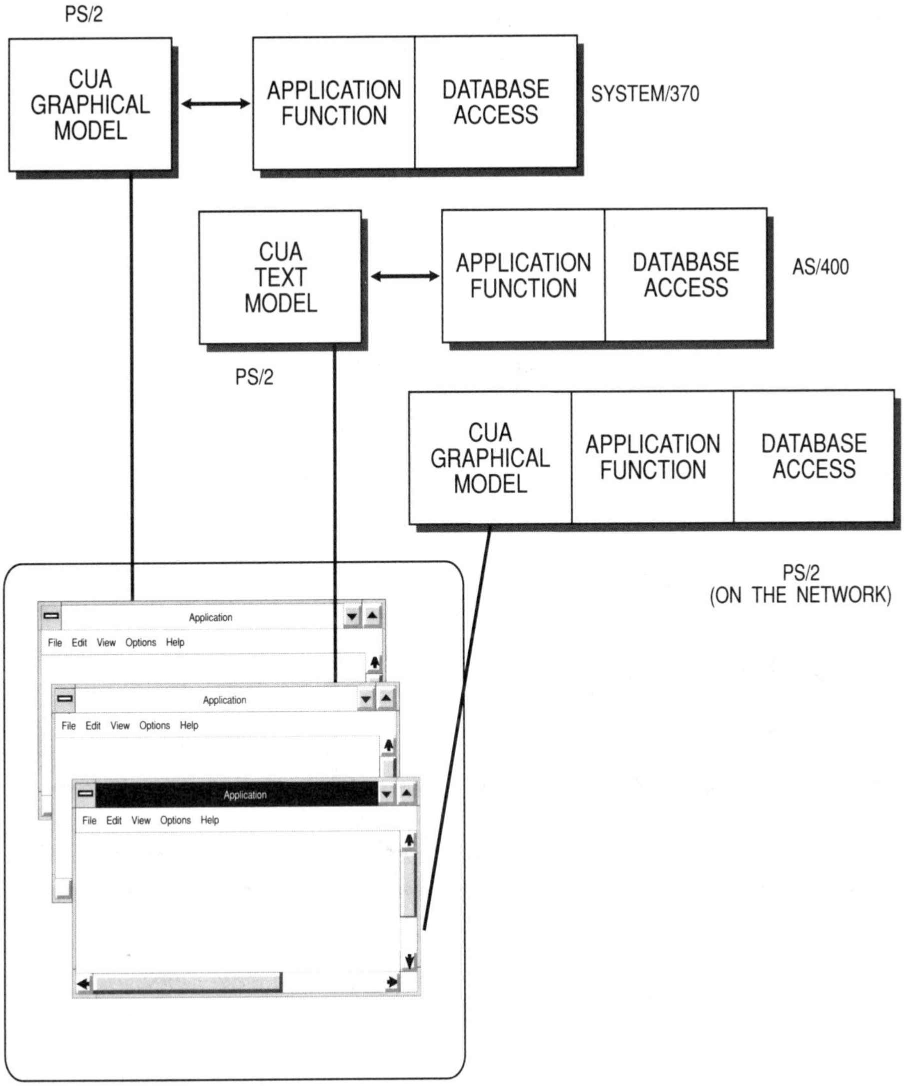

Figure II.23 Single-system Image to the User

In Figure II.22, the user is accessing three applications: the workstation emulated a 3270 to access a remote System/370; the workstation emulates a 5250 to access a remote AS/400; and the workstation runs a third application directly. With the proper implementing software at the workstation, the user would not have to learn different interface rules for the different systems and need not even know the physical location of those systems. Figure II.23 illustrates the use of CUA Graphical Model software on the PS/2 as a front end to those same systems. The reality of SAA is that while its definitions imply a single-system image, implementing this strategy using software available in the early 1990s requires a considerable degree of non-transparency to the programmer.

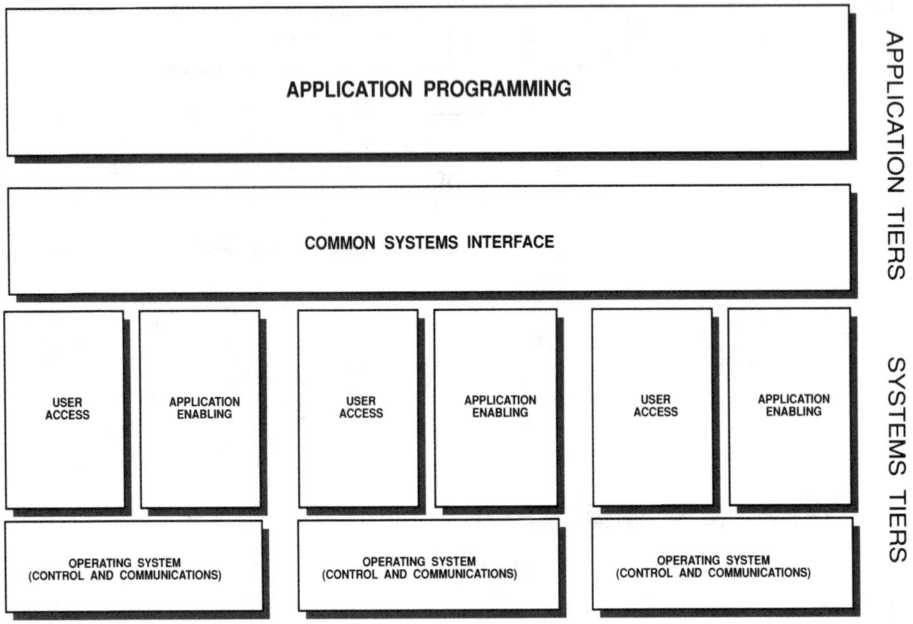

Figure II.24 Single-system Image to the Developer

Transparency to the programmer means that programs can be designed without regard to where they will operate and that co-routines and subroutines can be accessed without regard to where they reside (as long as they are accessible via the network). On the data side, it means having access to parts of the database located on different machines without the knowledge of the programmer. Only the System Administrator has to know where the data is in order to set up the required control tables. Some system software also comes close to providing this degree of transparency (CICS OS/2 for example), although almost always with some restrictions on environments supported (excludes AS/400 systems since they do not have CICS).

What the programmers need is a "common systems interface," exactly what the CPI is designed to provide. Figure II.24 portrays programs using the common system interface with different implementing products underneath. For example, IBM is addressing cross-system transparency in its relational data products. There are four different products (one for each SAA environment), all implementing the database element of the CPI. It will be several years, however, before all data can be read or written without specific regard to the system it resides on.

The main issue regarding transparency in SAA is waiting for the products that implement it.

12.3.1 A Conceptual Model of System Transparency

All of these SAA features help create an environment for distributed processing which is transparent to user and programmer. But is it enough? In their article "A Transparent Environment" in *Byte Magazine*, Walker and Popek define the following aspects of transparency:

- *Access transparency*: using the same system calls regardless of the resource's location. Two subsets are *device transparency* applying to data file access routines, and *process transparency* applying to process calls.

- *Location transparency*: the CPU on which a particular process resides is not embedded in the process name and can be changed without changing the call name.

- *Name transparency*: means that the same name used on different CPUs will access the same resource.

- *Performance transparency*: the overhead involved in referencing remote resources should be similar to that of accessing local resources.

The software implementing distributed and cooperative processing in SAA will eventually provide full access transparency and location transparency. Whether this software will provide an acceptable degree of performance transparency remains to be seen.

12.3.2 An Expanded Role for the PWS

The use of an intelligent workstation as an integral part of an application makes it possible to provide the application user with the most advanced and usable human-to-machine interaction available in information systems technology.

"Introduction to Systems Application Architecture," Earl Wheeler and Alan Ganek, IBM Systems Journal, Vol. 25, No. 3, 1988

When it comes to cooperative processing, not all workstations are created equal. The programmable workstation (PWS, a.k.a. advanced function personal computer) has come of age. Spurred by the shift to graphical user interfaces (GUIs), the PWS provides dedicated processing power at the user interface. It is the most cost-effective vehicle for providing processing power for highly interactive applications. Trying to do intensive spreadsheet manipulation via a 3270 and a mainframe-based spreadsheet product is both frustrating (from a response time point of view) and expensive. This is not to say that there won't be some uses for NPT access to mainframe systems (or even some use of mainframe spreadsheets for that matter). It is rather that the "friendliest" user interfaces (those with interactive graphics and imaging, and in the not too distant future, video and audio) will require dedicated processing power.

Regardless of whether you are distributing the processing or database portions of your application among one or many processors, the PWS represents the future terminal of choice for interactive applications. As prices come down over the next few years, PWSs (of varying capability) will completely replace non-programmable terminals.

IBM specifically announced its intentions in this regard in a separate announcement "Expanded Role for the Programmable Workstations in Systems Application Architecture" (*Programming Announcement 289-219*):

IBM introduces in Systems Application Architecture (SAA), an expanded role for the programmable workstation (PWS). The OfficeVision Family of office products uses the PWS to provide access to enterprise-wide function. The role of the workstation in SAA is further emphasized by extensions to the elements of SAA -- CCS, CPI, and CUA -- that more fully utilize PWS graphics and display capabilities.

To IBM, the PS/2 becomes the "window" into the enterprise computer network. To the user, the PWS provides a single-system image into what may be a myriad of local, distributed, and remote applications. Software to implement this concept includes CICS OS/2, AS/400 PC Support, and OS/2 Presentation Manager.

OfficeVision shows a "work in progress" toward a single-system image for distributed applications. Mainframe office applications such as electronic mail have been given workstation features which hide the location of the application from the user. The processing power of the PS/2 is used to provide that common view into a variety of applications running on a variety of processors.

[One of the uses of software tools like Easel is to put a front end on host applications so that the user sees a single-system image. In the short term, this is a very viable approach to solving this part of the transparency problem.]

12.3.2.1 A Dual Strategy: NPT and PWS

For the next several years, current users of non-programmable terminals ought to be able to continue using applications they are accustomed to. In the meantime, application developers can be working on new user interfaces following CUA. These new user interfaces will, of course, require the use of programmable workstations. If users want the new interface with its additional features, they will pay the cost of trading in their 3270s for PS/2s.

The other side of the dual delivery strategy is being able to use PWSs as terminals to existing host applications. Terminal emulation packages abound (3270 emulation for mainframes and 5250 emulation for AS/400) but they do little more than allow you to use expensive programmable workstations in place of inexpensive dumb terminals. More advanced features are beginning to show up in the next generation of terminal emulators, although these usually require some cooperation from the host system.

AS/400 PC Support is an example of this next generation of emulators. Among other features, it allows the PC user (both DOS and OS/2 EE) to transparently access both PC and AS/400 printers and files. It allows both PC and AS/400 programs to be initiated from the same menu. Easel is another example of a product allowing sophisticated programming in conjunction with terminal emulation. In general, these packages move PC users one step closer to a "single-system image" regardless of where their applications are actually running.

12.4 Distributing Data

Whether a distributed application is focused on distributed databases or distributed functions, some amount of data will show up on each of the computers which contain the various parts of the application. This means that almost every application developed over the next several years will have to deal with the issue of distributed data.

Different strategies may be employed for different types of data in the same application. In some cases, files may be entirely copied from one machine to another at the beginning of the day. In other cases, continuously updated data may be accessed a record at a time throughout the day. Whether you need high-speed or slow speed access, whether your data is static or updated in "real time," the distribution strategy you select will become a major factor in the success of your application.

12.4.1 Distributed Data Strategies

☛ *Issue: What are the trade-offs in distributing data among different platforms?*

☛ *Issue: When should a database server architecture be used?*

Data distribution strategies are many and varied. Each one's use is indicated in different situations depending on a variety of criteria. Four of the most important "strategy indicators" are:

■ Data access frequency: how often does an application make a request for data?

■ Data update frequency: how often is the database updated or changed?

■ Data currency: how up-to-date does the data need to be?

■ Transaction response time objective: is fast response time important?

■ Database size: how large is the database?

Major categories of data distribution include:

■ File copy: copying an entire file or database from one machine where it is stored to another where it will be used; this presents a "snapshot" of the file to the using application.

■ Manual data extracts: copying part of a file or database based on user or application specified criteria to a file on another computer; most often done between a host and a workstation and referred to as data "downloading."

■ Automatic data extracts: copying part of file or database to another machine when that part changes; may be synchronous or asynchronous; implies that the sending application (or some other system component) knows where all copies of its files are at all times.

■ Record level access: applications read or update individual records; variations depend on which processor decides which records to be accessed, the one running the application (in which case, processing is in the "distributed data" mode) or the one containing the database ("distributed data access," commonly referred to as a "client-server architecture").

In a partially inconsistent use of terminology, the first three strategies are often called "file server" strategies, and the fourth a "database server" strategy.

Strategy Indicator / Distribution Strategy	Access Frequency	Update Frequency	Data Currency Needs	Response Time Objective	Data-base Size
File copy	Low-HIGH	LOW	Low	FAST	SMALL-Med
Manual extract	Low-HIGH	LOW	Low-med	FAST	Med-LARGE
Automatic extract	Low-HIGH	Low-MED	Low-MED	FAST	Med-LARGE
Distributed database	Low-med	Low-med	Med-HIGH	Med-fast	Small-large
Typical client-server	LOW-med	Low-high	Med-high	SLOW-med	Small-large
High-speed server on high-speed network	HIGH	HIGH	HIGH	FAST	LARGE
Capitalized values are important indicators.					

Figure II.25 Data Distribution Strategies

Figure II.25 lists the data distribution strategies and presents a matrix showing the strategy indicator values that would be indicative of using a particular strategy. In most cells, a range of values is given since the particular distribution strategy can be used in a variety of situations.

In some cases, certain values (capitalized) would be highly indicative of using a particular strategy. For example, applications with low data update frequency and fast response time objectives would be candidates for the file copy strategy, particularly if the access frequency is expected to be high and the size of the database is small.

As in other aspects of distributed processing system design, it is only possible to provide rules of thumb. Exact formulas for deciding on a strategy have yet to be developed.

Keeping track of multiple updates to different parts of your database on different machines and ensuring that all have been successfully completed and synchronized is not a simple task. In creating a banking application where the debit goes to an account on one machine and the credit to an account on another machine, you have to make sure that both parts of the transaction have completed successfully before you can say that the database is correct and can let other users access it. Although some database server products claim to have the "two-phase commit" capability needed to accomplish this, there is almost always some restriction on its use. The result is that you have to add a lot of code yourself to ensure the integrity of the application's data.

File copy and extract strategies can be implemented by a variety of software products from IBM and others (IBM's DXT is one). Software that implements distributed data and client-server architectures is becoming more readily available in a wide variety of hardware and network operating environments. Performance characteristics and other features vary widely and require careful review.

12.4.2 Client-Server Architectures

The term "client-server architecture" refers to the use of database servers on a network to perform some (or all) of the work of accessing the database. The program requesting the access is the "client." In many applications, the client is implemented on a workstation and the server on a large machine or host. [Note that this usage, while more common, is the opposite of that used by the developers of the X Window System in which the individual workstation has the X Window "server" and the host is the "client."] It is the implementation of the "distributed data access" mode of distributed processing.

The reasons for employing a client-server architecture, rather than other types of distributed data solutions, e.g. file servers or distributed databases, are many:

- the data is controlled centrally (on the server) making security, access control, and database integrity more manageable;

- data access requests are processed on the server which can apply the most efficient performance enhancement techniques to all requests;

- as transaction volume increases, response time can be optimized without affecting individual client machines by upgrading the server hardware;

- as new releases of the database management system become available, they can be incorporated into the server, usually without affecting individual client machines;

- client-server architectures reduce network traffic by sending only the requested records to the client application (rather than an entire file);

- since individual workstations do not have to maintain copies of the entire database, they can have smaller (and less expensive) disk storage.

The importance of each factor has to be evaluated for your specific application. The overall efficiency claim made regarding client-server systems versus file server systems may not always apply. For instance, in a centralized accounting system with a major overnight update process, a workstation-based inquiry capability will provide better response time if a copy of the inquiry database is downloaded each morning than if every request has to go back to a database server across the network. There may be other reasons for choosing one architecture over another, but improved response time would not be one of them in this case.

12.4.2.1 Remote Data Services

Remote Data Services (RDS) is IBM's implementation of client-server distributed processing using relational data in OS/2 Extended Edition-based networks. The server must be an OS/2 EE system, but clients can be running either OS/2 EE or DOS. On OS/2 EE systems, SQL calls embedded in procedural languages (COBOL, C, FORTRAN) are "precompiled" into calls to the OS/2 Database Manager. The precompiler is not implemented under DOS, so applications must be precompiled on an OS/2 EE system and the modified source compiled for the DOS system. The object code can be downloaded and executed under DOS. Mixed DOS-OS/2 client-server computing does not currently provide transparency to either users or programmers.

12.4.2.2 Distributed Data Management

IBM's Distributed Data Management Architecture allows the implementation of a client-server system using flat, direct access, and indexed files.

The DDM architecture describes a set of verbs for accessing different types of files. Depending on the type of file and the specific DDM product being used to access it, a program can request individual records, specific or relative keyed records, or streams of data (a certain number of bytes beginning at a certain place in the file). Client programs can access multiple files on multiple servers using the same verbs, although not always transparently. If a local data management interface (LDMI) is available in the DDM product, it will interpret the request and determine where the file resides.

12.4.2.3 The X Window System

The X Window System, mentioned in the previous chapter, is more than a windowing standard. It provides, via X Network and X Protocol, a network independent mechanism for implementing client-server architecture cooperative processing. A user at a workstation running an X Window Server (each workstation runs the "server" software) sees an application (operating as a "client") as if it is operating on the workstation. [Remember that this terminology is the reverse of that used in discussing database client-server architectures.]

12.4.2.4 Third Party Client-Server Systems

The database server market has become one of the hottest for new products announcements, and the most hotly contested for claims of performance and interoperability. Some of the most popular entries are those from the Microsoft (based on software originally developed by Sybase), Gupta Technologies, ORACLE, XDB Systems, and, of course, IBM.

Although all of the client-server products implement SQL, there are acknowledged incompatibilities in the extension to SQL and in the additional control information that you have to provide to make them operate. Switching from one vendor to another is not transparent, and running two different databases on two different servers is a nightmare. Particularly if you expect significant growth in your application, you should carefully check the scalability of each vendor's offering (what different hardware platforms will they run on) or you may find yourself in a conversion project much sooner than you expect.

12.4.3 Database Design for Portability

Some issues in database design take on increased significance when that database may be moved from one computer to another as part of a growing distributed processing environment. These issues arise from internal code differences on different computers and restrictions in computer languages available in different environments. SAA is trying to standardize the computer languages to eliminate some of these issues, but code issues will exist for a very long time.

A simple example of a language difference is the number of characters allowed in a field name under SQL. The SAA CPI Database Interface specifies a 10-character maximum, the limit under the AS/400 Database Manager. If databases are developed under OS/2 or DB2, field names could be longer, but the database definition would not be portable without modification. Other restrictions in field naming apply to use of underscores and hyphens due to restrictions in the accessing languages on different machines. These issues should be reviewed before specifying new database designs.

There are also portability issues related to character coding. Data is stored using the ASCII coding scheme under OS/2 (and DOS), but using the EBCDIC scheme on both AS/400 and System/370 computers. [At least they are all byte-oriented machines; DEC has to deal with both byte and 36-bit word machines.] Not only are the codes for specific characters different (blank is 20 in ASCII and 40 in EBCDIC), but the collating sequence differs significantly (due to placement of upper and lower case alphabets and the numbers in the coding scheme). In EBCDIC, numbers follow upper case which follows lower case. In ASCII, lower case is last and numbers first with upper case in the middle. Database keys and reports which depend on sort sequence will look quite different if produced on these different machines. There are also representation and byte order differences for numbers which would result in erroneous results if files were moved directly from one machine to another.

12.5 Developing Distributed and Cooperative Processing Among SAA and non-SAA Applications

☛ *Issue: Can existing systems be adapted to distributed and cooperative processing?*

Almost every shop will have to address the issue of integrating existing non-SAA applications with SAA applications. Many times, this integration will take the form of creating a distributed processing environment where each application provides some of the functions required by the user. Several strategies can be followed to develop this environment in an orderly, structured way. All of them allow integration of both IBM-based and non-IBM-based applications. These are:

- creating a common front end for all applications ("single-system image");
- creating a common database system for all applications;
- creating a common communications system among all applications.

Each approach attacks the problem in a somewhat different way and has different benefits and costs. They all require writing code (TANSTAAFL at work). Applications which are already structured to separate either the user interface or database access or both from the main body of the application function are more likely targets for re-engineering into an SAA environment than others. [This will certainly be true if your shop adopts an "application architecture" approach to design.]

Figure II.26 depicts the common front end approach (this diagram is a variation of Figure II.22). Regardless of whether the underlying application is a new one designed with a user interface that follows CUA or an old one that does not, you can bring them together via a process running on an intelligent workstation. Several software tool developers (in addition to IBM) have obviously seen a market in this type of architecture since they have created a number of products to help you create CUA-conforming common front end applications. Some allow mixing communications modes so that applications using both IBM and non-IBM telecommunications protocols can be accessed simultaneously.

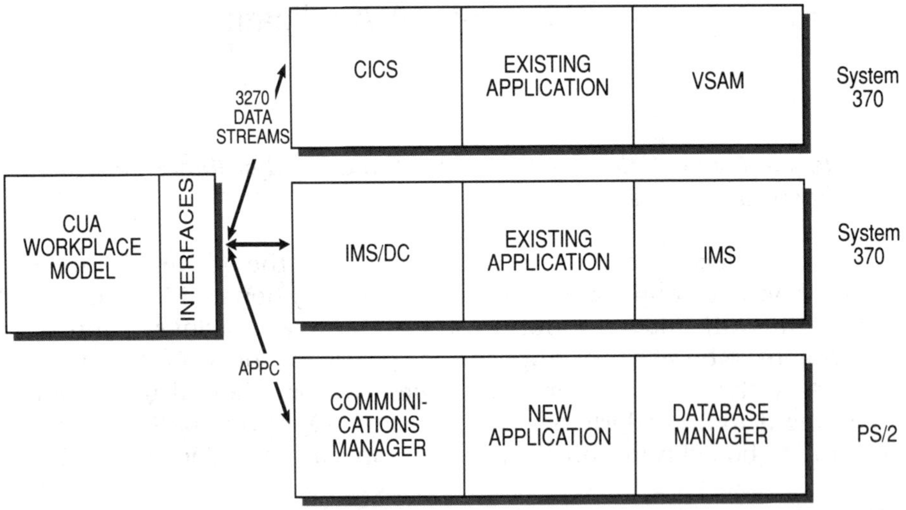

Figure II.26 Common Front End

A key characteristic of this approach is the ability to create a cooperative processing environment with little or no change to existing applications. Depending on the software tool you use, you may actually be creating CICS screen images out the back door of the workstation so that the host application does not even know it is communicating with a workstation. New applications could use APPC and LU6.2, while old applications use 3270 protocols and LU2.

If applications already isolate database access via an interface module, creating a common data access function across several applications is relatively straightforward. The database interface module can be modified to address a new host database management system or to direct its calls to a database server in a client-server architecture (see Figure II.27). Changes to existing applications are limited to this module, leaving the business function code intact. Obviously, if the existing application has database access code scattered throughout, this strategy may not be viable.

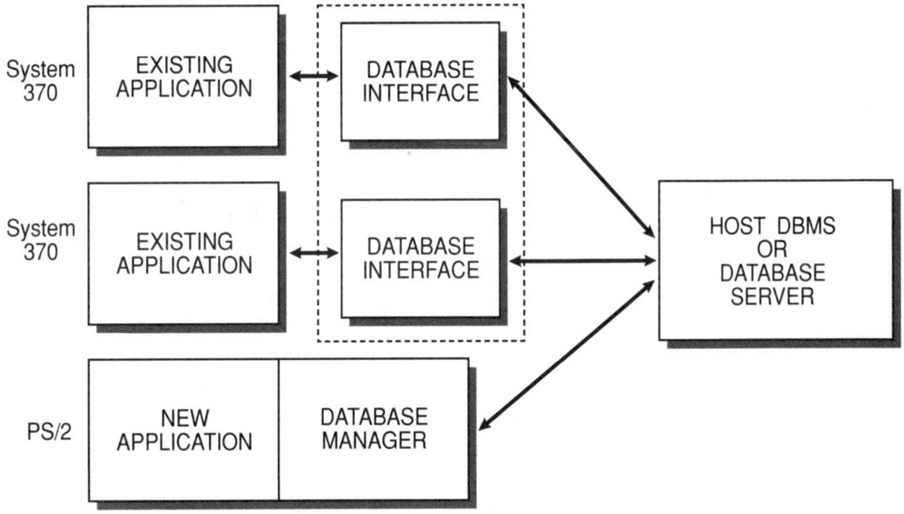

Figure II.27 Common Data Access

Some situations may allow you to make use of a common communications mechanism to create a cooperative processing environment. If old applications are already communicating with each other, you may be able to replace the communications interface module with one using APPC (or CPIC when it is more widely available) as shown in Figure II.28. IBM has licensed APPC to a number of vendors (particularly of UNIX systems) so this solution also allows integration of applications operating in several hardware environments.

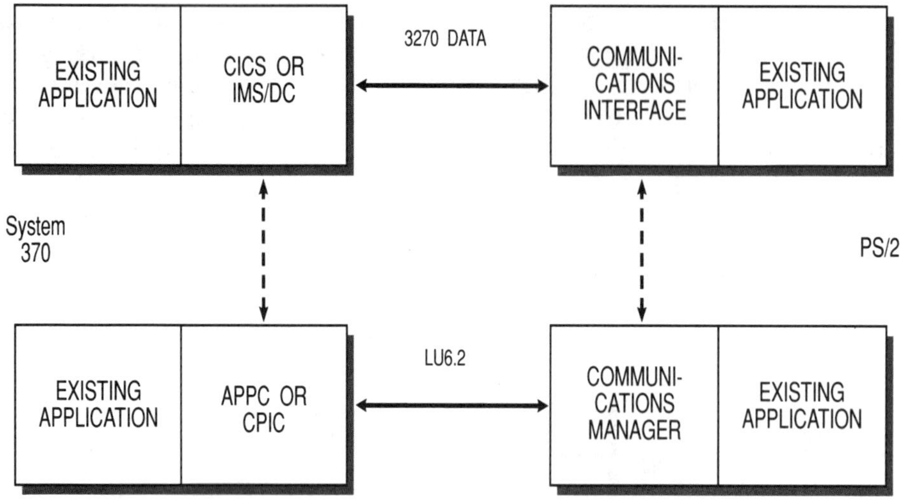

Figure II.28 Common Communications Interface

12.5.1 Cross-Vendor Solutions

Other major hardware vendors also provide software to implement distributed processing. Some of these are specific to their computer hardware (for example, Digital Equipment Corporation has extensive offerings), while some work in conjunction with IBM systems or add to them. These products make possible a variety of forms of cross-vendor distributed processing.

The most common mechanism for tying in with IBM systems is for another vendor to develop software that implements one of the IBM communications protocols. Programs on different machines can communicate in a distributed processing system using the same protocols, regardless of the equipment they are operating on. In the past, the most common approach was to send 3270 data streams using LU2. Everyone from Apple to UNISYS has announced or released such products. In the future, the most common approach will be to implement a distributed system using LU6.2.

Access transparency for the user of multiple hardware platforms from different vendors is also possible, although in limited form. Using front end user interface systems, applications which communicate on the same network can often be tied into the same user workplace, regardless of the underlying platform.

The variety of software and the possibilities they open up are increasing daily. All vendors are busily seeking out ways to tie their machines into an increasingly diverse enterprise computer network.

12.6 Using Distributed Functions in Enabling and System Software

The most obvious way to implement a distributed processing architecture is to *design* the application so that some functions and/or some data reside on the workstation and others on a mini- or mainframe computer. This is the most obvious way, but also the most complicated. It is far easier to design the application as if any part can reside anywhere and then to rely on the "enabling software" to do the rest. When the full SAA cooperative processing strategy is in place, operating system services will allow you to specify where different parts of the application and its data are. Other services will automatically handle communications and messaging. At the current time, only some of these capabilities are available and even those are not entirely transparent to the designer.

In a direct approach to distributed system development, you would call routines in the CPI for Communications in each part of your application to establish the appropriate communications dialog. [You would use APPC in those environments without an available CPIC product.] This implementation approach requires the programmers of both components of the system to understand fully the LU6.2 interface and the CPIC subroutine calls. While the result may be transparent to the user, it is hardly transparent to the designer and programmer.

Cooperative processing systems can be developed in a far simpler way using various IBM system control and enabling software modules. Database management products, such as DB2, allow you to distribute data among different platforms without changing the source program. Teleprocessing monitors, such as CICS, allow you to specify "links" to applications that are running on remote processors. In each case, the underlying software is itself implementing the communications dialog, thus relieving the application programmer from worrying about this aspect of the job.

For example, many levels of distributed database can be implemented using the capabilities to be provided by software delivering the SAA Database Interface (Database Manager, DB2, and SQL/DS). Each of the database managers on the SAA operating environments will eventually provide transparent access to data that is located remotely. Not all of the possible combinations of remote access are available at the current time. This is an obvious problem in designing an application that expects to use remote capabilities in the short run, although there are some current implementation alternatives from other vendors (Oracle, Microsoft, and Gupta Technologies, to name a few). In the long run, all capabilities will also be available from IBM.

12.6.1 Remote Procedures and Data in OS/2 EE

OS/2 contains several facilities for distributing both processes and data. Not all have been incorporated in the SAA CPI, but each represents a mechanism for developing certain types of distributed applications.

Database Manager, primarily used for accessing relational databases, provides a limited type of distributed processing transparency. Called the Database Application Remote Interface, this facility of the OS/2 EE Database Manager allows programmers to implement systems that cooperate across multiple OS/2 EE-based systems without any visible differences to the user. The programmer issues an explicit call which causes a procedure to be invoked on another machine. Several additional services would be required to make this process transparent to the programmer.

The Server-Requester Programming Interface (SRPI) is a set of subroutine calls in the Communications Manager which work with the System/370 Enhanced Connectivity Facility. Programs can be initiated on the host and databases accessed (both relational and flat file) to create distributed applications with the workstation.

Remote Data Services, also introduced in Release 1.2, adds capabilities to the Database Manager to access databases on other OS/2 EE machines. This is a fully transparent interface in that neither the user nor the programmer need to know the location of the database when they make a request or write a program.

All of these mechanisms have restrictions which limit their usefulness as general solutions for distributed processing. They show some of the capabilities that IBM has to sort out in providing a generalized mechanism across all platforms and databases.

12.6.2 CICS OS/2

CICS OS/2 Version 1.2 provides features for the production of SAA compatible applications that will be immediately useful to current CICS mainframe shops.

CICS is the most widely used mainframe teleprocessing environment. There are literally hundreds of thousands of applications developed for CICS, both by ISVs and by user organizations. With CICS OS/2, applications using command level CICS could be ported to the PS/2 with little or no effort (there are some differences in compilers and in the CICS APIs supported). With further effort, some portions of those applications could be ported to the PS/2 while some portions remain on the mainframe. The Distributed CICS Link capability allows transactions running on a PWS to link to CICS transactions running either on another PWS or on a host. Figure II.29 shows some of these possibilities. The equivalent capability on the mainframe can be used to start a program running on a PWS, even if it is unattended.

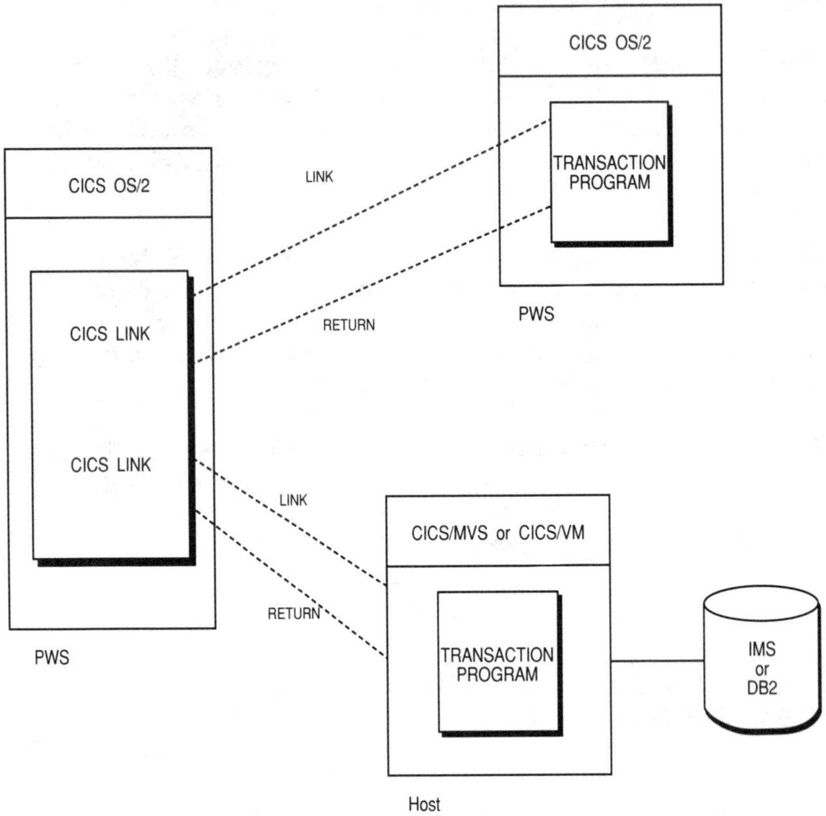

Figure II.29 Distributed CICS Link

If Distributed CICS Link does not provide enough flexibility, you can use APPC protocols in both host and PS/2 programs to create distributed processes. CICS OS/2 provides Distributed Transaction Processing

(DTP) commands to start such a conversation in either another CICS OS/2 equipped PS/2 or on a host running CICS with APPC support.

Another capability of CICS OS/2 is an enhanced transaction routing feature. Mainframe CICS transaction routing allows one CICS host to initiate a CICS transaction on another CICS mainframe (i.e., you can use CICS to cause a program to be run on another computer). The CICS OS/2 version similarly allows a CICS program on one PS/2 to cause a transaction residing on another PS/2 to be run. This opens up the strategy of using a PWS as a "transaction server," basically another processor to perform certain transactions.

For more limited distributed processing, function shipping allows you to issue CICS commands that access databases on remote systems.

The various modes of distributed processing via CICS OS/2 are summarized in Figure II.30.

Environment	PWS to PWS	PWS to Host	Host to PWS
Distributed CICS link	✓	✓	
Distributed Transaction Processing (DTP)	✓	✓	✓
Transaction routing	✓		✓
Function shipping	✓		✓

Figure II.30 CICS OS/2 Distributed Processing Capabilities

12.6.2.1 Software Updates via the Host

Although CICS OS/2 runs on a PWS, it is distributed to customers on a mainframe tape. This is in line with IBM's focus on controlling software distribution centrally. Program updates are applied to the mainframe libraries. Copies are then downloaded to the individual PS/2s licensed for the program.

An obvious next step in distributing software is for the PS/2 software to interrogate the mainframe to make sure it has the latest (or at least consistent) versions of the software. This might also be done automatically by CICS when a mainframe connection is made.

12.6.3 Program-to-Program Communications

☛ *Issue: Is it really necessary to switch to LU6.2 communications?*

IBM is building all its distributed processing software on the basis of a program-to-program communication paradigm. Distributed functions in the SAA CPI (specifically in the Database Interface) are implemented using LU6.2 communication. SNA Distribution Services and Management Services operate over LU6.2 sessions. Implementations of APPC to use LU6.2 are springing up for a wide variety of non-IBM environments, including UNIX environments (under license from IBM). LU6.2 is a significant step up from async and 3270-like communication. It requires a higher degree of sophistication to use, but products are already available which will make it simpler for the majority of situations. Its availability will help in creating cooperative processing applications by standardizing a wide range of communications tasks.

☛ *Issue: Should we wait for the CPIC or use APPC now?*

APPC and the SAA CPI for Communications are not exactly the same. Conceptually they derive from the same roots, but the specific verbs are different. CPIC is the newer, more efficient verb set. IBM has defined it to be the future standard for program-to-program communication.

APPC is available under OS/2, OS/400, VM, and MVS. Programs written using it will communicate with CPIC-written programs. This means that immediate conversion to CPIC is not necessary, although future conversion may be desirable. Certain LU6.2 functions are not provided in the CPIC and should be avoided in new LU6.2 programs. These calls are documented in the *SAA CPI Communications Reference.*

13. System Control Software

13.1 Issue Locator

13.2 System/370 Operating Systems

☛ *Issue: Does it matter which 370 operating system I use?*

Both of the major System/370 operating system environments are included in SAA. Whether you are a VM shop using CMS, or an MVS shop using TSO, you are working in an SAA environment. MVS, with the addition of a transaction processing monitor (CICS or IMS/TM), tends to be used for applications requiring a transaction-at-a-time type of interaction. VM is often used for decision support and inquiry applications which have more of a free form structure to their processing needs. Both environments are used for batch processing. The most important point is that IBM is promising to continue development of both operating systems and to bring identical SAA-defined components to each.

13.2.1 What About Batch Processing?

SAA is remarkably silent about batch processing. It is almost as if all aspects of a system were assumed to be performed in "real time," with the user sitting at a workstation waiting for the results. Obviously, this is not the case in the real world. Batch processing functions are performed in almost every system, whether you are talking about business systems with weekly payroll runs and monthly accounting closes, scientific systems crunching massive formulae against even more massive amounts of data, or transaction processing systems such as airline reservation systems which require overnight processing of everything from frequent flyer miles to matching ticket receipts. Batch processing is a necessary part of a complete information system, and at least some of the SAA standards should be applied.

In developing batch processing applications, you should be focusing on the use of products that implement the CPI. Languages included in the CPI are equally applicable in batch processing environments as they are in on-line or distributed environments (although different libraries and pre-compile steps are needed). The Database element of the CPI similarly defines the appropriate mechanism for batch processing access to relational databases. If your data is on another machine (acting as a database server), you should be using the distributed data features of DB2 and SQL/DS or the CPI for Communications, implementing a batch processing distributed process in the same way as one that is on-line.

In short, SAA may not be visible to the users of batch processing systems, but developers should be using SAA-implementing products throughout.

13.2.2 CICS and IMS/TM

CICS and IMS/TM (Transaction Manager, the new name for the data communications portion of IMS/ESA) are the two teleprocessing monitors that provide transaction processing capabilities to mainframe applications. Users enter transactions (a reservation request, a journal voucher to be processed, a database inquiry, etc.) and the application processes them, displaying the results (a positive acknowledgment, a list of errors, a portion of a database). The transaction monitor (CICS or IMS/TM) is called upon by the application to provide controlled sharing of processing and data resources to the simultaneous (or near simultaneous) requests from many users. The functions provided by the two monitors are similar enough so that development shops generally use one or the other for their applications. Since IMS/TM was first introduced with the IMS database management system, IMS/DB shops tend to use IMS/TM (although you can use CICS to control applications which reference IMS databases). Shops shifting to the DB2 database from IMS will also typically use IMS/TM rather than switching to CICS. Shops moving from CICS/VSAM systems to DB2 are more likely to continue to use CICS.

[In the current release of IMS/ESA (Release 3.1), IMS/DM (Database Manager) is a prerequisite to IMS/TM. IBM has packaged these as two separate products and appears to be moving in the direction of making them separately usable as well.]

CICS and IMS/TM run as subsystems under MVS (there is also a single user CICS under VM). Both are SAA environments. SAA does not include a multi-user transaction processing monitor under VM.

13.3 OS/400: An Object-oriented Approach

OS/400 is the system control program for the AS/400. To ensure upward compatibility with predecessor machines, it will operate System/36 and System/38 programs. It also provides a native programming environment unlike anything else in IBM's arsenal. Its native "object orientation" presents an approach to creating applications that integrates application code, enabling code, and operating system routines.

OS/400 is an SAA platform. However, there is less software available to implement SAA on the OS/400 than on any other SAA platform. Perhaps because of its heritage, perhaps because it is so different, OS/400 has lagged behind MVS, VM, and OS/2 in providing software to implement the CPI and CUA. This will be corrected in time, but you will have to wait a while before writing your totally transparent, distributed system with an AS/400 in the middle of your network.

13.4 The Strategic Role of OS/2 EE

The role of OS/2 has been debated since its introduction in 1987. Within SAA, its place is clear: OS/2 Extended Edition is *the* micro-computer environment targeted for full participation in the enterprise network. OS/2 EE is the system that IBM has put its strength behind in terms of both development and marketing. But does this mean that organizations wanting to implement SAA have to convert all their microcomputers to OS/2 EE? No, and that is what the issue is all about.

OS/2 Extended Edition and its sibling OS/2 Standard Edition are completely new operating systems. Their internal structure is similar to that of advanced mainframe operating systems and uses hardware facilities ("protected mode," full word address registers) not available in first generation PCs. EE differs from SE in its inclusion of an integrated Communication Manager and Database Manager and its associated Query Manager. These components are only available with OS/2 EE, although IBM and Microsoft have stated that "the two companies will work together to ensure that [they] are available to all OS/2 users" (*Programming Announcement 289-625*). OS/2 EE provides the full range of system control and application enabling services that developers need to produce advanced function distributed processing applications.

It is via the Communication Manager that OS/2 EE earns its place as the "window into the enterprise computing environment." This may seem a strange statement since it is the OS/2 Presentation Manager (also available under OS/2 Standard Edition) that actually provides the windowed user interface. It is the Communication Manager, however, that allows the OS/2 EE-based workstation to retrieve data and perform procedures in cooperation with other machines on the network. Whether you use the Communication Manager directly or indirectly (via the Remote Data Services capability in the OS/2 DBM), it is through its implementation of SAA Common Communications Support that the workstation takes on its strategic role.

13.4.1 Assessing OS/2

Personal computer operating systems provide five key functions:

- Memory management
- Storage management
- Database management

- Communications
- User presentation

The operating system (including any related "enabling software") should provide the level of capabilities you need in each area. Figure II.31 compares the four major environments for PC compatible hardware. In many cases, the level of capability is determined by the specific third party product that you buy in conjunction with the operating system. Obviously, the availability of different products in different environments (and their prices) will also affect your choice of operating system.

Operating System Capability	OS/2 Extended Edition	OS/2 Standard Edition	DOS with Windows	UNIX
Memory management	Swapping (Virtual)	Swapping	Expanded Memory System	Virtual
Storage management	HPFS	HPFS	FAT	UNIX File System
Database management	DBM	3rd party	3rd party	3rd party
Communications	CM	3rd party	3rd party	TCP/IP
User presentation	PM	PM	Windows	X Window System/ 3rd party GUI

CM = Communications Manager; DBM = Database Manager/2;
PM = Presentation Manager

Figure II.31 Comparison of PC Operating System Capabilities

13.4.2 OS/2 vs. DOS for Developers

☛ *Issue: What are the migration paths from PC-DOS?*

OS/2 is becoming the platform used by software developers. The advanced computer-aided software engineering (CASE) tools developers are starting to use are so feature-packed that they can barely be squeezed into the DOS environment. Two areas are particularly limiting: the 640Kb limit on directly addressable memory, and the lack of a multiprocessing capability.

The biggest limitation today in DOS is the way in which memory is addressed. Special software is needed to address more than 640Kb of system memory, a number that has become increasingly limiting. It is not unusual for even a spreadsheet application to require more than the available memory, particularly when other memory resident software is used ("terminate and stay resident" programs), such as notepads, DOS command shells, terminal emulators, and print queuing routines. Some software developers spend as much time figuring out how to squeeze their application into memory (or tricking the system to believe that it is there) as they do developing the functionality.

[Over 20 years ago, I thought the 4Kb memory address space available on a DEC PDP-8 was limiting and used an "expanded memory" management scheme to use 8Kb, "more than enough for any reasonable mini-computer application." Times have changed, almost by a factor of 1000, but expanded memory management is still needed.]

OS/2, written to operate on more advanced microprocessors than DOS (it requires Intel's 80286 or higher), is able to address up to 16Mb of real memory. Newer applications will use virtual memory schemes, the same as on mainframes, to address even more. Accessing this much memory in a straightforward way required both a new processor and a new operating system.

Another key feature used by application developers is multi-tasking. Developers perform multiple tasks at the same time in their work (one in the "foreground," and several in the "background"), and they build the same capability into their most sophisticated applications. For example, some of the functions today's CASE tools perform can easily be executed in the background (printing diagrams, checking models for consistency) while the designer or developer uses other functions in the foreground.

Every developer I have talked to who has made the switch from DOS to OS/2 is glad he or she did so. In spite of start-up problems, the increased productivity offsets the additional costs in just a few months.

13.4.3 OS/2 as a LAN Server OS

☛ *Issue: What operating system should be used on LAN Servers?*

Deciding to use OS/2 as the operating system on a LAN server is independent from deciding to use OS/2 on individual workstations. The advantages of using OS/2 LAN Server are due both to general characteristics of the operating system and to its LAN Server Application Programming Interface (API):

- Network applications written to the OS/2 LAN Server API are independent of the type of network they will be running on. Such applications will operate on networks using any of the lower level protocols supported by OS/2.

- API use has been endorsed by a wide variety of vendors, including 3Com (3+Open), Novell (which plans to have a version of its Netware product which will be based on OS/2), and DEC.

- The differences between Microsoft LAN Manager IBM LAN Server are being reduced by joint agreement of the two companies. This will expand the reach of OS/2 even further. Even now, they can service the same workstation software. Microsoft has also committed to release a UNIX version of LAN Manager, to be called LM/X.

- PC-DOS and OS/2 workstations can access a LAN Server network using their respective LAN workstation software.

Some of these same advantages are also available using other LAN server products. The increasing use of the IBM/Microsoft API will ensure that many applications are written for this environment first.

13.4.4 Installable File System

Another of many capabilities of OS/2 is the "installable file system" (IFS, introduced in Release 1.2). Via a command added to the CONFIG.SYS file (used at startup by the operating system to load optional routines and set parameters), you can specify which one of several file systems should be used to control the storage on one or more drives. Under DOS and early versions of OS/2, you had no choice -- the so-called "FAT" system was it. [The FAT is the File Allocation Table used to keep track of files in the standard DOS file system; it has become the moniker of this file system.] The introduction of IFS in OS/2 opens the door for better storage management of the increasingly large disks supplied with PWSs.

The High Performance File System (HPFS) supplied with OS/2 Release 1.2 is an IFS. HPFS was developed to address the needs of larger and "gigabyte" secondary storage devices and the correspondingly larger number of files that can be stored on them (it can be used on smaller disks as well). Disk caching, multi-threaded I/O (multiple read or write requests handled in an interleaved fashion), "write behind" logic (finishing the disk write while other processing takes place) all contribute to faster file access. File names as long as 254 characters, extended file attributes (file version number, type, creation history, etc.), and disk volumes larger than 32 Mb (the limit for the FAT file system until DOS Release 4.0) are features that enhance file management. In some situations, the availability of HPFS alone will provide a sufficient reason to use OS/2.

13.5 AIX and UNIX

☛ *Issue: Can UNIX and SAA operating environments coexist?*

Some parts of your organization may adopt AIX because of the existence of applications relevant to their mission. Using AIX (or some other UNIX implementation) may provide immediate advantages for some applications, e.g. multi-processing and distributed processing using relatively inexpensive graphical terminals. These systems can also be integrated with the organization's SAA approach.

From the point of view of the strategic computing plan, AIX provides an alternative to OS/2. [Although it is also implemented on the System/370, AIX is unlikely to be a significant competitor to MVS or VM.] It will also show up on mid-range systems from a variety of manufacturers (Digital Equipment, Hewlett-Packard, Sun, and dozens of smaller ones). The question is how to integrate UNIX and SAA systems into the "enterprise computing strategy."

There are four types of compatibility issues that need to be studied, and that IBM has addressed in its "interoperability" statement of direction:

- Programming language
- Database
- Communications
- User interface

There are many users and developers who are already familiar with UNIX-based systems, at the current time many more so than are familiar with OS/2. They will be able to create applications which cooperate with other SAA environments via implementations of compatible languages and operating system interfaces in all four areas. They can already develop database applications using SQL in the same programming language (C and COBOL) on both systems. While there are also many differences between UNIX and OS/2, the same principles of application design will apply.

Communication across a multi-vendor network has become much easier in the past year or two. Most UNIX systems use the TCP/IP network protocol on Ethernet networks. IBM has introduced products using this protocol and will be expanding them to its full range of systems. It has also licensed its proprietary LU6.2 program-to-program communications protocols to other vendors. Several are implementing LU6.2 communications packages for their UNIX systems. These packages will implement the SAA CPI for Communications, the subroutines you would call to transact an LU6.2 session. This means that applications running on AIX and other UNIX systems will be able to participate in a cooperative processing environment on the same footing as any other application running on an IBM-SAA platform.

The issue of a common user interface is somewhat more problematical. While IBM has hinted that it will develop a version of Presentation Manager for AIX, official announcements have not been made and no other UNIX vendor has said even as much. In fact, most vendors are committed to one of the other graphical user interface (GUI) standards, such as OSF/Motif and UNIX International's Open Look. Although there will be many similarities between such GUIs and CUA, they will not be the same. This could be a problem in an organization that has a variety of OS/2 and UNIX-based workstations.

Once again, the bottom line is that AIX and SAA are on parallel paths. But, those parallels seem to get closer and closer as time goes on. [Is IBM operating in non-Euclidean space?] Someday the only differences may be in the operating system kernels, and then who will care?

14. Computer Hardware

14.1 Issue Locator

14.2 Processors

Distributed processing means different things to different people. This has led to confusion about what it really is and what it is really needed for. The key purpose in distributing processing and data is to maximize the effective use of computing resources and to provide flexibility for future growth. With this in mind, you can begin to sort out the wide range of possible software and hardware strategies.

14.2.1 Distributing the MIPS

There are more MIPS sitting on desk tops than there are in computer rooms.

[Paraphrase of various marketing surveys]

☛ *Issue: What is the proper role for each type of hardware platform?*

In analyzing how to use your resources most effectively, you must first determine the appropriate role for each type of resource in your shop. As computer hardware capabilities have advanced over the years, certain specializations have shown up. While we may think of all of our computers as "general purpose," each performs certain tasks more efficiently than others. Mainframe computer architectures, such as the System/370 line, have been optimized to work on many individual jobs more or less simultaneously to maximize use of multiple internal hardware subsystems (disks, channels, processors, communications controllers, etc.). While one job is waiting for a relatively slow disk request to be filled, another job can usually make use of the CPU, and vice versa. This is the basis on which all modern operating systems have been developed, and which works well when the jobs conform to the expected mix.

If you were to put a number of CPU-bound jobs into a System/370 at the same time (i.e., jobs needing a large amount of processing power and only a small amount of disk or communication access), it would appear to bog down. In fact, it would simply be processing at CPU speed, with a certain overhead for operating system functions. For this job mix, a system with a less sophisticated operating system, or perhaps even several parallel processing units, would be more appropriate. And, of course, this is just what we see in today's supercomputers and vector processing attachments to general purpose mainframes.

To understand these issues, you need a "job mix" analysis across the computers and applications in your organization. Even when you are dealing with only the three classes of computers encompassed by SAA, answers where different applications should be operated may not be obvious. When you add the possibilities of other classes of machines, the "correct" answer is even more difficult to find.

In general, applications which require access to large databases, process large numbers of transactions in batch mode, or handle interactive applications which have a slow interaction rate (e.g. database inquiry as opposed to spreadsheet analysis) can best be handled by traditional mainframe machines. If the overall processing load is small enough, they could also be handled by the smaller processors in mid-range or mini-computers. This is not to say that a database application could not be done entirely on personal computers, and many, of course, are, but rather that certain characteristics of those applications make them more appropriate for a centralized environment. Chief among these is the need to share data among multiple people.

As the user interaction rate picks up, as it does dramatically in graphical applications, the applications need more dedicated processing power. "Personal" computers (PCs or more sophisticated workstations) become ideal dedicated processors to handle this load. The reason that VisiCalc was first commercialized on a personal computer (the Apple II) was that the authors couldn't "make it work" (from a user perspective) on the mainframe computer they also had available. They could not sustain the interaction rate, repainting all the cells on the screen every time one number was input, without a dedicated computer. This same need is why IBM is strongly recommending programmable workstations for user interface processing, regardless of what the mainframe or mid-range computer is doing. Personal computers provide the user with immediately available processing power for certain types of interactions which, when necessary, can be linked with even more processing power on a networked mainframe.

14.2.2 The Mainframe Will Still Be There

The reports of my death are greatly exaggerated.
Cable from Mark Twain to the Associated Press

Lest anyone forget, the workhorse applications currently run on mainframe computers can be distributed, cooperated, and split, but there will still be millions of computations left over to be performed in exactly the same way they are today. Mainframes will be around for a long time.

14.3 How Many Workstations Are Enough?

SAA strategy calls for a significantly increased role for programmable workstations versus non-programmable terminals. The question for hardware planning is how much of the computing workload in the organization calls for this type of capability, and, therefore, how many PS/2s will be necessary in the future. Additional requirements will also come from the IS development staff itself, which will require a more sophisticated development environment than they do today.

☛ *Issue: What percentage of new terminal or workstation requirements will be for CUA-usable systems?*

An analysis of this issue requires input from the strategic software plan. Without having some idea of the types of applications that are to be developed or re-developed in the next several years, it will be an impossible question to answer.

If the major activity for the IS department is maintenance of existing systems, PS/2s will be needed only when user interfaces are re-engineered. If re-development of the corporate accounting system is planned (complying with SAA, of course), many users will require PS/2s. Even in this case, sophisticated PS/2s may not be required in all situations. For example, an accounts payable data entry department with a lot of paper to push may find that fancy graphical interfaces does not buy it very much and decide to stick with NPTs.

☛ *Issue: What are the workstation needs of the IS department's development staff?*

New development tools will be needed to produce applications with CUA compliant interfaces operating in cooperative processing environments. These tools will require the use of PS/2s with large amounts of memory. Some IS departments have already begun using PS/2s, finding that the multi-processing capabilities of OS/2 increase the productivity of their staff even when developing traditional systems.

In general, it is reasonable to plan for the addition of PS/2s or the replacement of 3270s with PS/2s for all programmers developing new systems. Whether this process should take two, three, or four years will depend on the rate at which your organization can assimilate the change.

The move to PS2s raises the question of what to do about existing 3270s. Absent a significant "field installable" upgrade, 3270s will be relegated to very straightforward data entry tasks. You might also try selling your excess 3270s to those of your competitors not implementing SAA.

14.3.1 Workstation Configurations

I tested the [software] system using two SIVA 386/20 PCs from VNS America. Each had 8 megabytes of memory and a 300-megabyte SCSI hard disk drive connected to an Adaptec AHA-1540A/1542A controller. Each machine also had a 16-MHz 80837 math coprocessor. The network connection ran through a pair of Western Digital WD8003 Ethernet adapters. One system sported an Orchid ProDesigner VGA display adapter with 512K bytes of memory, and the other system had a Matrox PB-1281 34010-based graphics coprocessor. The Orchid VGA adapter drove a Seiko CM-1430 14-inch multifrequency monitor, and the Matrox was hooked to a 19-inch Mitsubishi Diamond Scan Model HL6905. Each system had a Logitech three-button mouse.

From a software product review in Byte Magazine, October 1989.

☛ *Issue: Should there be a standard workstation configuration and, if so, what should it be?*

Having standard PWS configurations for application users and application developers will generally simplify life for you and your workstation support staff (unless you get a thrill from dealing with hardware configurations like those in the quotation above). There will always be special cases, but even these can be kept to a minimum if the standard configurations are reasonable. Figure II.32 is a starting point.

[What do you mean "you don't have a workstation support staff?" Some organizations call them "PC gurus" while others are more formal with "Personal Computer Support Manager." Whether explicitly budgeted to do so or not, everyone has someone who helps people with their PC problems.]

CUA conforming applications using PWSs will require PS/2s running OS/2. Theoretically, only OS/2 Standard Edition is necessary (it includes the Presentation Manager), but many applications will require the additional capabilities of OS/2 Extended Edition. This is important since OS/2 EE requires a minimum of 3.5 megabytes (Mb) of system memory just to get started. OS/2 Standard Edition requires a minimum of 2 Mb. In both cases, you should plan for 2 Mb *above* these minimums if your users will be doing anything beyond dedicated applications.

Intended Use	Applications	Development
Processor	386SX	80386
Main memory	4 Mb [*] [OV +4 Mb]	8 Mb [*] [OV +4 Mb]
Display	EGA color	VGA color
Diskette	720 Kb 3 1/2"	1.4 Mb 3 1/2", 1.2 Mb 5 1/4"
Fixed disk	30 Mb [OV +7 Mb]	60 Mb local, 100 Mb on LAN [OV +20 Mb]
Pointing device	Mouse	Mouse
Note that all recommendations are *minimums*. [*] = OS/2 Release 1.3 will require 2 Mb less. [OV +..] = Additional for OfficeVision.		

Figure II.32 Standard PWS Configurations

[IBM and Microsoft have indicated their commitment to reducing the memory requirements for both flavors of OS/2. The reported OS/2 Release 1.3 (not announced as of this writing) will reduce memory requirements by 2 Mb. Even so, it will require much more memory than DOS, although DOS with Windows Release 3 needs 3-4 Mb to operate effectively. Both OS/2 and Windows have the characteristic that performance can be improved by adding more memory.]

If you are planning to use OfficeVision, you need "3.0 Mb memory minimum above prerequisite software requirements" with Release 1 and another megabyte for Release 2 (*Programming Announcement 289-201*). IBM is recommending a PS/2 Model 50Z as the minimum OfficeVision user machine.

Application developers will need even bigger workstations than users. A developer writing OS/2 EE applications will need a PS/2 Model 70 (the fastest one you can afford) with 8-12 Mb memory. For secondary storage, developers will need access to 100 Mb or more. Not all of that need be local to the workstation since some will represent shared files on the "development staff LAN."

With the differing needs of different staff members for workstation capability, you may have a distribution problem as people "trade up." Establishing an internal mechanism for transferring more and less powerful workstations among staff members is often a cost effective solution, although one fraught with administrative problems.

14.3.1.1 The 286 Is Dead; Long Live the 386

OS/2 Release 1.2 operates on PCs with at least an 80286 processor, the chip introduced in the AT-class PC. OS/2 Release 2, slated for release at the end of 1990, requires an 80386. DOS with Windows Release 3 will run on an 80286, but with certain functions crippled. An 80386 is recommended here, too.

OK, so the 80286 is a dead-end processor. But the 80486 is already appearing in commercial machines, so is the 80386 dying, too? Intel has stated its intention to support the 80386 architecture not only in the 80486, but also in the 80586 and 80686 -- in other words, for at least the next five years. These sophisticated processors (some already in the labs at Intel) add speed and capabilities, but do not change the basic 32-bit instruction set introduced with the 80386.

Spring for the extra dollars -- go 386. [Or at least go 386SX, its slower cousin.]

14.3.2 PS/2 vs. the Clones

As with earlier personal computers, manufacturers other than IBM are producing computers said to be software compatible with the PS/2. They will run DOS, they will run OS/2 Standard Edition, they will run Extended Edition. Since only IBM supplies OS/2 EE, you can generally verify such statements by trying to install OS/2 EE's latest version. If it boots and you can bring up the Database Manager and Communication Manager, it probably works. The problem is that there is no guarantee that the next release will work or that other vendor software will operate under OS/2 EE running on your "clone" machine. IBM is expected to license OS/2 EE to other hardware vendors, in which case this worry will go away, but it hasn't happened yet.

The operating system software for personal workstations has become so complicated that any change in configuration is cause for concern. Using a different graphics card is one obvious source of problems. Many of the early VGA-compatible products were barely compatible for displaying text, let alone color graphics. Even using different monitors sometimes causes problems. [No matter how unlikely this may sound, it is absolutely true. Many software vendors supply special modifications to their software, even under DOS, to deal with certain characteristics of supposedly compatible monitors. It is even worse under OS/2.]

IBM's decision to open up the specifications for OS/2 EE to other manufacturers will help this situation considerably. Until the clone makers get their OS/2 products to market (both software and hardware to run it on), you will have to exercise caution in using other than certified IBM equipment.

14.4 Secondary Storage

The big issue in planning for secondary storage is not how much (answer: it doesn't matter how much you plan for, people want more), but where. Personal computers, cooperative processing, network servers, and distributed databases all combine to confuse the answer to this question.

☛ *Issue: Where will data storage be provided, on local machines, servers, or the mainframe (acting as a server)?*

Centralized secondary storage requires sophisticated control mechanisms (both automated and manual), but also allows economic backup and recovery. Since backup is the primary problem with dispersed secondary storage (how many personal computer users in your shop regularly back up their hard disks?), there is a strong argument to be made for keeping most secondary storage centrally.

Unfortunately, life isn't quite that easy. The cost of a megabyte of storage on IBM's largest capacity disk (and therefore least expensive per Mb) is about $100. This compares with $10 per Mb on a typical PC hard disk (locally, or on a network server). Furthermore, new local area network "backup servers" are able to interrogate node machines and automatically back up files. Aside from the network traffic implications, this does obviate the issue of regular backup.

So, what's the answer? Use of local hard disks will increase faster than you think (or want), both to accommodate the dispersion (and possible duplication) of some databases and to accommodate the larger and more numerous programs that users will be using. You can try to force people to use diskless PCs and add more capacity on the mainframe, but this may not be economical. Multi-level storage schemes will continue to expand, particularly as controlling software becomes more sophisticated.

15. Application Development Environment

15.1 Issue Locator

15.2 Creating an ADE for SAA

Application development is no longer a paper and pencil activity and hasn't really been one for almost ten years. Designers and programmers need tools -- tools that were developed for their use and that work together to provide an environment conducive to productive work. Under the various rubrics of computer-aided software engineering (CASE), application development environments (ADE), integrated project support environments (IPSE), and a host of other names and abbreviations, automated tools are finding their way into the every day functioning of the IS department. Some of the tools you need to implement SAA-compliant applications are already in your toolbox, but some new ones will also be necessary.

The benefits of CASE have been debated endlessly over the past five years. For most of that time, IBM has been an observer. The AD/Cycle announcement in September 1989, was notable because IBM put its stamp of approval on the whole idea of integrated application development environments and the need to make a significant capital investment in the systems development process.

AD/Cycle is IBM's ADE concept and will eventually contain all the tools needed for implementing systems that comply with SAA. It doesn't have all those tools today, and in some ways is not much different from the home-grown ADEs put together by a number of large organizations for their own use. It illustrates two key points about CASE/ADE that will drive many decisions over the next several years:

- A central data repository with data shared via an "information model" will be the focal point of the ADE.

- Application development environments will themselves be sets of sophisticated cooperative processing applications.

Application software systems of any significant size are developed by teams of people. They are maintained by other teams of people for a decade or more. The information they produce, all the models, designs, program code, operations statistics, trouble reports, and whatever else, has to be accessible to large numbers of people. There must be a central place where the information about the system can be stored and accessed. Reconciling this need with the fact that some CASE tools are most appropriately provided on workstations and some on hosts leads to the implementation of CASE as a set of cooperative processing applications.

Of course, IBM's view of the world is not necessarily the correct one (or even being the correct one, necessarily the one that will happen), but in this case I and most other practitioners are in agreement. This chapter will explore these ideas and the issues you will face in creating an ADE for SAA development. For further information on implementing CASE or for a review of the general concepts, there are many seminars, magazine articles, and books (see, for example, *Making Software Engineering Happen* by Roger Pressman).

15.2.1 The Role of Methodology

☛ *Issue: What methodology should my organization be using in an automated development environment?*

Methodology gurus have debated (more or less endlessly) about the proper balance between a process orientation and a data orientation, between a system view and an organization view, between functional decomposition and architectural analysis, and now between modular programming and object programming. The bottom line is that most *good* analysts, designers, and programmers use a variety of methods, drawing bits and pieces from here and there, based on what works in their particular environment. The state of the practice is that very few organizations follow any *single* methodology consistently, but that is not necessarily bad. It is more important to follow *some* methodology (e.g. one that has been synthesized from several others) consistently and reliably than to follow any specific method half-heartedly.

The emergence of automated tool sets as an aid to system development and maintenance has served to emphasize this last point. Some tools support specific methods or methodologies. Others are more general and support a wide range of techniques, each of which is used in each of several methodologies (generally with slight variations).

For example, the concept of data modeling appears in most design methodologies (Figure II.33). It is the core of both information engineering and object-oriented design and is also used in most structured design methods. The symbols used may be a little different but the key concept, to create a model of the data, is the same. You ought to be doing data modeling, at a variety of levels (organizational, operational, decision support, individual applications, etc.), regardless of whether you have an ADE or not. CASE tools can help, but your staff should be trained in and using this technique anyway.

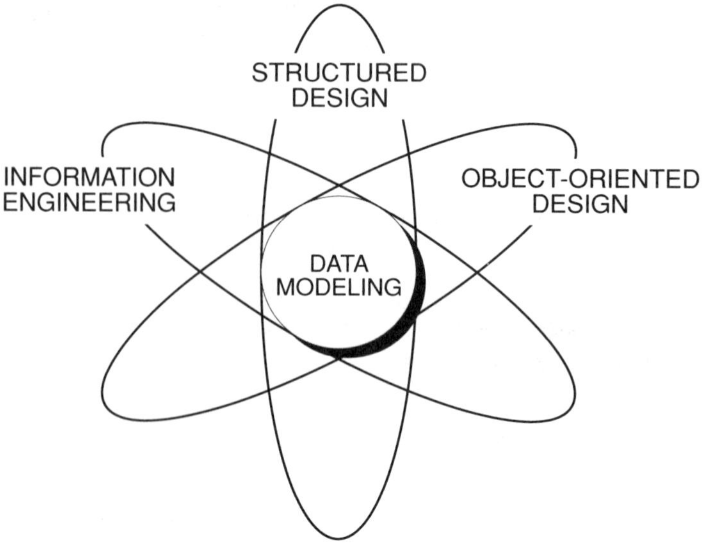

Figure II.33 Use of Data Modeling in Multiple Methodologies

Many other techniques have been developed for creating logical and physical system models and designs. Not all are useful in every situation. State transition diagrams, widely used in the development of real-time systems, are used in only a fraction of information system projects. They may be the perfect method for portraying the "state" of a person moving through the admissions process at a university or of an individual's overdue accounts being processed by a collection system, but have less relevance to tracking the flow of an accounting transaction through a general ledger system. Data flow diagrams may provide more information in this latter case, although they are wholly inadequate for specifying other classes of systems.

Having a wide variety of methods and techniques at your disposal is the best way of ensuring successful system development. "At your disposal" means that they have been codified (into a "methodology"), that your staff is trained in them, that there is some method of ensuring that they are used, and that your ADE supports them.

15.2.2 Are the Right Tools Available?

CASE/ADE is a dynamically changing field. In any six month period, at least a dozen tool vendors will introduce (or at least announce) new products, another dozen will come out with new releases, and probably another dozen will merge, consolidate, or go out of business. Answering the question as to whether the "right" tools are available in this type of atmosphere is difficult at best.

The short answer is that there are many tools available which, when used effectively, will result in improvements in your development and maintenance processes. It is also true that no specific tool would necessarily be universally accepted as the right tool for all situations. In particular, there are tools which will aid the designer in designing CUA and cooperative processing applications, the programmer in programming them, and the maintainer in maintaining them. It will be several years before tool vendors and users will have enough experience with these SAA development tools, however, to say what features the "right" tool should have.

The pragmatic view of introducing CASE (which I fully subscribe to) is that trying to select the right tool or the best tool may not be as useful as trying to use any tool; that ADEs will require some specialized tools or interfaces (read: "home-grown") for a long time into the future; and that, in general, using automated tools is generally better than not using them. Methodologies and tools: use them.

15.3 Role of the Repository

☛ *Issue: Do I need a central repository in the application development environment?*

Every development project creates a "repository," a place where the information generated during the project is stored. Pre-CASE, the repository was scattered over several media, with system designs in paper form, source code in on-line libraries, and operational information either on-line or on paper. With current technology, it is possible to have an automated repository as the focal point of your ADE. Even if some system information is stored separately, e.g. source code in a source code library system, the repository can be used to control access to that information as well. Ideally, a single repository can store information about all the projects and systems in an organization.

A common repository provides a number of obvious benefits:

- improved control over design and development information as it is being created;

- improved control over such information as it changes over time, as systems are maintained and upgraded;

- improved ability for automated tools to access such information using a common mechanism, i.e., a repository programming interface;

- improved ability for tools to work in tandem knowing that certain types of data will always be available in a common form (the "information model" of the repository);

Figure II.34 indicates how this might work. A CASE tool deals only with the repository manager software. It requests information from the repository and provides information to be entered into it. The repository manager determines (based on its own information model) where that data should reside, in the repository database directly or in some other place, such as a source or object library, and what the relationships are between that data and other data already present. All control and access information is kept in the main repository itself. The CASE tool also keeps some information stored locally for short periods of time to improve processing efficiency.

From another point of view, the central repository functions as a "library" for different CASE tools. Each tool puts some data in the repository in a commonly understood form. Other tools that need that data "check it out" for a period of time. They either modify that data or add additional data to the repository. In this way, tools that assist in performing different functions during the systems life cycle can draw upon the work developed by other tools operating in earlier phases. If the repository manager is sophisticated enough, tools can be notified or "triggered" when data of interest to them changes. For example, a consistency-checking program could be triggered automatically when changes are made to a system's data model. Figure II.35 depicts this "repository-based CASE" (R-CASE) concept.

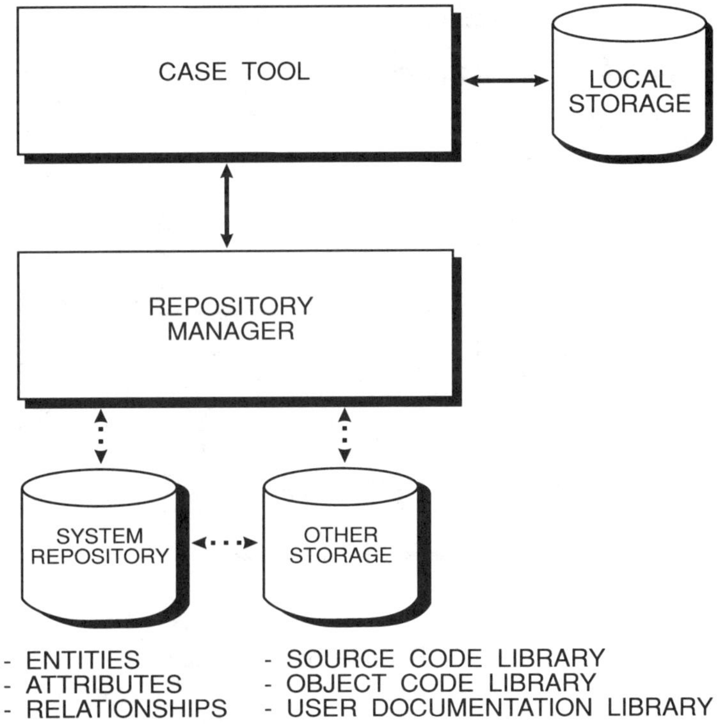

Figure II.34 Repository Management Concept

The repository is a common framework upon which tool developers can build a solution to the problem of providing integrated CASE environments -- and it provides more comprehensive facilities for doing this than have been seen so far. With a repository, tool developers will have better ways to sort out who has checked out which data, and why. With a repository, tool users will be able to establish procedures and standards for using CASE across large project teams. They will both need a "repository coordinator" (human being) to ensure that the integrity of the central repository is maintained. Database Administrators may have felt that their jobs were being distributed along with the distribution of CASE tools. What they may not have realized was that an expanded job was in the process of being created.

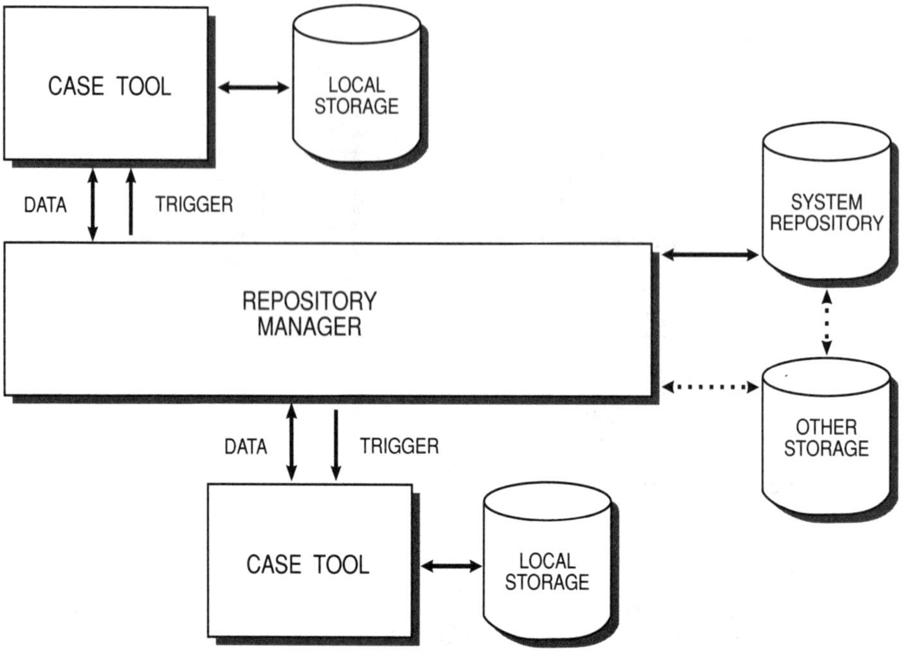

Figure II.34 Repository-based ADE

15.3.1 IBM's Repository

IBM's role in the marketplace guarantees that the IBM repository system (the Repository Manager, its associated information model, and other services) will have a significant role in ADEs of major organizations. By introducing Repository Manager/MVS, IBM has opened the door for repository-based ADEs. Using Repository Manager, various tools will communicate with each other via data stored in the repository. Prior to this, individual CASE tool vendors made "bilateral agreements" to establish an interface between their products. These arrangements are important, since it will be several years before the majority of tools include the capability to interface with Repository Manager.

Even then, there are significant questions about the workability of a "common information model." Will it really be possible for any CASE tool looking for, say, data model information to assume that it exists in a common form, regardless of which other CASE tool created it? The current state of the CASE market would indicate that this kind of transferability of information is a very long way off. The intense desire of many users of CASE tools, particularly in larger organizations, not to have to deal with existing incompatibility problems may force a quicker solution than would otherwise be forthcoming.

15.3.2 The Repository Is a Distributed Database

The Repository Manager has been announced in an MVS environment with VM and OS/400 versions to follow. The AD/Cycle announcement says that it is IBM's intention

> *to provide remote access [to the repository] from the Operating System/2 Extended Edition environment.*

In other words, much of the work of system development will be performed on the workstation using workstation-based tools, but the central repository for the development data will be on a host system. The process of system development will itself be a distributed process and its databases will also be distributed.

Creating a central repository does not in and of itself remove the need for local storage of information by individual CASE tools (as in Figures II.33 and 34). The implication, however, is that the problems of sharing information among many people working on the same project will not be immediately solved by the presence of IBM's (or anybody else's) central repository. The central repository will be just that: a central place to store information on a more or less permanent basis, as distinguished from local repositories which will exist on individual workstations (or LAN servers) for the convenience of staff members working on their particular tasks.

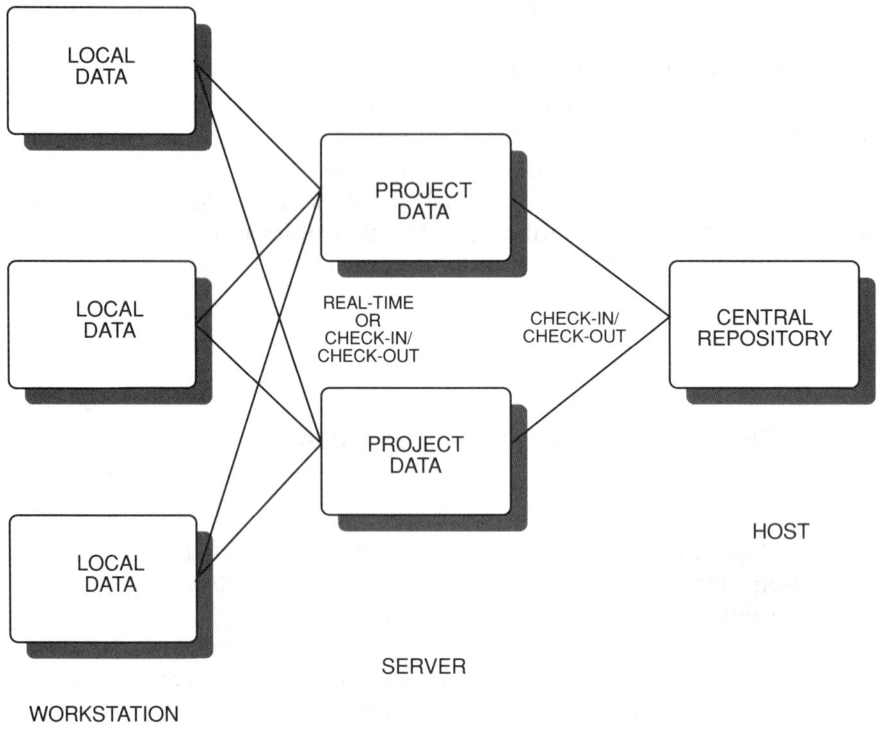

Figure II.35 Distributed Repository

The overall concept is that local repositories will act as a kind of "slow cache" for information checked out from the central repository. Designers and developers will ask for the information they need to perform a set of tasks (say a data flow diagram and the associated process and data flow descriptions), work on them for a period of time (maybe an hour, perhaps as much as a day), and then return the updated information to the central repository. Figure II.36 shows one possible multi-level (including a project level) set of repositories. The CASE tools, referencing repository data via Repository Manager APIs, will have to deal with the access and data integrity control enforced by the Repository Manager.

Could the central repository, which is implemented in DB2, directly handle the day-to-day access needs of multiple project team members? Not if they were working with the highly interactive design tools included in AD/Cycle. These tools (Index Technology's Excelerator, Knowledgeware's Information Engineering Workbench, and Bachman's Re-engineering Toolset) require high-speed (sub-second) access to large numbers of entities in the design database to provide the level of interaction demanded by analysts and designers. A typical design diagram and related repository entries (data flow or data model) might contain as much as 50 Kb of data. There is currently no way to provide an effective response from a host database to such a workstation request, given the amount of data to be moved, the number of relationships to be checked, and the associated processing to be performed. Someday, perhaps, the Repository Manager will operate in an environment and use a database manager capable of totally replacing each CASE tool's workstation-based data, but not for now.

15.3.3 The Repository in Configuration Management

One of the problems facing application designers and developers is how to keep track of changes. Each portion of the design will go through many revisions before the application is turned over to the developers -- and some design information will be revised even further before the system finally goes live. To ensure the integrity of the design, you must keep track of revisions individually and collectively, and carefully monitor the impact of a change to one part of the design on another. An obvious example is when a change to the number of digits in an organization code causes a redesign of screens and reports that use it and of programs that manipulate it. Keeping everything in sync is called "configuration management." Source code, object code, and test data must also be "configuration managed" to ensure that all the pieces of the application work together.

Repository Manager provides many functions needed for configuration management, but cannot by itself be called a configuration management system. Its expandable Information Model allow you to create any entities, attributes, or relationships that will assist in the configuration management process; for example, audit trail entities to be attached to different parts of your application design. Its "policies" and "object methods" allow you to create any number of integrity controls; for example, "if entity A is changed, then all entities directly related to entity A must also be changed." Its provision for multiple logical views into the same data allows you to create "versions" of a design that include different revisions of different entities. But the general burden is on you (the tool builder or user) to create the configuration management constraints. Perhaps some enterprising tool builder will come up with a standard set of policies, methods, and views that can be grafted on to any user's repository Information Model to add full configuration management.

15.3.3.1 The Source Code Library Manager

Configuration management for source code is handled by the Library Services component of AD/Cycle which is implemented by the Source Code Library Manager (SCLM) of the mainframe ISPF/PDF product. SCLM provides true configuration management services, facilitating the creation of and automatic access to multiple versions of an application system. For example, multiple test versions of a system can be accessed simultaneously, each incorporating certain new modules with the production version of others. Testers would have their own views into the source code libraries based on a "version hierarchy model" determined in advance (and stored by the SCLM).

With the Workstation Platform for OS/2 feature, tool builders and users get access to host-based libraries in a cooperative processing mode. Since this feature was first delivered in the spring of 1990, it is too early to tell whether it completely solves the problem of source code configuration management across PCs and host-based development environments.

15.3.3.2 VM/Software Engineering

VM/Software Engineering (VM/SE) is an IBM "Program Offering" (developed by IBM in conjunction with others) which provides configuration management services to software developers. It controls source, object, and documentation in a "central repository." Developers can define rules for accessing the repository and for creating "versions" and "releases" of software and documentation. These facilities should be of great benefit both to organizations internally and to ISVs.

VM/SE only operates in the VM environment and currently uses its own repository (not the one controlled by Repository Manager). It is a practical solution in the short term for VM users, but look to its eventual replacement by components of AD/Cycle.

15.3.4 Relation to the IRDS Standard

IBM's announcement of the Repository Manager has this to say about the American National Standard for an Information Resource Dictionary System:

> *While the Repository Manager/MVS product does not fully conform to the ANSI standard on Information Resource Dictionary Systems (X3.138-1989), it does provide most of the services and capabilities required for conformance to the standard... IBM is actively involved in the ANSI X3H4 committee which defines the Information Resource Dictionary System standard.*

As has sometimes been the case with other standards, IBM's version of the repository may do for the industry what no official but generally unimplemented standard can, namely, bring the idea of a common, centralized repository closer to reality. IBM has clearly been influenced by the work of the ANSI committee, and vice versa. As ANSI begins work on an expanded version of the IRDS standard, it ought to be possible for these two organizations to get their act together and bring the official and unofficial standards into convergence with each other, one way or another.

15.4 An Application Development Environment

15.4.1 An ADE Architecture

An application development environment consists of tools, methods, and databases (the repository).

At one level, Figure II.35 portrays an ADE architecture. The repository provides storage for design and development data and the repository manager provides access to that data for the various CASE tools in the environment. Figure II.37 adds one more dimension, depicting the different components of the systems life cycle for which tools are available. Within each component, there may be as many as a dozen or more individual "tools" or functions, although many of these will be packaged into a single product. This may seem like an enormous number of tools for a system developer to learn (50 to 100 is a reasonable estimate for a fairly complete ADE), but it does represent the range of tasks that are performed in developing and maintaining systems.

In today's marketplace, you have to create your own ADE. Some vendors provide tools that cross life cycle phases, but no one produces a complete repository-based ADE as pictured. [This isn't too surprising, given that the cost of developing a full ADE has been estimated at over $100 million.] In the absence of commonly available tools interfacing with IBM's Repository Manager (or anybody else's for that matter), your ADE system diagram may look more like a bowl of spaghetti than the nice, neat picture of Figure II.37.

This is the reality of ADE today. As application developers and tool users, we can only hope that (and apply pressure on) the tool builders see the light and latch onto standard interfaces and information models. Maybe the next edition of this book will be able to report that integrated ADEs can be created directly from commercially available building blocks.

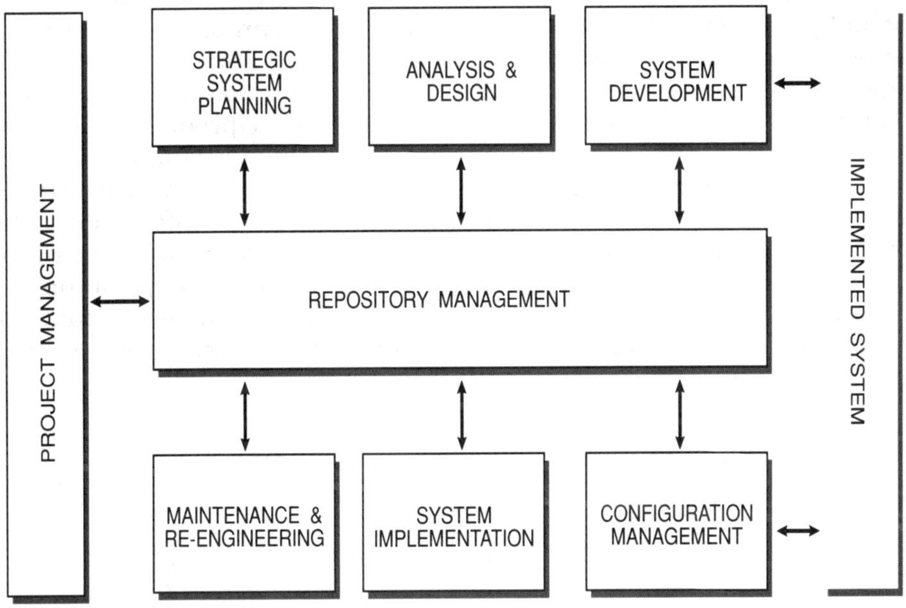

Figure II.37 Repository-based ADE Architecture

15.4.2 Where Do You Do Development?

☛ *Issue: Do I have to develop a system in the same operating environment as it is targeted to operate?*

For most of the history of data processing, the conventional wisdom was that you should develop a system using the same hardware and operating system as that system was targeted to run on. In other words, the development environment and the target environment should be the same. This encouraged tool builders to stick to one environment, creating some very effective and now widely used products. This was particularly true in the mini-computer world, which was always oriented to on-line development activity (look at the tools used in typical VAX, HP-3000, and AS/400 shops versus those used in S/370 shops). For totally different reasons (although both related to hardware limitations), very few tools for development of large micro-computer applications are available in the PC environment, and tools for development of mainframe applications in the mainframe environment can at best be called primitive.

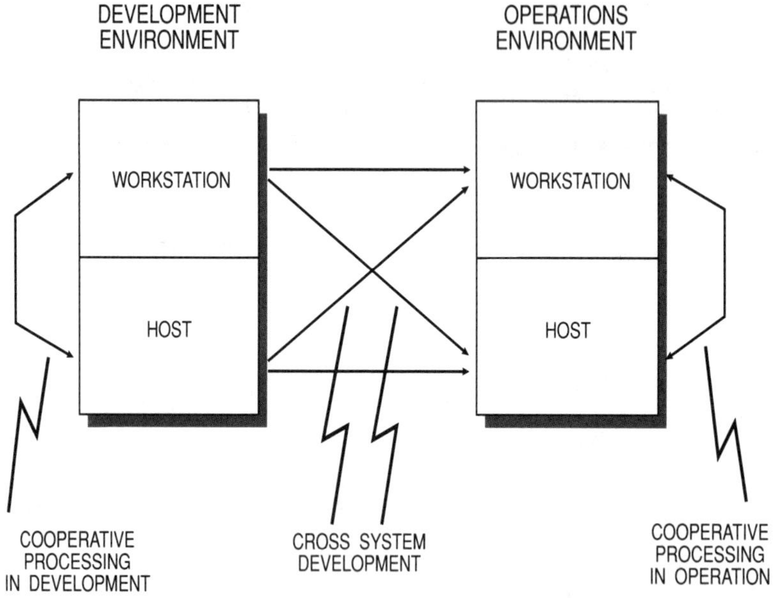

Figure II.38 Development vs. Target Operating Environments

What was (and is) needed was a way to develop tools on whatever platform or operating environment was best suited for those tools and to target the resulting system to whatever platform or operating environment was best suited for the system, as Figure II.38 shows. This concept applies to development and operation on different computers as well as on different DBMSs, teleprocessing monitors, or operating systems. [It is interesting to note that most real-time systems are developed in this way. Real-time computers are just not suited for application development.]

Several vendors, including IBM, developed application generators that allow you to develop (design, code, generate) in an on-line environment, say VM/CMS, and target operation to CICS/VSAM or IMS DM/TM. When MicroFocus came out with its COBOL Workbench for the PC, developers could do all their coding and most of their testing in that environment and be (reasonably) assured that their applications would work when recompiled under COBOL on a mainframe. The age of cross-system development has arrived.

The key advantages to cross-system development relate to the availability of specific tools. If all tools (including a common repository) were available in all environments, the issue of where to develop would not be of such importance. At the moment, the better analysis, design, and planning tools exist on personal computers. Most of the popular application generators have development systems available on both PCs and mainframes, although typically their PC-based versions are more interactive and somewhat easier to use. [IBM's Cross System Product is no exception to this rule, with its PC-based application development component introduced in Version 3.3.] Testing tools are available on both PC and mainframe environments, with PC tools able to assist in debugging both PC and mainframe systems. So far, common repositories are all mainframe based. Figure II.39 (repeated from Chapter 7) shows one view of which phases can be performed on either mainframe or workstation or both, given current tool availability. [Don't infer, however, that all tools will ever be available in all environments; the hardware differences still exist.]

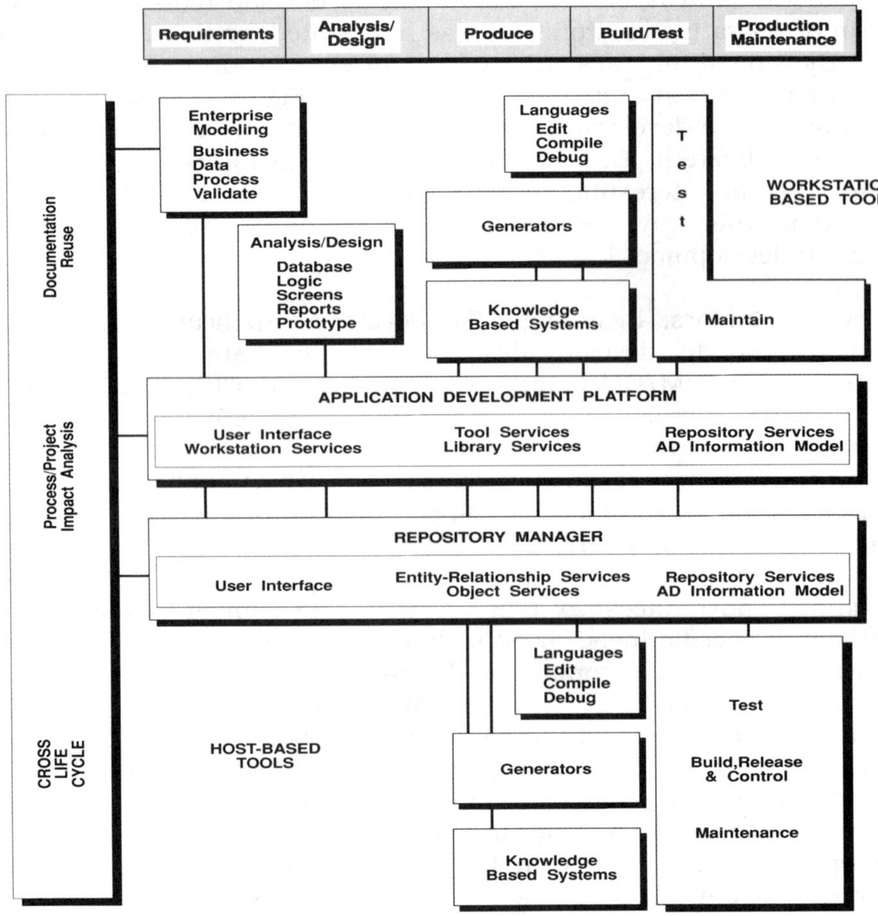

Figure II.39 AD/Cycle Application Development Environment

15.4.2.1 ASCII to EBCDIC and Back Again

One of the difficulties in cross system development is the difference in coding structures between PCs and IBM mainframes. These differences were discussed in the section on Database Design for Portability. Exactly the same issues exist for programs which are going to manipulate that data. Coding issues, sort sequences, accuracy, etc. are all related to the coding structure used on a particular computer. Some cross-system development tools provide a "transparency" feature while others leave it up to you.

15.4.3 Selecting Your Tools

☛ *Issue: What types of tools do I need in an ADE?*

One of the questions to deal with in creating an application development environment is what type and how many tools to include. If you needed a different tool for each task we have to perform, you would be in a lot of trouble. Depending on the level of detail provided in a life cycle task list, there can be anywhere from 50 to 500 individually differentiated tasks. Luckily, many tasks often relate to the same development function (there may be as many as 20 tasks related to database design) and can be performed using the same tool. You want to make sure, however, that you have a sufficient number of tools to help with most tasks in most phases.

There are several ways of analyzing what tools do and where they are applicable. These are by life cycle phase, by design/development entity dealt with, and by function.

Function	Life Cycle Phase
Enterprise Modeling	Requirements
Analysis/Design	Requirements, Analysis/Design
Languages	Produce, Build/Test
Generators	Produce, Build/Test
Knowledge Based Systems	Produce, Build/Test
Test, Build, Release, Control, Maintenance	Build/Test, Production Maintenance
Process/Project Impact Analysis, Documentation, Reuse	Cross-life Cycle

Figure II.40 AD/Cycle Tools Classification Matrix

IBM, in its AD/Cycle announcements lists tools according to the phase of the life cycle and the overall function supplied by the tool (see Figure II.39). It portrays the tools in AD/Cycle as performing a certain function in a certain life cycle phase (see list in Figure II.40). While these are not necessarily the phase names or functions you might use, the idea of classifying tools by the life cycle phase and function is a good one. It allows you to see if you have tools appropriate to each phase and if some tools are used in several phases.

There are, of course, other ways to classify the different tools you need. For example, there are tasks in every phase of the life cycle relating to the analysis and design of the system databases. Similarly, there are tasks relating to modeling, designing, and building the processes that the system performs. Data and processes are two of the fundamental things, or "entities," you work with in developing systems. One classification of tools is, therefore, according to the entities they deal with. See if you have tools which deal with each of the following six broad entity types:

- Data
- Processes
- Screens and reports
- Procedures
- Tests
- Documentation

In analyzing the types of tools you need, look both at the phases of the life cycle and entities you are dealing with. In most cases, the work you perform in one phase builds on the work performed in an earlier phase. Often, the tools you use are the same, but you use different features, or you go back and modify or add to the entities created in an earlier phase.

In other words, do you have data modeling tools (graphics and dictionary), process design tools, screen generation tools, procedure building tools (procedures languages), test verification tools, documentation production tools, etc.? For each tool in your application development environment, specify its use by life cycle phase, design/development entity worked with, and function performed. Figure II.41 shows the three lists you can use for this purpose.

Life cycle phase	Entity Class	Function
System Concept (objectives, requirements, analysis, system model)	*Data*	*Text editing*
	Processes	*Graphics editing*
General design (user design, logical data model, application architecture)	*Screens and Reports*	*Dictionary*
	Procedures (manual and automated)	*Matrix manipulation*
Detailed design (physical data model program specifications)	*Tests*	*Automated analysis*
	Documentation	*Programming*
Development (programming, testing)		*Code generation*
System Implementation (installation, conversion, training)		*Testing*
		Debugging
Post-implementation Support (enhancement, modification, maintenance)		*Configuration management*
		Project management

Figure II.41 Tools Classification Criteria

15.4.3.1 AD/Cycle Tools to Implement SAA

AD/Cycle includes tools developed by IBM and by some of its business partners. All of these software packages provide capabilities useful in accomplishing some tasks in the systems life cycle. Some needed capabilities are missing, however, forcing you to bring non-AD/Cycle tools into your ADE. [You may also want to use alternative packages for some of the functions provided by AD/Cycle tools, but that is a matter of choice, not necessity.] It is not the purpose of this book to review the field of CASE tools (which would be impossible anyway -- it changes too rapidly to be done in a book), but rather to discuss how they help implement SAA. CASE tools that integrate with AD/Cycle and the repository are necessary, but not necessarily sufficient, for automating the full range of tasks to be performed in implementing SAA-compliant systems.

Implementing SAA means following CUA, architecting for distributed and cooperative processing, and using the CPI. These three criteria can be added as a fourth column in Figure II.41 to help in evaluating the completeness of your ADE. Figure II.42 shows the classification of the current components of AD/Cycle. Your job in creating a complete ADE is to find tools which supply the missing functions for the indicated entity groups for all the life cycle phases for your SAA implementation needs. That is also IBM's job, either by developing tools themselves or by encouraging CASE software tool vendors to do it for them.

Life Cycle Phases **AD/Cycle Tools and Classification Criteria**	SC	GD	DD	Dv	SI	PI
■ Application Development Productivity System Entities: all Function: project management SAA: N.A.	✓	✓	✓	✓	✓	✓
■ Source Code Library Manager Entities: code Function: configuration management SAA: N.A.				✓	✓	✓
■ IEW/Planning Entities: data, processes Function: text editing, graphics editing, dictionary, matrix manipulation, automated analysis SAA: distributed processing	✓	✓				
■ DevelopMate Entities: data, processes Function: automated analysis SAA: N.A.	✓	✓				

[CONTINUED] **Life Cycle Phases** **AD/Cycle Tools and Classification Criteria**	SC	GD	DD	Dv	SI	PI
■ PC Prism Entities: data, processes Function: dictionary, matrix manipulation, automated analysis SAA: distributed processing	✓	✓				
■ IEW/Analysis Entities: data, processes, screens and reports, procedures Function: text editing, graphics editing, dictionary, automated analysis SAA: distributed processing		✓	✓			
■ Excelerator Entities: data, processes, screens and reports, procedures Function: text editing, graphics editing, dictionary, automated analysis SAA: distributed processing		✓	✓			
■ Re-engineering Product Set Entities: data Function: graphics editing, dictionary, automated analysis, code generation SAA: CPI (database)		✓	✓	✓		
■ Cross System Product Entities: data, processes, screens, reports Functions: programming, code generation, testing, debugging SAA: CPI (application generator)			✓	✓		✓

SC = System Concept
GD = General Design
DD = Detailed Design
Dv = Development
SI = System Implementation
PI = Post-implementation Support

[CONTINUED] **Life Cycle Phases** **AD/Cycle Tools and Classification Criteria**	SC	GD	DD	Dv	SI	PI
■ Easel Entities: processes, screens Functions: programming, code generation SAA: CUA, distributed processing			✓	✓		✓
■ Synon/2E Entities: data, processes, screens, reports Functions: programming, code generation, testing, debugging SAA: CUA			✓	✓		✓
■ Third generation language compilers Entities: data, processes, screens, reports Functions: programming SAA: CPI (languages)				✓	✓	
■ The Integrated Reasoning Shell Entities: data, processes Functions: code generation SAA: [none]			✓	✓		✓
■ Workstation Interactive Test Tool Entities: processes, screens, reports Functions: testing SAA: CPI				✓		✓
■ Software Analysis Test Tool Entities: processes Functions: testing, debugging SAA: CPI (PL/I)				✓		✓
■ Structuring Facility Entities: processes Functions: re-engineering SAA: CPI (COBOL)						✓

Figure II.42 AD/Cycle Tools

16. Education and Training

"Is that a bus?" "No, dad, it's a cow bell."
Rebecca Miriam Grochow, Age 10, in conversation with the author

The true nature of a thing is not always obvious. A key purpose of an SAA education program is to make the concepts and strategies of SAA understood at all levels in the organization. The managers and executives who will approve the hardware and software budgets require as much grounding in these ideas as the programmers who will be working with SAA's myriad standards and implementing software products. These too have to be taught, but it is in teaching the concepts that you will create lasting understanding of the true nature of SAA.

16.1 Issue Locator

16.2 SAA Education As an Ongoing Process

The key to implementing SAA is education, and a lot of it. Users and developers alike need to understand how systems and procedures will change with the introduction of SAA compliant systems. They need to understand the changes that will take place in the development cycle and their respective roles in it. If they are to accept these changes, they need to understand the benefits that SAA will provide both to your organization and to each individual in it. This is not a "one shot" seminar -- education in SAA will be an ongoing process.

Training will take many forms, from classroom courses to workshops to self-paced tutorials. Based on the SAA Statement of Direction for your organization, you can decide on the appropriate topics for both general and detailed training sessions. There is so much material to be covered that an entire curriculum can be developed, with basic, mid-level, and advanced sequences. Different courses and tutorials will also be necessary to address the needs of different audiences, from senior management to users to system developers. Since SAA will be changing over time, materials will have to be revised to keep up with the latest information.

During the early stages of implementing SAA, training for most people will focus on overall concepts. Those few systems people involved in early development work will need special training in the particular tools and methods they will be using. As SAA becomes more a part of the day-to-day environment, training needs will also become more routine, with users and developers needing refreshers and updates.

Throughout the process of instilling the SAA approach in your information systems and user departments, there will be an important role for a direct support organization. In some shops, the required "hand holding" will be supplied by the Development Center (to developers) and the Information Center (to users). In other shops, a special unit (with highly trained experts) will be more appropriate. Either way, the people providing this kind of one-on-one support and problem solving will need a special level of education, training, and experience.

16.3 Developing a Common Curriculum

☛ *Issue: What courses are needed to train IS staff in SAA concepts and implementation?*

☛ *Issue: What courses are needed to train user staff in SAA concepts and implementation?*

Developing a curriculum for SAA should follow a fairly standard approach. You must begin by identifying the types of people to be trained and classifying their training needs. Figure II.43 is a first cut at this process. It identifies six categories of staff, from senior management to programmers to users. It divides their training needs two ways:

- Overview versus detailed information.

- Concepts (e.g. CUA) versus standards (e.g. CUA rules for the Graphical Model) versus specific implementing product (e.g. PM or Easel).

SAA Training Matrix	**Concepts**	**Standards**	**Products**
Senior Management	O		
Information Systems Management	D	O	O
Technical Specialists	D	D	D
Design Staff	D	D	O
Programming Staff	D	D	D
Users	O		
O = Overview; D = Details			

Figure II.43 Curriculum Planning Matrix

This chart can be used as the starting point for analysis of your organization's training needs.

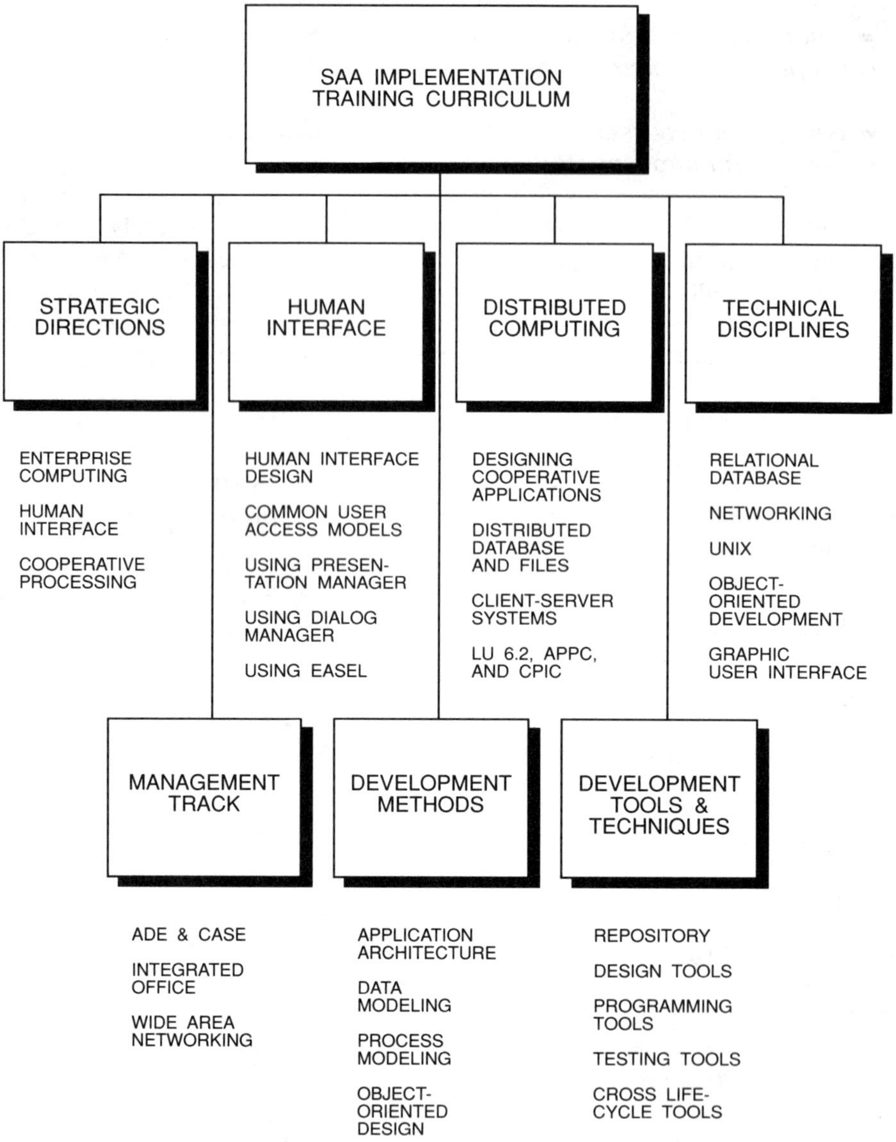

Figure II.44 SAA Training Curriculum

Figure II.44 shows the courses you might offer. Each title represents a possible course. Courses are grouped by subject area (i.e., Strategic Directions, Human Interface, etc.). Depending on the size and needs of your organization, some of the individual "courses" might be treated as mini-courses, perhaps only single lectures or portions of a day in a larger course covering the entire subject area.

In creating your curriculum, some courses should be "required" and some optional. The required courses will vary significantly depending on the approach you are taking to SAA implementation. If you are diving into cooperative processing and graphical user interfaces via direct implementation of LU6.2 communications and CUA, courses in APPC or CPIC and in Presentation Manager will be necessary. If you are approaching these areas via the facilities provided in enabling software or CASE tools, then courses in distributed relational database products, Easel, or Dialog Manager will be more appropriate. The specification of the training curriculum must follow the specification of the SAA implementation plan or you might be spending a lot of time learning the details of topics of marginal direct value.

Some of the courses in your curriculum will be available from IBM. There are also several major training and consulting organizations offering similar subjects. Given the relatively short time that these topics have been addressed, you should be sure to investigate the credentials of your training supplier very carefully.

16.4 SAA Publications

As the References section of this book shows, most of the literature on SAA comes from IBM. Many of the manuals listed provide an excellent overview of a topic area and can be used as a prerequisite for more formal training. There are also many product-specific manuals that form a reference library for the programming staff. [The References section is generally limited to manuals targeted to a broader audience. Any manual with the words "general information" in its title is a basic overview of its subject.] Most of these are available with a subscription service which automatically provides you with updates as they are published.

For the serious student, there are many general reference materials on concepts relevant to SAA implementation. These range from books on human-interface design to C coding techniques. There are literally hundreds of books that will provide some information useful to your SAA implementation project. The References section only listed a few of these.

In a rapidly advancing field such as this, you must also give significant time to reviewing periodicals for articles of interest. Two in particular, *BYTE Magazine* and the *IBM Systems Journal*, often have articles covering the major conceptual underpinning of SAA as well as (in the case of *BYTE*) timely product information. Key issues of these journals are listed in the References. [The *IBM Personal Systems Developer* is also excellent; it is available on a limited basis through IBM.]

Finally, someone has to keep up to date on IBM product announcements. In addition to one or two big splashes every year (such as the ones for OfficeVision and AD/Cycle), IBM is always announcing SAA enabling products, or discussing how new releases of old products implement SAA compliance. These announcements are an excellent source of information and will help you to keep your training curriculum up to date.

16.5 SAA Support Organization

☛ *Issue: Is an ongoing support function necessary?*

In addition to providing training and publications on SAA, you will have to actively support those of your staff actually implementing SAA applications. The combination of your Development Center and Information Center (or similar organizations) has to become the focal point for expertise. Developers and users need someone to talk to (quickly) about their questions and problems and these groups must provide that someone. The questions they will have to deal with range from very high level issues (what distributed processing strategy is best for a particular application?) to very detailed ones (why doesn't a particular PM function call do what I think it is supposed to?). In some cases, your Development Center and Information Center staff will only be acting as a referral service to other experts in the organization (or in IBM or an outside consultant).

Regardless of who actually does the work, experience has shown time and again the importance of having a clearly identified support organization with responsibility for introducing new technology. And SAA is definitely "new technology."

17. What About the Future?

The magic robot had something electric in its hand...
Joshua Abraham Grochow, Age 5, unpublished essay

Whether the evolution of SAA follows an orderly course or involves some form of magical transformation remains to be seen. What is clear is that it will continue to evolve, to follow emerging standards, to add functionality, to provide more sophisticated system interfaces for developers and users.

17.1 Filling in the Holes

The Systems Application Architecture framework has holes. In some cases, the holes result from IBM's "don't include it until you can provide it in all appropriate environments" policy. In other cases, the holes are there because IBM's design teams were unable to agree on what strategy to follow in some area or other -- so they put those areas aside. And in some cases, the holes were not obvious at all -- someone had to start using SAA before they could see what was missing. [This section deals with "architectural holes." Missing (unannounced or incomplete) enabling software does not constitute a hole in the architectural strategy, although it may result in one for your implementation strategy.]

By tracing back to the basic goal of SAA, i.e., to develop a set of standards and interfaces for application development in an enterprise environment, you can begin to find some of the missing pieces. Many of these will undoubtedly be filled in as SAA evolves over the next several years.

17.1.1 Common User Access

Much of CUA is oriented to the creation of "office" software. For obvious reasons, the designers of IBM's first SAA-compliant product, OfficeVision, must have worked closely with CUA's designers and provided significant input to its contents. There is nothing wrong with this, but one way to "fill in the holes" is to expand CUA's models to deal with broader classes of applications. [Whether this needs to be done will be debated by CUA designers who believe that the current CUA is more universally applicable; major portions of it are -- but that shouldn't stop its expansion in areas where it isn't.]

As the enterprise moves into a cooperative processing environment, PWS user interfaces will front-end many of the mainframe applications accessed today from 3270s. These applications span a very wide range, including high volume data entry, database inquiry, decision support, customer service, order entry, accounting, engineering, etc. Some of these types of applications are not suited to the "pull-down -- pop-up" format that characterizes the advanced CUA models and are not improved significantly by the basic CUA models. Can you imagine what would happen to the airline reservation business if a reservation operator had to use a mouse to select and reposition windows on the computer screen to answer your questions about schedules, fare, and availability? Using the fastest PS/2 available, operations would grind to a halt. CUA designers will have to look at these and many other types of applications to satisfy the demand for comprehensive user access standards in the future.

And while we are on the subject of mice: there must be some better way to gain the flexibility of "point and shoot" manipulation than having to allocate a square foot of desk space to a marginally usable rolling rodent that requires you to have better eye-hand coordination than a tennis pro. With today's emphasis on productivity, I am sure we will see a significant improvement in CUA's approach to command input and graphic manipulation.

And, of course, CUA has to be expanded to deal with the presentation of images, voice, and even interactive video. The hardware is here to display (or play) information in all these modes; so is some of the software. Now we need the standards, before applications lose their common look and feel all over again.

17.1.2 Common Programming Interface

The CPI specifies six languages and seven services. This is too few by a factor of two. Languages were picked for the CPI because they were already in wide use (if not on one platform, then on another; if not in the United States, then elsewhere in the world). CPI service elements were identified to provide standard interfaces to specific operating system and enabling software. The CPI of the future should lay out a general framework for programming interfaces across a broad spectrum, regardless of current usage. IBM could then make a commitment to create them over a longer period of time. This approach would provide the IS community with a much better idea of the long term goals of the CPI architecture.

In the language area, artificial intelligence and object-oriented constructs are becoming increasingly important. The AD/Cycle framework already hints at the addition of artificial intelligence languages ("fifth generation") to SAA. Object orientation is a major theme of both OS/2 Presentation Manager programming and the Repository Interface. Articles in the computer press have quoted "reliable sources" as developing CPI elements for both C++ and Smalltalk, two object-oriented languages. Common languages in both object-oriented and artificial intelligence programming will be needed to meet the needs of future system developers.

Just adding more languages to the CPI, however, is not the only way to make the CPI more useful. There are hundreds of "problem specific" languages in use today and there is no reason to believe that number will decrease -- nor is there reason to add them to the CPI. What is really needed is a CPI specification for linking programs together, regardless of the language they are written in. A "universal procedure call" would significantly expand our ability to provide compatible systems in a broad range of problem areas. And what could be a more appropriate part of the "common" programming interface?

A procedure call specification should also allow access to remote procedures. IBM has announced that it will begin to include the technology from the OSF Distributed Computing Environment in SAA to provide the functions necessary for full "remote procedure call." This should include a capability for standardizing the "registration" of applications and databases with the network (so that system software can provide transparent access to them), and, for that matter, the registration and management of anything (person, hardware device, or software) over a wide-area network. [This use of OSF specifications will also bring SAA and the UNIX world even closer together.] Sitting on top of an expanded list of Common Communications Support protocols, a remote procedure call mechanism in SAA will begin to provide a "single-system image" for applications developers as well as for application users.

In the services area, the CPI could be expanded to provide facilities for screen definition (the Dialog Tag Language only handles text screens), report definition, and database definition (any kind, not just relational). It could add (and, therefore, make "common") services that programmers are always creating over again, services such as application security control (beyond that provided by the operating system and its extensions), user error notification, and data entry and correction.

There is a lot more to programming than just the procedure division, and the CPI cannot begin and end at the level of system subroutines. If we really want to achieve "any to any" connectivity in applications and systems (any language. any operating system, any hardware), the CPI has to expand in a variety of ways.

17.1.2.1 Non-relational Databases

The Database Interface deserves a separate comment. Reading the SAA CPI, you would think that there is only one kind of database -- relational. In spite of IBM's best efforts (as well as those of a number of smaller companies), relational databases do not hold the majority of the world's data and are unlikely to do so in the near future, if ever. [The relational approach may even be superseded by object-oriented databases, perhaps resting on a variety of data access mechanisms.]

The database element of the CPI should include specifications for "any-to-any" interfacing among databases. Any-to-any interfacing means that a database call made by an application should be satisfied wherever that data resides on the network, and in whatever form it may reside in.

Any-to-any access in the relational world is clearly in IBM's plans. Recent announcements of DB2 and OS/2 Database Manager capabilities indicate that, although it may be several releases of these and other products before full cross-system relational database access becomes a reality. Now the CPI should be updated to provide the necessary services (e.g. transparent directory services across the different database management systems).

The CPI could be taken even further. Data stored in other types of databases and files could be made more generally accessible. Why do we have to program different calls to deal with direct access files, indexed files (e.g. VSAM), hierarchical databases (e.g. DL/I), and relational database access (i.e., SQL)? What we need is some way to ask for data that is independent of the storage mechanism. This will require a "higher level" interface than is provided by current APIs. By expanding the CPI to move the physical aspects of the access to an even lower level, it will be easier to produce consistent, portable, distributed applications.

17.1.3 Common Communications Support

Communications media and protocols are continuing their very rapid evolution. Higher speed networks operating over fiber optic cables will use the Fiber Distributed Data Interface (FDDI) protocols. Wide-area networks will begin to use the Integrated Services Digital Network provided by telephone companies. OSI protocols will find their way into more and more networks. All the while, the venerable Ethernet and TCP/IP protocols will continue to be used -- and expanded.

If SAA is to make good on its promise of "what should be common, will be common," then CCS will be in for significant expansion as well.

17.1.4 Environments

The big debate about SAA environments at the current time is over the "ins" and the "outs." The definition of an "SAA environment" has to do with IBM's long term commitment to implement in each environment not only the current definition of SAA, but new CPI elements as well. It is confusing, however, to say that an operating system is not an SAA environment *today*, even if most components of the CPI and CCS are implemented and if applications using them become indistinguishable from those developed for the official SAA platforms. These definitions need to be clarified.

The AIX/SAA distinction is also one that needs re-thinking. Digital's Application Integration Architecture and Network Applications Support is designed to create enterprise networks of computers running VMS, UNIX, and PC operating systems. The AIX/SAA interoperability strategy is also designed to allow similar enterprise networks, yet SAA and AIX are portrayed as being on separate tracks. This creates, rather than reduces, confusion. [One recent article reported a rumor that IBM will include Apple Macintosh machines in a future expansion of SAA -- I think I'll wait and see about that one.]

It is not that SAA needs to be expanded to include more operating environments. It is that the designations and categorizations need to be cleared up.

17.2 SAA and Open Systems

"Open systems" has quickly become an over-used industry buzzword. Under the most popular definitions of "open," SAA is closed. It was developed by IBM for IBM hardware with no review and approval other than from IBM employees and whomever they chose. In that sense, SAA *is* a closed architecture. However, IBM has already shown its interest in making SAA open, at least to the extent of widely publishing all the SAA standards, licensing the various protocols (such as LU6.2 and External Source Format), and, in general, encouraging software developers to use or at least coexist with SAA technology. The scope of IBM's customer and software developer councils and assistance programs also indicates a very strong interest in getting input from the users of its software.

Another aspect of openness is willingness to use national and international standards. IBM has always been a participant in standards-making bodies, but has often taken an "I'm going my way so you better follow me" attitude. This also is changing, as evidenced by the inclusion of ISO standards in SAA, and by IBM's acceptance of the OSF standards. In many ways, IBM is now more driven to comply with outside standards than are some of the smaller computer manufacturers.

SAA should remain open to remain vital. If IBM keeps on its present course, and resists the temptation to retreat into the security blanket of totally proprietary operating systems, it may have the most open systems of all.

17.3 Future Architectures

SAA does not define a complete application architecture. As the figures in Section 10.2 show, SAA barely scratches the surface of the "application tier" functions. One way that SAA can grow is by including interfaces for more and more application functions (a horizontal expansion of the CPI). This approach will eventually bog down as the expanding needs of different types of applications become more diverse. Another way to continue is to recognize differences in application function on an industry-by-industry basis and to add CPI elements for the specific types of applications seen in each industry (a vertical expansion of the CPI). There are indications that IBM is on both tracks, vertical and horizontal, and may be moving toward "industry-specific architectures" to complement SAA.

Industry-specific architectures would include not only new CPI services, but also data models for each industry (pre-loaded in the AD/Cycle Repository Manager, of course). One press report stated that IBM has identified 17 industry areas for this type of approach. If this approach succeeds, it may be that the application system of the future is no longer thought of in terms of source code and object code, but rather in terms of information models and application generators.

One possible architectural approach puts the emphasis on common ways of specifying the "high level design" for applications (in terms of data, process, and other types of models), and hiding the CPI in the internal workings of sophisticated application generators. The tools to implement this approach are not all that far away -- some independent software vendors are already beginning to follow this strategy. They deliver components of their applications in conjunction with CASE tools with pre-loaded dictionaries and specialized generators. They are, in effect, creating their own industry-specific application architectures -- but each one using a different implementation approach.

IBM has an opportunity to capitalize on the combined strategies of SAA and AD/Cycle to create the next generation of application architectures, i.e., fully populated repositories based on robust industry-specific information models. If IBM follows this path, it will be helping to change the definition of what constitutes an application system from "delivered code" to "delivered repository (and generated code)." Whether this is the next step for SAA remains to be seen.

17.4 Future Outlook

SAA has its share of skeptics and at least some of what they say is correct. There is no doubt that IBM had a healthy degree of self-interest in mind in formulating the SAA strategy. There is also no doubt that it has a long way to go in fully implementing that strategy. But regardless of the self-interest and not-yet-completed picture, isn't SAA exactly what we need? We certainly do not need incompatible hardware and software -- not if we are going to deliver the next generations of application solutions to solve our users' problems.

Standardization, compatibility, flexibility, interconnectivity, ease of use: these are the words and phrases heard over and over again in private and public forums. If SAA is IBM's best shot at delivering on these concepts, then we have to sit up and pay attention. If it is lacking, then we have to let IBM's people know directly, for it is these people who will eventually make the changes.

Throughout this book, I have attempted to provide as complete and accurate a picture of Systems Application Architecture as possible. The opinions and speculations are, of course, my own, but they are borne from the viewpoint of someone working in the midst of large-scale application development across a wide range of application areas, industries, and environments. One way or another, we have to live with and respond to Systems Application Architecture. So do you.

References

Books and Journals

Albrecht, A. J. and J.E. Gaffney, Jr., "Software Function, Source Lines of Code, and Development Effort Prediction: A Software Science Validation," *IEEE Transactions on Software Engineering*, Vol SE-9, No. 6, 1983.

American National Standards Institute, *American National Standard for Information Systems - Information Resource Dictionary System (IRDS)*, ANS X3.138-1988.

Apple Computer, *Human Interface Guidelines: the Apple Desktop Interface*, Addison Wesley, 1987.

Best, Laurence J., *Application Architecture*, John Wiley & Sons, 1990.

Black, Uyless, *Data Networks: Concepts, Theory, and Practice*, Prentice Hall, 1989.

Bouldin, Barbara, *Agents of Change*, Yourdon Press Computing Series, Prentice Hall, 1989.

BYTE Magazine, issue on object-oriented programming, Volume 11, Number 8, August 1986.

BYTE Magazine, issue on distributed processing and graphical user interfaces, Volume 14, Number 7, July 1989.

BYTE Magazine, issue on Applications Architectures, Volume 15, Number 4, April 1990.

Connect, The Journal of Computer Networking, special issue on client-server computing, 3Com Corporation, Volume 2, Number 4, 1989.

Dunfee, W.P., J.D. McGehe, R.C. Rauf, and K.O. Shipp, "Designing SAA applications and user interfaces," *IBM Systems Journal*, Vol. 27, No. 3, 1988.

Forman, F. and M. Hess, "Form Precedes Function," *Computerworld*, September 5, 1988.

Grady, Robert B. and Deborah L. Caswell, *Software Metrics: Establishing A Company-Wide Program*, Prentice Hall, Inc., 1987.

Hartson, H. Rex and Deborah Hix, "Human-Computer Interface Development: Concepts and Systems for Its Management," *ACM Computing Surveys*, Volume 21, Number 1, March 1989.

Hess, M., "Information Systems Design in Industrial Practice," *Concise Encyclopedia of Information Processing in Systems and Organizations*, A. P. Sage, Editor, Pergamon Press, 1990.

International Function Point Users Group, *Counting Practices Manual, Release 2.0*, 1988.

Jones, Capers, *Programming Productivity*, McGraw-Hill, 1986.

Killen, Michael, *IBM: The Making of the Common View*, Harcourt Brace Jovanovich, 1988.

Lorin, H., "Distributed Processing: An Assessment," *IBM Systems Journal*, Vol. 18, Number 4, 1979.

Loucks, L.K. and C.H. Sauer, "Advanced Interactive Executive (AIX) operating system overview," *IBM Systems Journal*, Vol 26, No 4, 1987.

Martin, James, and Kathleen Chapman, *SNA - IBM's Networking Solution*, Prentice Hall, Inc., 1987.

Microsoft, *Microsoft Windows Application Style Guide*, Microsoft Corporation, 1987.

Microsoft Systems Journal, published monthly by Microsoft, New York, NY.

Open Software Foundation, "The OSF/Motif Unified User Environment," Cambridge, MA, 1989.

Pressman, Roger, *Making Software Engineering Happen*, Prentice Hall, 1988.

Rodgers, Buck, *The IBM Way*, Harper and Row, 1986.

SAAage Newsletter, Systems Educational Associates, Inc., Oak Brook, IL.

Sammet, Jean, *Programming Languages: History and Fundamentals*, Prentice Hall, 1969.

Scherr, A.L., "Structures for networks of systems," *IBM Systems Journal*, Vol. 26, No. 1, 1987.

Scherr, A.L., "SAA distributed processing," *IBM Systems Journal*, Vol. 27, No. 3, 1988.

Schneiderman, B. *Designing the User Interface*, Addison-Wesley, 1987.

System Development, special issue on function points, Applied Computer Research, Volume 9, No. 8, August 1989.

Walker, Bruce J. and Gerald J. Popek, "A Transparent Environment," *BYTE Magazine*, Volume 14, Number 7, July 1989.

Wheeler, E.F. and A.G. Ganek, "Introduction to Systems Application Architecture," *IBM Systems Journal*, Vol. 27, No. 3, 1988.

Yourdon, Ed (Editor), *American Programmer*, special issue on "object-oriented observations," Vol. 2, Nos. 7-8, Summer 1989.

IBM Publications

[All items listed in this section are available from IBM.]

[Items marked with an [*] are included in the IBM SAA Library listed below.]

Brooks, A.P., "Introduction to SAA CUA Concepts Applicable in Mainframe Environments," *Technical Report 21.1268*, IBM Data Systems Division, 1988.

IBM, *AIX Family Definition Overview*, IBM GC23-2002.

IBM, *Advanced Architectures: APPC, SNADS, DIA, and DCA*, IBM GG22-9105.

IBM, *Application Development Project Support General Information*, IBM GH19-8109.

IBM, *Application System/400 System Concepts*, IBM GC21-9802.

IBM, *Bookmaster Release 2.0 General Information*, IBM GC34-5006.

IBM, *Character Data Representation Architecture: Executive Overview*, IBM GC09-1392 [In publication].

IBM, *CICS OS/2 General Information Manual*, IBM GC33-0637.

IBM, *Concepts of Distributed Data*, IBM SC26-4417.

IBM, *Cross System Product Version 3 General Information*, IBM GH23-0500.

IBM, *Data Extract Version 2 General Information*, IBM GC26-4241.

IBM, *DevelopMate General Information*, IBM GC26-4641.

IBM, *Distributed Data Management Level 3 Architecture: General Information*, IBM GC21-9527.

IBM, *Distributed Relational Data Base Architecture Reference*, IBM SC26-4651 [In publication].

IBM, *Introducing the OfficeVision Family: An SAA Application*, IBM GH21-0448.

IBM, *NetView Distribution Manager General Information*, IBM GH19-6587.

IBM, *Office Information Architectures: Concepts*, IBM GC23-0765 [OBSOLETE].

IBM, *Open Systems Interconnection within Systems Application Architecture*, IBM G511-1137.

IBM, *OSI/Communications Subsystem General Information*, IBM GL23-0184.

IBM, *OSI/File Services General Information*, IBM GH19-6636.

IBM, *OS/2 Office Programming Interfaces*, IBM SH21-0446.

IBM, *OS/2 Office Application Integration*, IBM SH21-0447.

IBM, *Query Management Facility: General Information*, IBM GC26-4299.

IBM, *SAA Applications: A Value Guide*, IBM G320-9804.

IBM, SAA Library (20 manuals listed with an [*]), IBM SBOF-1240.

IBM, *Software Analysis Test Tool General Information*, IBM GC26-4671.

IBM, *Systems Applications Architecture: A Guide for Evaluating Applications*, IBM G320-9803.

IBM, *Systems Applications Architecture: AD/Cycle Concepts*, IBM GC26-4531 [*].

IBM, *Systems Applications Architecture: An Overview*, IBM GC26-4341 [*].

IBM, *Systems Applications Architecture: The Framework for an Enterprise Information System*, IBM G580-4005.

IBM, *Systems Applications Architecture: Writing Applications*, A Design Guide, IBM SC26-4362 [*].

IBM, *Systems Application Architecture Common Communications Support: Summary*, IBM GC31-6810 [*].

IBM, *Systems Application Architecture Common Programming Interface Applications Generator Reference*, IBM SC26-4355 [*].

IBM, *Systems Application Architecture Common Programming Interface C Reference*, IBM SC26-4353 [*].

IBM, *Systems Application Architecture Common Programming Interface C Reference - Level 2*, IBM SC09-1308 [*].

IBM, *Systems Application Architecture Common Programming Interface COBOL Reference*, IBM SC26-4354 [*].

IBM, *Systems Application Architecture Common Programming Interface Communications Reference*, IBM SC26-4399 [*].

IBM, *Systems Application Architecture Common Programming Interface Database Reference*, IBM SC26-4348 [*].

IBM, *Systems Application Architecture Common Programming Interface Dialog Reference*, IBM SC26-4356 [*].

IBM, *Systems Application Architecture Common Programming Interface FORTRAN Reference*, IBM SC26-4357 [*].

IBM, *Systems Application Architecture Common Programming Interface PL/I Reference*, SC26-4381 [*].

IBM, *Systems Application Architecture Common Programming Interface Presentation Reference*, IBM SC26-4359 [*].

IBM, *Systems Application Architecture Common Programming Interface Procedures Language*, IBM SC26-4358 [*].

IBM, *Systems Application Architecture Common Programming Interface Procedures Language Level 2 Reference*, IBM SC24-5549 [In publication].

IBM, *Systems Application Architecture Common Programming Interface Query Reference*, IBM SC26-4349 [*].

IBM, *Systems Application Architecture Common Programming Interface Repository Reference*, IBM SC26-4684 [*].

IBM, *Systems Application Architecture Common Programming Interface RPG Reference*, IBM SC09-1286 [*].

IBM, *Systems Application Architecture Common Programming Interface Summary*, IBM GC26-4675 [In publication].

IBM, *Systems Application Architecture Common User Access Advanced Interface Design Guide*, IBM SC26-4582 [*].

IBM, *Systems Application Architecture Common User Access Basic Interface Design Guide*, IBM SC26-4583 [*].

IBM, *Systems Application Architecture Common User Access Panel Design and User Interaction*, IBM SC26-4351 [OBSOLETE].

IBM, *Systems Network Architecture: Concepts and Products*, IBM GC30-3072.

IBM, *Systems Network Architecture: Technical Overview*, IBM GC30-3073.

IBM, *The Integrated Reasoning Shell General Information*, IBM GH21-1005.

IBM, *Transaction Programmer's Reference Manual for LU Type 6.2*, IBM GC30-3084.

IBM, *VM/Software Engineering General Information Manual*, GH21-0012.

IBM, *Workstation Interactive Test Tool General Information*, IBM GC26-4670.

IBM Communications Systems Bulletin, *Advanced Architectures: APPC, SNADS, DIA and DCA*, IBM GG22-9105.

IBM Developer Assistance Program, *IBM Personal Systems Developer* (periodical), IBM G362-0001-nn.

IBM Enterprise and Application Enabling Systems Support Center, *SAA CUA Application Design Guidelines for CICS BMS*, IBM GG66-3115.

IBM International Technical Support Centers, *SAA and LU6.2 Considerations on CICS/MVS Applications*, IBM GG24-3295.

IBM International Technical Support Centers, *An Introduction to Advanced Program-to-Program Communication (APPC)*, IBM GG24-1584.

IBM International Technical Support Centers, *APPC/PC User Application Interface*, IBM GG24-3025.

IBM International Technical Support Centers, *Architectures for Object Interchange*, IBM GG24-3296 [OBSOLETE].

IBM International Technical Support Centers, *IBM CUA 1989 Evaluation*, IBM GG24-3456.

IBM International Technical Support Centers, *Information Interchange Architectures*, IBM GG24-3503.

IBM International Technical Support Centers, *Introduction to Distributed Relational Data*, IBM GG24-3200.

IBM International Technical Support Centers, *SAA Portability Guidelines, Phase 1*, IBM GG24-3354.

IBM International Technical Support Centers, *Writing IMS SAA Applications - A Design Guide*, IBM GG24-3324.

IBM Marketing and Services, *SAA Customer Briefs*, SAA Marketing Department, Atlanta, GA.

IBM Systems Journal, Vol. 27, No. 3, 1988 (issue on SAA), IBM G321-0091-00.

IBM Systems Journal, Vol. 29, No. 2, 1990 (issue on AD/Cycle), IBM G321-0099-00.

IBM Washington Systems Center, *SAA CUA Application Design Guidelines for CICS BMS*, IBM GG66-3115.

IBM Announcements

[All items listed in this section are published by IBM as Programming Announcements. The second and third digits of the reference number indicate the year of publication.]

287-088 Systems Application Architecture

Announcement of SAA, "a collection of selected software interfaces, conventions and protocols..."

287-099 IBM Operating System/2, Standard Edition

The first release of the new generation of operating systems for personal computers.

287-100 IBM Operating System/2, Extended Edition, Version 1.1

The first release of Database Manager, Communications Manager, on top of the first release of OS/2 Standard Edition (Release 1.1) which included the Presentation Manager.

287-471 CICS/MVS and IMS/VS Data Communications Included in SAA

Describes the role of CICS and IMS/DC as "participating" environments for the host part of cooperative applications.

287-499 Operating System/2 Extended Edition Version 1.1 and New Version 1.0

The first usable version of OS/2 EE including Communications Manager, Database Manager, and Presentation Manager (Version 1.1).

288-289 AS/400 System Environment of IBM SAA

Announcement of the AS/400 series of computers and how they support SAA.

288-336 OS/400 in SAA

Announcement of OS/400 features and capabilities; also introduces RPG to the SAA CPI and distributed file management via the introduction of Distributed Data Management to the SAA CCS.

288-456 VSE Relationship to SAA

Announces that a subset of SAA CPIs will be provided in VSE and that the primary function will be as a CICS cooperating environment.

288-490 Open System Interconnection Protocols Included in SAA Common Communications Support

Addition of key OSI protocols to the definition of SAA CCS.

288-528 Cross System Product Version 3 Release 2 Modification 1

Announces CSP application execution for OS/2 and OS/400.

288-545 Distributed Relational Data in SAA

Concepts of Remote Unit of Work and Distributed Unit of Work defined for SAA databases.

288-547 DATABASE 2 (DB2) Version 2 Release 2

The first release of DB2 to include Distributed Relational Data.

288-600 Object Interchange Architectures

Protocols for transmitting various objects (text, graphics, images) among different applications.

288-609 IMS/ESA Version 3 Release 1

Separates IMS into two products, Database Manager and Transaction Monitor.

288-611 CICS Operating System/2 Version 1.1

CICS subset implemented for OS/2 EE; includes COBOL command-level API and "function shipping" to a host-based CICS transaction via LU 6.2; a subset of this product will operate under PC-DOS and use LU 2 communications.

289-041 Cross System Product Version 3 Release 2 Modification Level 2

Update of CSP Version 3 Release 2 which adds External Source Format to allow application definitions to be imported and exported to other development tools.

289-044 Application Development Project Support

A mainframe-based CASE product initially marketed by IBM World Trade.

289-200 IBM OfficeVision Family

Overview of OfficeVision series of products. Announcements of individual products are 289-201 through 289-207.

289-215 IBM Data Interpretation System

A cooperative processing application for graphically analyzing data; based on software from Metaphor Corporation; while not currently CUA compliant, this package is thought to provide a preview of possible CUA extensions.

289-216 Easel for Operating System/2 Extended Edition

A CASE tool for developing CUA-compliant systems, either standalone or in a cooperative processing mode (using 3270 data streams); produces code in the Easel language (not SAA); licensed from Interactive Images, Inc. which also markets a PC-DOS version (see 289-247).

289-217 Operating System/2 Extended Edition Version 1.2

High Performance File System; Dialog Manager including Dialog Tag Language Compiler; Presentation Manager enhancements; SNA extensions including gateway, X.25, and Ethernet; Database Manager extensions including Remote Data Services, referential integrity, Query Manager callable interface, SAA language support.

289-218 OS/2 Standard Edition Version 1.2 and OS/2 Programming Tools and Information Version 1.2

Version 1.2 of SE includes HPFS, enhanced PM, and other improvements; adds Dialog Manager to OS/2 SE Programming Tools.

289-219 Expanded Role for the Programmable Workstation in SAA

Statement of direction regarding expanded role for PWS in SAA as the terminal for providing access to enterprise-wide functions. Discusses extensions to Common User Access for Entry, Graphical, and Workplace models.

289-220 AS/400 PC Support Extended with OS/2 Support

Programs to allow AS/400 users to use PS/2s with OS/2 as terminals (Workstation Function). Also provides file transfer (including data conversion) and shared menus, printers, and folders.

289-222 IBM GDDM-OS/2 Link

User can run GDDM applications in OS/2 PM windowing environment.

289-241 Interactive System Productivity Facility (ISPF) Version 3 for MVS

Includes SAA Dialog Tag Language for defining screens; C and REXX support.

289-242 ISPF Version 3 for VM

Includes SAA Dialog Tag Language for defining screens; C and REXX support.

289-418 IBM C/400

Announcement of full SAA Level 2 C for the AS/400 series of machines.

289-420 AS/400 TCP/IP Connectivity Utilities

Software which allows AS/400 systems to participate in TCP/IP networks, typically in multi-vendor environments.

289-424 AS/400 Programming Languages and Utilities

Adds functionality across the board, specifically bringing COBOL/400 up to the SAA CPI (and adding an "SAA compatibility" switch), and bringing the first hint of CUA to existing development tools ("significant use of Entry Model rules").

289-456 AD/Cycle

Announcement of a strategy for creating a comprehensive application development environment; also included announcement of the addition of PL/I and Repository Interface to the SAA CPI.

289-457 Repository Manager/MVS Version 1 Release 1

The core component of AD/Cycle, the Repository Manager provides a central control point for "information and functions in support of application development, systems management, and other data processing activities."

289-458 Dictionary Model Transformer Release 1

A program for converting IMS Data Dictionary contents into a form suitable for input to the Repository Manager/MVS.

289-459 Interactive System Productivity Facility/Program Development Facility Version 3 Release 2 for MVS

An upgrade to ISPF/PDF noted for inclusion of the Workstation Platform for OS/2 feature, a key component of the AD/Cycle Application Development Platform.

289-461 Cross System Product Version 3 Release 3

Adds an advanced function development facility on the PWS.

289-465 Cross System Product/370 Runtime Services

Product to generate COBOL code from CSP definitions for IMS applications; includes a run-time component.

289-479 Statement of Direction Network Definition Program that uses IBM Repository Manager/MVS

Another intended use of Repository Manager: to store network configuration data and to underlay network management software.

289-528 IBM Computer Integrated Manufacturing (CIM) Architecture

The CIM Architecture defines interfaces and functions common to CIM applications. The CIM Architecture will be made available on both SAA and AIX platforms. Development will be supported by AD/Cycle and development data will be stored via Repository Manager.

289-620 CICS OS/2 Version 1.20

Adds new features to CICS OS/2 for SAA compatibility, including C language support, ability to use Presentation Manager, and expanded function shipping and transaction routing for implementing cooperative processing applications.

289-623 OS/2 Local Area Network Server Version 1.2

Add functionality to LAN Server, particularly by adding APIs already provided by the Microsoft OS/2 LAN Manager; also adds DOS LAN Requestor as a component of the LAN Server package.

289-625 Statement of Direction for DOS, OS/2 and LAN Offerings

A joint statement by IBM and Microsoft of their intentions to coordinate development for different environments. IBM LAN Server and Microsoft LAN Manager will be made compatible. DOS/Windows and OS/2 PM will not. DOS/Windows was defined as the environment of choice for small to medium PCs only. Furthermore, both companies agreed to release new versions of software first under the OS/2 environment, clearly a big boost for OS/2.

289-696 The Integrated Reasoning Shell Product Family

Knowledge-based system development tool available under OS/2 and AIX (developed applications can also run under MVS or VM). Included in AD/Cycle for the development of artificial intelligence applications.

290-068 AIX Version 3 for RISC System/6000

A new version of AIX, initially operational only on a new hardware platform, including enhanced compatibility with POSIX, X/Open, and other UNIX standards.

290-069 AIX Family Definition Enhancements

Statement of direction for enhanced functionality, including distributed relational database compatible with SAA relational databases, LU6.2 support, C and FORTRAN compliance with the SAA CPI.

290-070 Interoperability for SAA and AIX Environments

Formal statement of relationship between SAA and AIX, specifically addressing communications connectivity, network management, distributed database, shared files, presentation services, mail exchange, and common languages.

290-071 AIXwindows Environment/6000

Graphical user interface for AIX on the RISC System/6000 based on OSF/Motif and the X Window System; includes Enhanced X-Windows which will support application "clients" running locally or on any X Window system available via a local area network.

290-072 AIX NextStep Environment/6000

Graphical user interface for AIX on the RISC System/6000 is equivalent to Release 1 of the NeXT version of NextStep; includes a desktop manager, a graphical interface builder, and an object-oriented C compiler.

290-077 RISC System/6000 Connectivity

Specifies optional AIX programs for SNA connectivity, 3270 emulation, and SNA network management.

290-141 EASEL Version 1.1 for Operating System/2 Extended Edition and Statement of Direction

Announcement of new features in EASEL (APPC support, enhanced CUA compatibility); inclusion of EASEL as an Analysis/Design phase tool of AD/Cycle; statement that EASEL can be used to develop standalone applications as well as cooperative processing applications.

290-185 IBM OfficeVision Family Revised Availability

Announces a delay in the introduction of OfficeVision Release 2; adds Release 1.1 and Release 2.1.

290-300 IBM's Open System Interconnection Position Statement

Extends IBM's commitment to support OSI communications protocols, both in SAA and AIX.

290-363 SAA Distributed Relational Data Architecture

Extends Common Communications Support functions to provide the underpinnings for access to remote relational databases.

390-034 Information Interchange Architecture

Architecture extending the Object Content Architectures for office document interchange.

390-072 Systems Application Architecture Common User Access Enabling Direction

Explicitly recognizes the primacy of the PWS for providing user access to applications systems; commits the implementation of the Presentation Interface only on the PWS; indicates that the Dialog Interface will receive only limited future attention.

390-076 Statement of Direction: IBM Fiber Distributed Data Interface

Statement that IBM intends to offer FDDI local area networks, and interconnection with token-ring and Ethernet.

Abbreviations Glossary

ACSE **Association Control Service Element**; an OSI application layer standard which defines how applications can control the transfer of information across different systems.

AD **Application Development**; used to indicate one of the components of CSP, as in CSP/AD; used in the name of the SAA CASE environment, AD/Cycle.

ADE **Application Development Environment**; a set of software development tools, methodologies, and architectures; meaning varies.

ADPS **Application Development Project Support**; CASE tool developed by IBM and initially marketed in Europe, included in AD/Cycle.

AE **Application Execution**; used to indicate one of the components of CSP, as in CSP/AE.

ALF **Application Load File**; the machine-independent pseudo-code produced by CSP/AD.

AIA **Application Integration Architecture**; Digital Equipment Corporation's software architecture for portability and interoperability.

AIX **Advanced Interactive Executive**; IBM's version of UNIX.

ANSI — **American National Standards Institute**; national body which promulgates standards in a variety of industries, including computer hardware and software.

API — **Application Programming Interface**; recent jargon for the syntax definition for a computer language or special purpose subset, such as the "communications API."

APPC — **Advanced Program to Program Communication**; communication protocol using LU6.2 from which CPIC is derived.

AS/400 — **Application System/400**; IBM's line of mid-range computers.

ASCII — **American Standard Characters for Information Interchange**; definition of the binary-equivalent values for letters, numbers, and special characters; used extensively in personal computer and mini-computers; contrast with EBCDIC.

Async — **Asynchronous Communications**; a simple protocol generally used for slow speed communications over telephone lines between mainframes and PCs or among PCs.

AT — **Advanced Technology**; a class of personal computers, as in PC/AT.

BCD — **Binary Coded Decimal**; a way of encoding the decimal digits in binary; see EBCDIC.

C — [Not an abbreviation] Name of a programming language first developed as part of the UNIX project at AT&T, but now widely used by personal computer software developers; part of the SAA CPI; successor to the "B" programming language.

CAE — **Common Applications Environment**; standards for UNIX hardware and software developed by the X/Open Company, Ltd., an industry consortium.

CCS **Common Communications Support**; a major component of SAA.

CDRA **Character Data Representation Architecture**; a data stream architecture included in CCS to handle the transmission of graphic characters across systems.

CI **Callable Interface**; refers to the ability to use the Query Manager via a program call in an SAA language.

CICS **Customer Information and Control System**; the most common teleprocessing environment in use on IBM mainframe systems.

CIM **Computer Integrated Manufacturing**; refers to the family of applications used in manufacturing organizations; IBM announced a CIM Architecture on top of SAA.

CM **Communications Manager**; part of OS/2 EE.

CMS **Conversational Monitor System**; see VM/CMS.

COBOL **Common Business Oriented Language**; name of the programming language.

CPI **Common Programming Interface**; specification of SAA computer language constructs and system support routines.

CPIC **Common Programming Interface - Communications**; the SAA CPI for communications, based on APPC.

CPU **Central Processing Unit**; on a mainframe, the computation unit; on a personal computer, the "chip."

CSP **Cross System Product, the SAA Applications Generator.**

CSP/AD **Cross System Product/Application Development**; the development component of CSP.

CSP/AE **Cross System Product/Application Execution**; the execution component of CSP.

CUA **Common User Access**; SAA specification of user interface standards.

DB2 **DATABASE 2**; IBM's relational database for MVS and VM systems.

DC **Data Communications**; used to indicate a component of IMS, as in IMS/DC.

DCA **Document Content Architecture**; defines a protocol for specifying the formatting of documents to be exchanged between applications; two types of DCA are part of SAA Common Communications Support.

DCE **Distributed Computing Environment**; Open Software Foundation specification of protocols and tools to implement distributed applications; SAA and AIX will include components of DCE.

DDM **Distributed Data Management**; an "application services" architecture for distributed record oriented files; do not confuse with the more general concept of "distributed data."

DEC **Digital Equipment Corporation**; another large computer manufacturer.

DDM **Distributed Data Management**; architecture which deals with the sharing of files and records within files; one of the SAA CCS application services.

DFD **Data Flow Diagram**; a type of diagram used in structured system design which shows individual system processes and the data flowing among them.

DFM **Distributed file management**; refers to IBM's strategy for distributed access to record-oriented files (non-relational).

DFT **Distributed Function Terminal**; protocol for communication between a communication controller and an intelligent terminal which allows multiple simultaneous sessions.

DIA **Document Interchange Architecture**; specifies how documents are to be transmitted and processed across systems in a network; one of the SAA CCS application services.

DISOSS **Distributed Office Support System**; office application environment for MVS and VSE.

DL/I **Data Language/I**; the subroutine calls used to access IMS databases.

DM **Dialog Manager**; programming system for creating user interactive programs.

DOS **Disk Operating System**; original name for one of IBM's mainframe operating systems; shorthand for popular personal computer operating system; see DOS/VSE, PC-DOS, MS-DOS.

DOS/VSE **Disk Operating System/Virtual System Executive**; IBM's low end mainframe operating system; not a full SAA environment.

DP **Data Processing**; as in Data Processing Department; often used as a synonym for Information Systems.

DRDA **Distributed Relational Data Architecture**; an application services layer protocol included in CCS to permit access to remote relational databases.

DSU **Distribution Service Unit**; a node in the SNA/Distribution Services network which handles SNA/DS traffic.

DTL **Dialog Tag Language**; language for defining panel layouts and dialogs; based on the ISO Standard Generalized Markup Language.

DTP **Distributed Transaction Processing**; CICS OS/2 feature allowing transactions running on one machine to control transactions running on another machine.

DXT **Data Extract**; an IBM product for extracting portions of databases on one machine and sending them to another.

EBCDIC **Extended Binary Coded Decimal Character**; an 8-bit character format used on the ESA/370 line of computers.

ECF **Enhanced Connectivity Facility**; MVS and VM products which allow PC access to host data.

EDI **Electronic Data Interchange**; evolving standards for transmitting business information electronically, typically among different organizations.

EE **Extended Edition**; as in OS/2 EE.

EGA **Enhanced Graphics Adapter**; one of several color graphics schemes employed on personal computers; considered "standard" on AT-class machines.

EHLLAPI **Emulator High Level Language Application Programming Interface**; service routines for performing 3270 data stream communications.

ESA **Enterprise System Architecture**; new suffix for operating systems, e.g., MVS/ESA.

ESA/370 **Enterprise System Architecture/370**; the new name given to IBM's extended line of mainframe computers.

ESF **External Source Format**; externally available data format for CSP definitions.

EZ-VU [not an abbreviation] PC implementation of ISPF with additional facilities for creating panels.

FAT **File Allocation Table**; the file management system used under PC/DOS; see HPFS.

FD:OCA **Field-formatted Data:Object Content Architecture**; a CCS object protocol which defines data attributes to be included along with data fields and structures in a data stream.

FORTRAN **Formula Translator**; name of a programming language for scientific and engineering applications.

FTAM **File Transfer, Access, and Management**; an OSI application service standard for file transfer across systems.

GDDM **Graphical Data Display Manager**; service routines for creating graphics, typically on NPTs attached to a host; foundation for Presentation Manager.

GML **Generalized Markup Language**; tag language used in a variety of text and data transfer applications; also used in CSP External Source Format files; see SGML.

GUI **Graphical User Interface**; generic term for programming systems which provide CUA-like user interfaces, such as Windows, X Windows, PM, New Wave, etc.

HLLAPI **High Level Language Application Programming Interface**; short for EHLLAPI.

HPFS **High Performance File System**; an installable file system supplied with OS/2 Release 1.2 which features fast access to very large disks and file names of up to 254 characters.

IBM [not an abbreviation] derived from the former name, International Business Machines Corporation, of a large computer manufacturer.

IEEE **Institute of Electrical and Electronic Engineers**; professional society which includes a large number people in the computer field; organization that promulgates data processing standards, notably including POSIX.

IFS **Installable File System**; a feature of OS/2 (introduced in Release 1.2) which allows you to specify alternative file control systems for each device; see HPFS.

IMS **Information Management System**; IBM's hierarchical database management system for mainframe computers.

IPDS — **Intelligent Printer Data Stream**; one of the SAA data stream protocols, typically used for communicating between large computers and attached laser printers.

IRDS — **Information Resource Dictionary System**; ANSI standard for a common CASE data repository.

IS — **Information Systems**; as in Information Systems Department.

ISDN — **Integrated Services Digital Network**; networking services offered by common communication carriers for both voice and data; communications protocols for such services include functions across the three lower levels of the OSI model.

ISO — **International Standards Organization**; international body which promulgates a wide variety of standards, including many for the computer industry.

ISPF — **Interactive System Productivity Facility**; programming system for creating user interactive programs whose current release implements the SAA Dialog Interface on the System 370.

ISV — **Independent Software Vendor**; a software manufacturer other than a unit of a hardware manufacturer.

Kb — **Kilobyte(s)**; 1024 bytes.

LAN — **Local Area Network**; method of attaching a number of computers of varying types and sizes in a local work group.

LDMI — **Local data management interface**; routine which intercepts a file I/O request and determines where the file resides on the network; part of the Distributed Data Management Architecture.

LU6.2 — **Logical Unit 6.2**; IBM's program-to-program communications protocol; a key element in the CCS.

MAU — **Multistation Access Unit**; a wiring control box used in token-ring networks to establish electrical connections in a circular topology.

Mb **Megabyte(s)**; 1,048,576 bytes; 1,024 Kb; often rounded to 1,000,000.

MCGA **Multi-color graphics array**; one of several color graphics schemes employed on personal computers; introduced by IBM on some mid-range models of the PS/2.

MIS **Management Information System**; one of a class of computer applications used in the administration or business operation of an organization.

MIT **Massachusetts Institute of Technology**; a trade school in Cambridge, MA; home of the Laboratory for Computer Science (formerly Project MAC); developer of (1) Multics, grandfather of UNIX (2) X/Windows GUI for UNIX (3) other advances in software concepts and technology too numerous to mention.

MO:DCA **Mixed Object:Document Content Architecture**; a specification for document interchange involving text, graphic, and image components; component of SAA CCS.

MSL **Member Specification Library**; stores CSP application specifications.

MS-DOS **Microsoft Disk Operating System**; generic version of PC-DOS which Microsoft markets to PC-compatible manufacturers.

MVS **Multiple Virtual Storage**; current series of operating systems for ESA/370 computers; indicates that multiple independent virtual storage spaces are created; successor to SVS (single virtual storage) operating system.

NAS **Network Application Support**; Digital's enabling software for implementing portable applications based on AIA.

NLS **National Language Support**; refers to the ability of SAA software, e.g., the Dialog Manager, to use and display languages other than English.

NPT **Non-programmable terminal**; e.g., 3270.

NPW — **Non-programmable workstation**; see NPT.

ODA — **Office Document Architecture**; high level protocol for exchanging documents among applications; an OSI Layer 7 protocol.

OOD — **Object-oriented Design**; methodology used to design object-oriented systems.

OODB — **Object-oriented Database**; a kind of database management system said to help in implementing OOPS; too new to have a standard definition.

OOP — **Object-oriented Programming**; a model for program construction which encapsulates data with the program that controls how it can be accessed; Presentation Manager can be used to create object-oriented user interface programs.

OOPS — **Object-oriented Programming System**; system developed using OOD and OOP.

OS/2 — **Operating System/2**; a new personal computer operating system first introduced with the PS/2 series of computers; comes in two flavors, Standard Edition and Extended Edition.

OS/400 — **Operating System/400**; the operating system for the AS/400 series of computers.

OSF — **Open Software Foundation**; an industry group developing components of a standard operating system for the UNIX environment based on specifications from X/OPEN and POSIX and core technology from AIX; initial members were Apollo Computer, Groupe Bull, DEC, Hewlett-Packard, IBM, Nixdorf, and Siemens, now numbers over 100.

OSI — **Open System Interconnection**; a set of international standard protocols for data communications.

PC — **Personal Computer**; refers to a type of computer first introduced for standalone, personal use; obsolete concept.

PC-DOS — **Personal Computer - Disk Operating System**; IBM's version of MS-DOS.

PDF **Program Development Facility**; an add-on to ISPF that provides such functions as program editing, library management, and tools invocation.

PL/I **Programming Language/I**; a language developed by IBM, initially as a successor to FORTRAN, then a general purpose third generation language.

PM **Presentation Manager**; service routines for creating user interface programs; OS/2 PM implements the CPI Presentation Interface.

POSIX **Portable Operating System Interface**; a UNIX variant being developed as a standard by the IEEE and adopted by OSF.

POWER **Performance Optimization With Enhanced RISC**; as in "RISC System/6000 POWERstations." [Previously used in the name of a VSE spooling product, VSE/POWER, Priority Output Writers, Execution Processors, and Input Readers.]

PROFS **Professional Office System**; office support software for VM.

PROM **Programmable Read-only Memory**; type of non-volatile computer memory typically used to store programs which control the operation of some part of the hardware.

PS/2 **Personal System/2**; IBM's current line of personal computers, PS/2.

PU2.1 **Physical Unit 2.1**; a physical node (hardware) in a network that is capable of establishing a connection with another node, e.g., a programmable workstation or a mainframe computer; the SAA CCS networking protocol.

PWS **Programmable Workstation**; e.g., PS/2.

QMF **Query Management Facility**; software for accessing relational databases.

R **Release**; as in R2, Release 2 [definition copied from IBM SAA Marketing Competency Center publication].

RDS **Remote Data Services**; capability of OS/2 EE Database Manager which allows transparent access of remote data.

REXX **Restructured Extended Editor**; originally developed for VM, the basis for the SAA Procedures Language CPI.

RFT:DCA **Revisable Form Text:Document Content Architecture**; protocol which specifies a text document which can be further edited; one of the SAA CCS data streams.

ROM **Read-Only Memory**; fast memory used to store commonly used functions, such as parts of the operating system.

RPG **Report Program Generator**; the most popular language on IBM mid-range computers.

RRAS **Remote Relational Access Support**; feature in SQL/DS supporting access to data on other SQL/DS databases.

SAA **Systems Application Architecture**; the subject of this book.

SDLC **Synchronous Data Link Control**; low level communication protocol used for managing synchronous communications.

SGML **Standard Generalized Markup Language**; ISO standard for defining panels and other user presentation formats; basis for the Dialog Tag Language of the SAA CPI Dialog Interface.

SNA **Systems Network Architecture**; IBM's model of communications protocols for heterogeneous networks; basis for SAA CCS.

SNA/DS **SNA Distribution Services**; messaging service available to applications on an SNA network; one of the SAA CCS application services.

SNA/MS **SNA Management Services**; refers to the SAN applications services for controlling a network, i.e. problem management, performance and accounting, configuration and change management; SNA/MS problem management is one of the SAA CCS application services.

SQL **Structured Query Language**; now an ANSI standard language for accessing relational databases, also the SAA CPI for database access.

SRPI **Server-Requester Programming Interface**; OS/2 facility for using Enhanced Connectivity Facility on the System 370 to write distributed applications.

TANSTAAFL **There Ain't No Such Thing As A Free Lunch**; economic concept, often referenced in explaining why seemingly positive and unexpected events often have hidden or future negative results associated with them.

TCP/IP **Transmission Control Protocol/Internet Protocol**; networking protocol developed initially for the Department of Defense Advanced Research Projects Agency (DARPA); widely used on UNIX networks.

TM **Transaction Manager**; as in IMS/ESA TM, one of the two components of IMS (the other being the IMS Database Manager).

TSO **Time-Sharing Option**; an interactive user environment available as an option to the MVS operating system.

UNIX **[Not an abbreviation]** Name of a popular operating system noted for its ability to be easily transported to a variety of hardware environments; modeled after the Multics time-sharing system developed by MIT, Bell Labs, and General Electric (now Honeywell); UNIX is "'one of' whatever Multics was 'many of'."

UOW **Unit of Work**; in SQL, the statements executed between database "commit" points.

V **Version**; as in V1.1, Version 1.1 [definition copied from IBM SAA Marketing Competency Center publication].

VGA **Video Graphics Array**; one of several color graphics schemes employed on personal computers; now considered the high-end standard.

VM — **Virtual Machine**; software simulated computer; a major operating system for IBM mainframe computers which simulates multiple independent computers.

VM/CMS — **Virtual Machine/Conversational Monitor System**; a user interface for VM systems which provides directly a simple conversational operating environment.

VTAM — **Virtual Telecommunications Access Method**; mainframe communications software implementing SNA protocols.

WYSIWYG — **"What You See Is What You Get;"** refers to a highly intuitive user interface which displays information in exactly the same form as it would be printed; used in word processors and some graphical applications.

X.25 — ISO designation for definition of packet-switched network protocol.

X.400 — ISO designation for definition of electronic mail protocol.

X.500 — ISO designation for a network directory standard supporting the naming and specifying of various system resources.

X/OPEN — [Not an abbreviation] Consortium of computer vendors developing a standard definition of the UNIX operating system.

XNS — **Xerox Network Services**; network protocol used over Ethernet networks.

Index

Author's Biography

Jerrold M. Grochow is a nationally noted consultant, speaker, and author on software engineering. His broad experience ranges from operating systems development at MIT's famed Project MAC to application systems development at American Management Systems, Inc., where he is currently Vice President, Corporate Technology Group. His responsibilities encompass a variety of programs for software productivity and quality improvement. For the past three years, he has been responsible for AMS's strategic and developmental plans for compatibility with IBM's Systems Application Architecture and other industry standards.

Dr. Grochow received B.S., M.S. and Ph.D. degrees from MIT. He resides with his family in the Washington, D.C. area.